Animals in
Emergencies

Animals in Emergencies

Learning from the Christchurch earthquakes

Annie Potts
Donelle Gadenne

First published in 2014 by

CANTERBURY UNIVERSITY PRESS
University of Canterbury
Private Bag 4800, Christchurch
NEW ZEALAND
www.cup.canterbury.ac.nz

Text copyright © 2014 Annie Potts and Donelle Gadenne
Appendix I © 2014 Steve Glassey

The moral rights of the authors have been asserted.

Unless otherwise specified, all photographs appearing in this book were supplied by the organisations, agencies or individuals alongside whose stories they appear.

ISBN 978-1-927145-50-0

A catalogue record for this book is available from the National Library of New Zealand.

This book is copyright. Except for the purpose of fair review, no part may be stored or transmitted in any form or by any means, electronic or mechanical, including recording or storage in any information retrieval system, without permission in writing from the publishers. No reproduction may be made, whether by photocopying or by any other means, unless a licence has been obtained from the publisher or its agent.

Page and cover concept design by Working Ideas
Page and cover layout by Quentin Wilson & Associates, Christchurch, New Zealand

Typeset in Melior
Cover image: Alex Hubert
Printed by The Caxton Press, Christchurch

Annie Potts thanks the Pufendorf Institute for Advanced Studies, Lund University, Sweden, and the LMK Foundation for their support while completing this book.

Contents

vi	Dedication
vii	Preface
ix	Acknowledgements
xi	List of abbreviations
xii	Map
1	Introduction: Animals in emergencies
21	**PART ONE: RESCUE, SHELTER AND ADVOCACY**
23	Chapter 1: Front-line responders
71	Chapter 2: Shelter and advocacy
105	**PART TWO: ANIMAL EARTHQUAKE STORIES**
107	Chapter 3: Feline tales
149	Chapter 4: Canine tales
179	Chapter 5: From turtles to hedgehogs: other species affected by the quakes
221	Chapter 6: Those most vulnerable
231	Conclusion: Learning from the Christchurch experience
248	Postscript
249	Appendix I: Guide to protecting pets during disasters (Steve Glassey)
253	Appendix II: Online resources
255	References
262	Further reading
264	Contributors acknowledge their supporters
267	Index

Dedication

Annie and Donelle dedicate this book with love to Screech (1997–2014) and Bear (1998–2007).

Preface

As a consequence of the magnitude 6.3 earthquake that struck Christchurch at 12.51pm on 22 February 2011, 185 people lost their lives and thousands of others were abruptly, profoundly and extensively affected. Within moments, the direction of the city and its inhabitants changed forever. Loved ones were gone, homes were ruined, jobs terminated and families displaced. Parts of Christchurch and its environs would remain unrecognisable. More than three years on and the situation for the city's human population is still precarious; the long-term accommodation arrangements and livelihoods of many remain uncertain. In local and national media, updates on the battles of frustrated home-owners with the Earthquake Commission (EQC) and insurers dominate. Debate over demolition or restoration of heritage buildings is also fraught. More positively, the rebuilding of Christchurch's central business district (CBD) is anticipated with excitement, while the Gap Filler project demonstrates the creative initiative of the city's citizens. Community stoicism and resilience are phenomenal; stories of courage and determination in the immediate aftermath of tragedy and in the face of continued instability and adversity are evident in local reports and the QuakeStories accessible via the University of Canterbury's CEISMIC Digital Archive.[1] People have shown tremendous empathy towards strangers as well as towards close family, friends and neighbours.

Importantly, thousands of non-human lives have also been deeply affected by the major earthquakes and aftershocks of the past few years. While stories have circulated about the city's creatures – domestic and wild – few of these have been documented in detail. Those broadcast in newspapers and online tend to represent the most extraordinary accounts of, for example, cats returning home after long absences or dogs predicting aftershocks. This book aims to present some of these unusual stories alongside the more everyday descriptions of how diverse species – from lions and horses to hedgehogs and parrots – responded to the seismic activity in the city. As might be expected, cats and dogs feature prominently, but tales of rats, turtles, chickens and lemurs are also included.

---

1 See Canterbury Earthquake Images, Stories and Media Integrated Collection (CEISMIC): www.ceismic.org.nz

The accounts presented here – of animal welfare experts and companion animal guardians – were collected over three years via interviews, email correspondence, online archives and media reports. We have structured the book so the highly specialised roles of animal rescuers and shelter workers are represented in the first part. Because these professionals led efforts to ensure animal welfare after the quakes, they have unique experiences of the reactions of animals and people in the immediate aftermath of these events. The second part of the book focuses on personal stories of animal survival (and sometimes loss) following Canterbury's seismic activity, and demonstrates the remarkable devotion of humans to their companion animals and to the other creatures inhabiting the city.

More than anything, this book is a testament to the bravery and resilience of the animals and people of Christchurch and its environs, and a tribute to those who protected, sheltered and cared for the city's multi-species inhabitants after the quakes. It is also a plea for us to take the life and death of every being seriously when disaster strikes.

Acknowledgements

This book has been made possible because of the tremendous support, guidance and commitment of Catherine Montgomery, publisher at Canterbury University Press. We are grateful to editor Katrina Rainey for her constructive feedback on the manuscript and to Quentin Wilson for his effective design. We thank Rachel Scott, former publisher at Canterbury University Press, for first seeing the potential in this book proposal.

A project such as this is a collective achievement. We have been humbled by the generosity of all those who contributed directly or indirectly in the development of *Animals in Emergencies*. We thank the people and animals of Christchurch for their contributions and for reminding us all how important meaningful cross-species relationships are in both normal and extraordinary times. Special thanks to Steve Glassey, Hayley Squance, Bridget Vercoe and Leonie Waayer who have provided strong mentorship and encyclopaedic advice in the area of animal welfare in emergencies. The authors are also indebted to Chloe Geoghegan and Karen Saunders for their conscientious and speedy transcription of interviews; photographer Jo Moore and all those who supplied images to illustrate their stories; Alex Hubert for generously contributing our cover image; Douglas Horrell for kindly preparing numerous images for use in the book; Kim Buchanan, Arnja Dale, Sacha Dowell, Kirsty Dunn, Nikki Evans, Nathan Hawke, Chris Hawker, Barry Helem, Bob Kerridge, Hans Kriek, Nichola Kriek, Lois Lang, Tania Lee, Charmaine McLaren, Jennifer Miles, Jamie Muller, Drina Sisarich, James Smithies, Christina Stachurski, Geoff Sutton and Mark Vincent, for their assistance with various aspects of this project; and the College of Arts Internal Research Grants Committee 2012 for funding research travel. We sincerely thank Paul Millar, Head of the School of Humanities and Creative Arts, for his ongoing support of Human–Animal Studies (HAS) at the University of Canterbury; and all the members and associates of the New Zealand Centre for Human–Animal Studies for their continued inspiration.

The bulk of *Animals in Emergencies* was completed while Annie Potts was seconded to Lund University in Sweden to work at the Pufendorf Institute for Advanced Studies on a project entitled 'Exploring the Animal Turn'. Annie is grateful to Therese Karlsson and the LMK Foundation for funding this fellowship, the Pufendorf Institute for providing a positive interdisciplinary research environment, and her colleagues in Sweden for sharing their knowledge and companionship: in particular Amelie Björck, Tobias Linné, Helena Pedersen, EvaMarie Lindahl, Eva Persson, Ann-Sofie Lönngren, Kristina Jennbert, Sune Sunesson, Bengt Pettersson, Sture Forsén, Kurtis Boyer and Ally McCrow-Young.

Annie has had the honour of serving as the New Zealand Companion Animal Council's representative on the National Animal Welfare Emergency Management (NAWEM) advisory group since 2011. Her experience as part of this group has been invaluable in providing a deeper understanding of the issues affecting animals in emergencies. She wishes to acknowledge with great respect chairpersons Bridget Vercoe and Wayne Ricketts; and NAWEM members Les Dalton, Ritchie Dawson, Paul Molloy, Roger Poland, Mark Ross, Hayley Squance and Leonie Waayer.

On a personal level, Annie is immensely grateful to Donelle Gadenne, co-author extraordinaire and awesome friend. Special thanks also to Ola Roff, Jill Vosper, Harry Kerr, Roxane Vosper, Verity Kerr, Justine Roff; as well as Ross Gibbs, Erin Harrington, Tobias Linné, Sharon McFarlane, Karen Saunders, Anna Smith, Christina Stachurski and Shelley Trueman. In the aftermath of the quakes Annie's partner Philip Armstrong and their furry, hairy, feathered and scaled house companions provided solace, security, distraction and affection; each day they all remind her of what makes life truly special. Annie's cherished friend and colleague in Cultural Studies, Howard McNaughton, died during the last month of work on this book. A champion of the marginalised, Howard was Annie's mentor for over 12 years. Along with his partner Christina, he was also the proud guardian of two cats – and once upon a time, several Flemish giants. In light of his affection for cats, chapter 3 (Feline tales) is dedicated with love to Howard.

Donelle would like to thank Annie Potts for being an inspirational mentor and a cherished friend. She is grateful to her for giving her the opportunity to collaborate on this book with the assistance of the University of Canterbury's invaluable Summer Scholarship Programme.

Donelle credits her late mother, Kaye, with being her moral compass. Without such role models, we might never come to realise that animals are our equals. Donelle owes her passion for companion animals and their welfare in large part to her own departed team-with-tails, Max, Harley and her brave chihuahua, Bear.

List of abbreviations

AABH	Animal and Bird Hospital
ARU	Animal Rescue Unit
AWERT	Animal Welfare Emergency Response Team
CARA	Christchurch Animal Research Area
CBD	central business district
CDEM	Civil Defence Emergency Management
CEISMIC	Canterbury Earthquake Images, Stories and Media Integrated Collection
CPIT	Christchurch Polytechnic Institute of Technology
CPL	Cats' Protection League
CTV	Canterbury Television
EQC	Earthquake Commission
HUHA	Helping You Help Animals
MCDEM	Ministry of Civil Defence and Emergency Management
MPI	Ministry for Primary Industries
NAWEM	National Animal Welfare Emergency Management
NAEAC	National Animal Ethics Advisory Committee
NZCAC	New Zealand Companion Animal Council
NZCAR	New Zealand Companion Animal Register
NZVA	New Zealand Veterinary Association
PETS	Pets Evacuation and Transportation Standards
PGC	Pyne Gould Corporation
PTSD	post-traumatic stress disorder
RNZFB	Royal New Zealand Foundation of the Blind
SAFE	Save Animals From Exploitation
SPCA	Society for the Prevention of Cruelty to Animals
TNR	trap–neuter–return
UCR3	University of Canterbury's Centre for Risk, Resilience and Renewal
USAR	Urban Search and Rescue
VERT	Veterinary Emergency Response Team
WSPA	World Society for the Protection of Animals (to be renamed World Animal Protection, WAP)

Map showing key locations

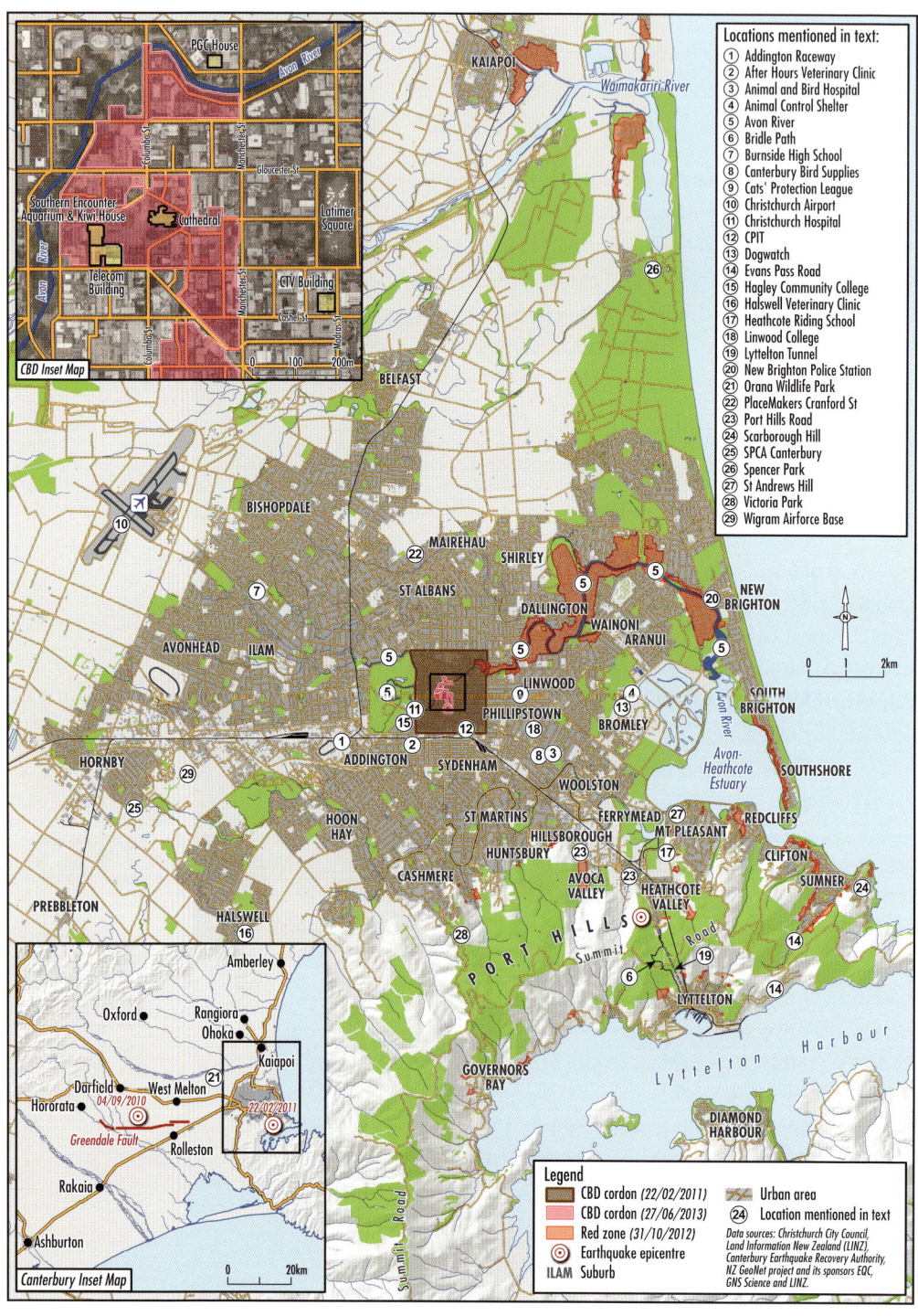

Introduction
Animals in emergencies

This book serves two key purposes. First, it stands as an accurate historical record of what occurred in Christchurch with respect to the rescue, shelter and follow-on care of animals affected by the major Canterbury earthquakes of 2010 and 2011. To this end, first-hand accounts have been collected from professionals at the front line of animal protection, rescue and welfare during this time (Part One), as have personal stories from those whose companion animals were affected by the quakes (Part Two). Second, the book provides an introduction to the specialised area of animal welfare management during emergencies. Drawing upon lessons learnt in the wake of Canterbury's earthquakes (and in the aftermath of Hurricane Katrina in the United States), we also discuss effective ways in which to plan and prepare for companion animals in the event of future natural or human-induced disasters. When disasters strike it is of course not only our companion animals who are at risk: other domesticated animals (those on farms, for example), as well as animals kept in laboratories, zoos and wildlife parks, and all the wild creatures of the city and its environs are affected. The book also outlines some of the important issues associated with managing the safety and welfare of these animals in disasters.

We begin here by emphasising the special place companion animals hold in our lives. Because so many animals may disappear or die as a consequence of unforeseen disasters, we explain how the loss of beloved companion animals affects humans. Bereavement for non-human species remains trivialised and underestimated in Western anthropocentric culture; such disenfranchised grief is further complicated when it occurs as a consequence of catastrophic events which may also have taken human lives and permanently destroyed properties and communities.

The book reviews previous research in the field of animal welfare management during emergencies. Prior to the Canterbury earthquakes, those at the forefront of animal rescue and shelter during crises, both nationally and internationally, had learnt much from the devastating loss of human and animal life in the wake of Hurricane Katrina, which struck New Orleans in the summer of 2005. In response to the American tragedy, as well as to local predicaments such as snow storms, flooding and volcanic activity, concerned agencies in New Zealand initiated the National Animal Welfare Emergency Management (NAWEM) advisory group in 2006; its role, as its name suggests, is to offer guidance on matters pertaining to animal welfare following natural and human-induced disasters. In large part thanks to lobbying by NAWEM, New Zealand is on the brink of important new legislation aimed at improving outcomes for animals – and their humans – when future disasters occur (for more on this, see the conclusion to this book).

Companion animals: love and loss

New Zealand boasts the highest level of companion animal guardianship per capita in the Western world. A survey undertaken by the New Zealand Companion Animal Council (NZCAC) in 2011 provides some fascinating information on human–animal relations in this country: we are clearly a nation of multi-species homes and families. There are approximately 5,000,000 companion animals in New Zealand; 68% of households contain one or more 'pets'. This figure exceeds companion animal statistics in the United States (where 62% of homes contain at least one pet) and the United Kingdom (47%). Globally, we have the highest rate of cat guardianship, with 48% of households containing an average of two cats (the pet cat population is estimated to be around 1.419 million). Nearly a third of homes house at least one dog (with 700,000 dogs estimated across the nation). Fish outnumber cats and dogs, however (at 1.678 million), with 11% of households containing on average nine fish, a statistic no doubt reflecting the rise of apartment living in New Zealand (NZCAC, 2011).

Interestingly, 60 or so years ago, those who 'kept pets' were more likely to be viewed with some bemusement or suspicion: pets were trivialised as substitute children, 'accessories' to show off, or quirky hobbies (Serpell, 1986). People who demonstrated close relationships with pets – treating them as valued members of the family, for example – were thought to be unusual (sometimes even deficient in some way), either lacking the social skills to communicate or relate well with other humans (hence the assumption they favoured interactions with other species), or asumed to be looking to replace a missing person with an animal. Even children's relationships with animals were less valued than today. Pet-keeping was criticised for being an 'extravagance', a practice that did not contribute to the economy or to social improvement in any substantial way (Potts et al., 2013).

This outdated perspective still persists today, but to a lesser extent, and it has been robustly challenged by the well-recognised emotional, social and physical (and economic)[1] value of our companionable connection with other species. In psychology, this connection is called 'the human–animal bond', which, as Barbara Meyers (2002) points out, is not a substitute or replacement for human companionship, but rather one of the many kinds of relationships we are capable of fostering and enjoying. 'The human–animal relationship stands on its own, possessing unique properties that distinguish it from others. It is not more or less important than other relationships; it is simply different – worthy of affirmation, validation, and respect' (Meyers, 2002, p. 252). Sharkin and Knox (2003) describe this as a 'pure' bond, one based on a genuine and consistent sense of unconditional love and acceptance: 'Animal companionship can provide a sense of "non-judgemental" social support, a form of support that can be difficult for people (including supportive spouses or friends) to provide' (p. 415). This sense of total acceptance comes from the fact that 'animals do not discriminate' (Meyers, 2002, p. 252); they do not withdraw their affection when the object of that affection falls sick, grows old or unattractive, or goes 'broke' – or even if they have a disagreeable personality!

Today the immense and varied benefits of animal companionship are well researched and readily acknowledged. The widely accepted changes in terminology – from 'pet' to 'companion animal', and from 'owner' to 'guardian' – reflect how much societal attitudes towards human–companion animal relationships have shifted in the popular consciousness (Franklin, 1999). By far the majority of people who live with animals consider these companions to be bona fide members of the family (Glassey, 2010; NZCAC, 2011). In a recent study, young adults even reported a closeness to companion dogs they felt was equal to their emotional bond with their mothers, best friends, siblings and significant others (Kurdek, 2008). Medical, psychological and sociological research from the 1980s onwards has shown the direct physiological benefits and stress-buffering effects of close bonds and interactions with animals. For example, living with a companion animal is associated with increased rates of recovery and survival following heart surgery or disease (Friedman et al., 2000), and decreased occurrence of depression (Wells, 2009). It has also been shown that elderly people who share their lives with animals make fewer visits to doctors (Allen et al., 2002).

Companion animals also have a calming effect on people, contributing to feelings of safety and comfort. Controlled studies demonstrate that the physiological responses of those under psychological pressure

---

[1] In 2011 New Zealanders spent approximately 1.6 billion dollars on pet food, veterinary visits and other products for their companion animals. An estimated 766 million dollars per year is spent on food alone for pets in New Zealand (NZCAC, 2011).

are moderated more by the presence of a pet dog than by that of a supportive human friend (Allen et al., 2006). It is not even necessary to have a personal bond with an animal in order to benefit from his or her company; physically ill or emotionally distressed people show improvements in health even after spending time with unfamiliar animals. Following the terrorist attacks on the World Trade Center in Manhattan, dogs were brought to Ground Zero and placed in a rest zone for rescue workers who could visit them for hugs and comfort. It was recognised that their presence would help relieve the emotional exhaustion and distress of officers involved in this harrowing recovery work (Hall et al., 2004). Even low-key interactions are health giving: watching fish, for example, can reduce blood pressure and produce a state of relaxation. Positive effects have also been noted in studies where participants merely observe images of animals (Beck & Katcher, 1996).

Importantly, the misconception of the mid-20th century that those who lived with pets were inadequate in their relationships with humans has been debunked by contemporary research, which reveals that the reverse is actually the case: empathy towards animals is demonstrably connected to a more compassionate attitude towards other humans. Those living with companion animals are also found to score higher than non-pet-owners on measures of 'interpersonal trust', and, at least in the case of older women, to have more close confidants (Hyde, Kurdek & Larson, 1983). In fact, it seems increasingly clear that our connections with animals actually *teach* us empathy for our fellow human beings. Children participating in an animal-focused humane education programme showed on completion of the course (and continued to show, one year later) more empathy towards humans (as well as animals) than children who had not undertaken the training (Ascione & Weber, 1996). Likewise, a positive relationship in childhood with a companion animal has been found to coincide with concern for both human well-being and animal welfare later in life (Paul & Serpell, 1993).

Unfortunately, New Zealand is a nation plagued by daily disrespect for, and neglect, abuse and manipulation of animals (Potts et al., 2013). Each year the Society for the Prevention of Cruelty to Animals (SPCA) releases its *List of Shame*, which publicises the worst acts of cruelty towards animals during that year. Violence is perpetrated every day towards the most vulnerable: those animals who are confined, exploited, unwanted and disregarded. While we know that close, affectionate companionship between humans and other species brings positive benefits to humans, we can but hope that these benefits are reciprocal. However, research into the link between domestic violence and animal abuse indicates that companion animals may enter into human–human dynamics by providing distraction or diversion from family conflict, or, conversely, by becoming the target of anger meant for or related to another family member (Cain, 1991; see also www.firststrike.org.nz). The behaviour of pets can therefore be a 'barometer of the family atmosphere, patterns of interaction, and emotional undercurrents such as anxiety, conflict and tension' (Cusack, 1988, cited in Sharkin & Knox, 2003, p. 416). During times of high stress – such as natural disasters – when tension in relationships is exacerbated, animals are even more likely to bear the brunt of domestic discord. Both the negative and positive sides of human–animal relationships following a natural disaster are evident in the stories of rescuers and others recounted in this book.

The death or disappearance of a beloved companion animal is a life event many of us endure. While it is now recognised as having a similar impact to the loss of a close human family member or partner (Quackenbush & Glickman, 1984; Podrazik et al., 2000; Thomas, 2009), grief for an animal friend may be experienced even more intensely. This is because our relationships with companion animals are unique in nature: their lives are naturally shorter than our own, and although we expect this, it is a fact we carry unhappily throughout our animals' lifetimes, watching them grow older and more frail ahead of us. We are also often faced with the distressing decision to end an animal's life in order to reduce suffering. As with grief for humans, people who lose beloved animals may be preoccupied with memories of them and can experience diminished concentration, changes in appetite and patterns of sleep, as well as feelings of guilt, remorse and anxiety (Chur-Hansen, 2010). Acceptance of death may be complicated by the circumstance in which an animal dies: suddenly or following chronic disease; in old age or as the result of an accident; and of course, whether or not euthanasia was involved (McCutcheon & Fleming, 2001). When companion animals go missing, grief can be protracted and complicated.

One of the ways in which the earlier denigration of close human–animal relationships continues to manifest nowadays is through our culture's propensity still to trivialise or diminish the sense of deep loss and despair associated with an animal's death or disappearance. The profound bereavement experienced by many for absent loved animals is a form of 'disenfranchised grief' as it is not readily acknowledged or validated in wider society, including our workplaces. A failure to appreciate the significance of companion animal loss can occur at many levels, and in diverse situations, but is fundamentally the consequence of a culture that places human–animal relationships in a hierarchy under, or in competition with, human–human ones. Thus, when something occurs that threatens or impacts on a human–animal relationship, people may offer less sympathy, or less-sincere sympathy, than if the relationship were traditionally held in high esteem and respected within the culture. Meyers (2002) argues that: 'the narrow definition of who deserves sympathy and understanding is responsible for inflicting pain on the bereaved that is often greater than the loss itself. It is what isolates and disenfranchises such grievers' (p. 253).[1]

The fact that Western culture diminishes the importance of animal death may exacerbate the sense of despair when a companion animal dies, especially for more vulnerable people experiencing extreme stress. Given the extraordinary quality of our relationships with companion animals, it stands to reason that they figure even more significantly during periods of illness, bereavement, separation and divorce, and most importantly for the subject of this book, during recovery from natural disasters and other catastrophes. Therefore, the death, disappearance or forced relinquishment of a special animal friend as a consequence of a major earthquake inevitably compounds the trauma associated with this event.

At the time this book is going to press, extensive in-depth studies on the emotional impact of animal loss in the Christchurch context post-earthquakes have not yet been published (although see Nikki Evans and Maria Perez-y-Perez's, 2013, analysis of the implications of loss and resiliency within human–animal relationships for social workers). There is, however, a wealth of research derived from elsewhere on the subject of pet loss and adjustment following natural and human-induced disasters. While reports are still emerging following the tsunami that devastated northeast Japan in March 2011 (Goldman, 2011), many studies have already been completed in the United States post-hurricanes, flooding, hazardous chemical spills and the terrorist attacks on New York City. In emergencies, grief for companion animals is complicated by many factors, including whether a bereaved person is coping with multiple losses at once (home, job, family and animals), their age (older and younger people are more vulnerable, as well as those who live with and rely on 'service' animals), and household circumstances (a single person with one companion animal may be affected more profoundly

---

1   Meyers also discusses how erroneous assumptions can be made about a particular individual's capacity to 'healthily' grieve for a lost animal. She cites the example of an elderly woman whose cat dies, and how others may assume she is suffering excessively because she lives alone and the cat provided her company. Instead, it may be the case that this woman has lived through many deaths in her lifetime and is quite resilient and adaptable. Meyers says: 'The perception of the old woman whose cat has died – a pathetic, friendless, fragile person who will fall apart – is a knee-jerk conclusion that more accurately represents other people's attitudes about older people than it does about human–animal relationships' (p. 259).

than a larger family living in a home with many animals) (Podrazik et al., 2000). Hunt et al. (2008) showed that those who lost a companion animal due to Hurricane Katrina experienced similar levels of depression, post-traumatic stress disorder (PTSD) and anxiety as those who had lost their homes; and in some cases, pet loss was a better predictor of depression than was losing a home – both home loss and pet loss caused stress but only pet loss resulted in higher levels of depression and PTSD. Moreover, those who lost both homes and pets experienced levels of psychological distress similar to those felt by people who had lost pets but not homes.

Already we can see the importance of evacuating companion animals alongside their human guardians in emergencies, and, if for some reason this is not achievable at the time, the need to rescue those animals that have been left behind as soon as possible after the evacuation. Although this may seem straightforward, the reality of animal rescue is more complex, in large part because of how companion animals are represented in legal and everyday discourses. Sarah Brackenridge and colleagues (2012) describe the shift in the past 50 years from viewing 'pets' as 'possessions' to seeing companion animals as non-human 'social actors', albeit 'vulnerable dependents', in a similar domain to our children (p. 235). As vulnerable dependents, companion animals influence people's decisions regarding evacuation and shelter during disasters. If companion animals are our valued dependents and we want to shelter and care for them during crises, then it follows that people will not leave their homes if there is not adequate provision for their pets. However, while companion animals may be viewed by many as legitimate members of the family – and as vulnerable dependents – they remain *under law* simply 'possessions', the 'property' of individual 'owners'. As such, they fall under the status of 'things' and are at risk of being treated as 'things' or 'objects' under official civil defence and emergency legislation (some, of course, will also be treated as 'property' or 'things' by their 'owners', as the SPCA's annual *List of Shame* demonstrates). Thus, as Brackenridge et al. (2012) point out, it continues to be difficult to evacuate and shelter companion animals effectively 'due to regulations and customs that relegate pets to the status of possessions' (p. 236).

Hurricane Katrina: lessons learnt from the American experience

To date there is a substantial and growing global body of research into the effects of disasters on animals and our relationships with them. Most studies focus on the impact of natural or human-induced catastrophes on companion animals and their human guardians, although sociologist

Leslie Irvine (2006) has also examined the risks and dangers specific to captive or confined animals living on farms or in zoos, laboratories and pet shops (see also chapter 6).

Brackenridge et al. (2012) provide a useful overview of companion animals and disasters in the context of the United States in the last decade or so. They categorise American research in this field into key eras. The first era (pre-Hurricane Katrina) is characterised by investigations into evacuation and re-entry decisions made by human guardians of companion animals. These studies suggest that failure to evacuate during disasters is linked more to homes containing pets than to other types of homes; likewise, people are more likely to attempt risky re-entries into hazardous areas if they have had to leave pets behind. This was the case in Christchurch when worried people breached cordons in order to retrieve companion animals from the central business district (CBD) red zone following the earthquake on 22 February 2011 (Burgess, 2011). For these reasons, it is vital that disaster management plans and practices take into account the importance of animal family members.

The second era of research into animals and disasters in the American context coincides with the calamity of Hurricane Katrina, which hit Southeastern States on 29 August 2005. A day earlier, the Mayor of New Orleans had ordered evacuation of the city (mandatory evacuation orders had already been given to much of coastal Louisiana and Mississippi). Most residents of New Orleans left, but out of a population of 485,000 it is estimated that around 50,000 people remained – for varied reasons, although the plight of the impoverished and most vulnerable was especially inexcusable and tragic (Giroux, 2006; Bullard, 2010). In scholarship on disaster management, this relates to a model called 'the vulnerability paradigm', which asserts that 'disasters' are not merely extreme events caused by external forces beyond our control; rather, they are 'disasters' precisely because they tend to impact differentially on those who are most at risk in a society where inequality already exists amongst certain groups. In other words, those already marginalised are also those most vulnerable in calamitous situations. Factors that affect people's options and choices in everyday life include ethnicity, gender, age and socioeconomic status; these same factors impact on risk and vulnerability during adverse events.

While there are no official figures detailing how many people stayed because of companion animals, the tremendous number of abandoned animals post-Hurricane Katrina indicates that many citizens chose to leave without their animals, despite widespread television and radio coverage advising people not to abandon pets (Irvine, 2007). Additionally, media coverage showed that many who *had wanted* to take animals with them had been forced to leave pets behind by those ordering evacuations. These converging scenarios resulted in an unprecedented catastrophe for the animals of the city and its affected environs.

One incident captured by media conveyed the heart-wrenching separation of a boy from his dog. America was appalled to watch the now infamous footage of a little white dog, Snowball, being taken from his young friend's arms as the boy was pushed onto a bus leaving the city. Mary Foster from the Associated Press reported: 'Pets were not allowed on the bus, and when a police officer confiscated a little boy's dog, the child cried until he vomited' (cited in Irvine, 2007, p. 23). This image became an iconographic representation of the inadequacies (and indeed the cruelties) of disaster management at that time, which failed to recognise and act on the significant emotional bonds between humans and animals (Zotarelli, 2010), nor did it recognise or value the fundamental suffering of other living beings. Animals were not permitted on the evacuation transport or in welfare centres, such as the Superdrome (which was used as a 'shelter of last resort' in New Orleans), nor did most motels or other forms of accommodation accept animals accompanying human evacuees.

The horrors of animal abandonment, suffering and death were inescapable when viewing American newscasts: numerous reports and televised accounts showed National Guardsmen releasing panicking cats and dogs while their human companions watched on helplessly (Irvine, 2007). As Brackenridge et al. (2012) write: 'images and stories of animals in dire circumstances and pets taken by threat of force from children and the elderly have become part of the collective memory of Hurricane Katrina' (p. 237).

In all, more than 50,000 pets were stranded due to forced abandonment during the evacuation of New Orleans and 80–90% of these animals subsequently perished (Shiley, 2006). Of those remaining, around 15,000 pets were rescued as a result of the largest animal welfare rescue mission in United States history to date (Anderson & Anderson, 2006; Irvine, 2009). Of these, fewer than 3000 pets were reunited with their human guardians, leaving many animals requiring new homes or facing termination, after everything they had already endured. In addition to the companion animal deaths, more than 600,000,000 'production' animals – the overwhelming majority of these were intensively farmed chickens – suffered and died in horrific circumstances (Irvine, 2009).

An international poll of 3000 people conducted a few weeks after Hurricane Katrina confirmed what authorities had failed to realise earlier: 49% of adults surveyed stated they would refuse to evacuate if they could not take pets with them (67% of people polled who lived with animals reported they would refuse, compared to 24% of those polled who did not live with animals) (Zogby International, 2005). Given the salience of companion animals' plight in the wake of the hurricane, and inspired by the story of Snowball, Democrat Congressman Tom Lantos from California proposed the Pets Evacuation and Transportation Standards Act (PETS Act) to the House of Representatives, which would require all states seeking Federal Emergency Management Assistance to ensure pets and service animals were included in their disaster plans, particularly in strategies for evacuating residents from properties. The bill passed with an overwhelming majority on 22 May 2006 – Lantos claiming that he received more support for the PETS Act than for any other legislation in his 25-year tenure in office (Leonard & Scammon, 2007) – and was signed in law by President George W. Bush in October of that year. The PETS Act also allocated federal funds to the development of emergency shelters for pets. The passing of this legislation marked the beginning of the current era, where the welfare of animals in disasters is recognised and officially monitored in the United States.

The experience of saving humans and animals post-Hurricane Katrina highlighted the complex multiple factors and issues at work during effective emergency management. Human differences such as age, gender, ethnicity, physical ability, and socioeconomic status, the closeness of specific human–animal relationships, and factors such as whether or not an animal is classified as a 'pet' or as a 'working animal' (guard dog, service dog) all impacted on decisions about animal welfare. For example, the American experience showed that the elderly, who are already more vulnerable in disasters, were less likely to voluntarily evacuate when a beloved animal's welfare was in question (Laska & Morrow, 2006), while those in homes with children were more likely to leave a disaster zone (Lindell et al., 2005). As Zotarelli (2010) points out: 'Hurricane Katrina demonstrated the complicated nature of disasters and that the quick-acting, single-event models do not account for situations in larger, more complex disasters with varied-timed and forced evacuations and multiple, widespread impact zones' (p. 112).

Importantly, the PETS Act was instigated in the United States primarily as a way to improve outcomes for *humans* caught in disasters: 'The impetus [was] not animal welfare; rather, it focused on evacuating and sheltering pets as a means to improve human evacuation response' (Brackenridge et al., 2012, p. 231). As sociologist Leslie Irvine (2009) points out, traditional emergency management discourse is ultimately anthropocentric, with animals featuring or mattering only to the extent that their welfare impacts on humans' safety and well-being. We would argue, along with many readers, that animals are worthy of protecting and saving in their own right, regardless of whether or not they have a human companion who needs or cares for them. We are now in an age of abundant ethological and physiological research that conclusively demonstrates the diversity and complexity of other species' perceptive, sensory, cognitive, emotional and social worlds (see, for example, Evans & Evans, 1999; Evans, 2002; Horowitz, 2010; Plec, 2013). Although the Cartesian model positing that non-human animals are merely machine-like bodies incapable of serious suffering remains influential in certain domains (vivisection and factory farming, for example), it has more generally been discredited and abandoned as newer and more progressive scientific studies emerge (Allen & Bekoff, 1999; Bekoff et al., 2002; Bekoff & Goodall, 2003; Wise, 2003; Balcombe, 2006; Balcombe, 2010).

Leslie Irvine (2007) argues: 'the primary lesson to be drawn from Katrina's animal response is that animals are part of the human family. They cannot simply be left behind with promises of rescue sometime in the future. Emergency response plans at all levels *must* incorporate pets to avoid the tragedy of New Orleans' (p. 119). Again, in the American context, Sebastian Heath's (1999) extensive research has demonstrated that households containing children are more likely to evacuate during emergencies than those without children; while households containing companion animals are less likely to evacuate than households without companion animals (Heath, 1999; Heath et al., 2001).

We might question why, given Brackenridge's theory that both children and animals fit into the category of 'vulnerable dependants', families with children evacuate more readily than those with companion animals. One key factor influencing non-evacuation of homes containing animals is likely to be a lack of options for those taking animals with them. Traditionally, shelters for humans have not accepted animals. Other factors contribute to and complicate 'failure to evacuate' scenarios. For example, Heath et al. (2001) have found that the more cats a household has, the greater the likelihood that people in that home will decide to stay put, largely because cats are difficult to catch and transport, and because multiple cat households are not always equipped with enough carriers for every cat.

Canterbury's earthquakes: the New Zealand response

The first significant earthquake to strike Canterbury in recent times occurred at 4.35am on Saturday 4 September 2010 and measured 7.1 on the Richter scale, its epicentre situated 40 kilometres west of the city (10 kilometres southeast of Darfield) at a depth of 11 kilometres. This quake lasted 40 seconds and was felt across the South Island and as far north as New Plymouth. It is generally reported that no direct loss of life was associated with this quake; however the tremor did result in power outages, as well as in damage to water and power supplies. New Zealand's National Crisis Management Centre in the basement of the Beehive in Wellington was immediately activated, and Civil Defence declared a state of emergency for Christchurch, and for Selwyn and Waimakariri districts. The New Zealand Army was deployed to assist in the worst affected areas. As a consequence of this event, New Zealand's Earthquake Commission (EQC) received around 157,000 insurance claims; the scale of damage included 12,000 severely damaged homes and 300 resident evacuations to six Civil Defence welfare centres across the city (Glassey & Wilson, 2011). Most people, however, remained in their homes or went to stay with relatives or friends, and because of the lower scale impact on homes, many animals were not affected as much as they were to be in the February earthquake five months after.

Several companion dogs are known to have died following the 2010 event, however; one dog, left behind by his owners when they evacuated, was found dead from a heart attack on their return (Bellis, 2010). Another dog was treated for poisoning after contact with contaminated flood water, and a cat had to be rescued after becoming trapped in a wall while trying to escape (Binning, 2010). A number of injuries were also incurred by animals fleeing homes and other buildings (Muir, 2010). One evacuee reliant on a disability (hearing) support dog was reportedly refused entry to a Civil Defence welfare centre, with staff attempting to separate the dog from this person (Glassey & Wilson, 2011, p. 53).[1] The relatively low rate of human and animal injury and displacement is largely attributed to the fact that this earthquake occurred during the night while many were in bed sleeping rather than undertaking daytime activities.

As outlined in the New Zealand Civil Defence Emergency Management Act 2002, the Animal Control division of Christchurch City Council assumed the lead for companion animal affairs during emergencies. Under this plan, evacuated animals (including species other than dogs) were sent to an animal control facility, with any overflow accommodated at the local SPCA shelter (Glassey & Wilson, 2011). In the days that followed the September earthquake, SPCA Canterbury took the lead in reunification of lost and found pets through their Track

---

[1] This was in breach of Section 75 of the Dog Control Act 2002, which included the proviso that Disability Assist Dogs be given access to public places (Glassey & Wilson, 2011). Since then, the Ministry of Civil Defence and Emergency Management has partnered with the Disability Assist Dog certifying organisations to develop a tag that will be used by all Disability Assist Dogs under the Dog Control Act. The presence of this identity tag signals that the dog is to accompany his or her human guardian into all venues, including Civil Defence welfare centres.

A Pet service, and they also launched a disaster appeal for people with companion animals whose lives had been adversely affected. SPCA Canterbury reported 460 pets registered as lost for the month following the September 2010 quake, compared with 77 for the same period the previous year (Glassey & Wilson, 2011).

National emergency management expert Steve Glassey and geologist Tom Wilson have studied rescue responses and outcomes in order to build a better picture of lessons learnt from the 2010 event in Christchurch, as well as from the New Orleans' experience. Earlier in 2010 Glassey had published a report outlining vital amendments to legislation and practices needed for the emergency management of animals caught in disasters in New Zealand (Glassey, 2010). Combining findings from this pre-quake report with those of a co-authored post-quake study, Glassey and Wilson (2011) proposed the following key recommendations to minimise adversity for animals (and their humans) in future catastrophic events: micro-chipping companion animals (as this facilitates quick and easy reunion with guardians); a single coordinated approach to listing lost and found animals (problems occur when multiple systems are used); the enlistment of veterinarians on Welfare Advisory Groups convened by Civil Defence Emergency Management authorities (to ensure animal welfare matters are included and veterinary clinics involved in local response plans); the need for veterinary clinics themselves to have up-to-date disaster plans in order to be able to deal effectively with inpatients at the time of disaster and with any later influx of injured animals from the community; and the need for all homes to devise plans for evacuation of animal members of the family (including procedures for capture and transport, and knowledge of suitable alternative temporary accommodation).

Glassey and Wilson also asserted the necessity to evacuate companion animals alongside their human guardians, as otherwise both animals and humans are placed at greater risk. They pointed out how, during international disasters, failure to include animals in Civil Defence emergency evacuation plans resulted in 'evacuation non-compliance' (people refusing to leave their homes without pets), illegal re-entries to dangerous areas (when people go back to retrieve animals), and detrimental psychosocial outcomes stemming from forced abandonment and separation.

Steve Glassey – expert on animal welfare in emergencies

Steve Glassey says he prefers not to be typecast as 'the animal disaster man', but he has certainly earned this title in New Zealand. His childhood interests and career trajectory demonstrate a passion for reducing harm to animals, whether this harm is caused by human cruelty towards other species, or by natural disasters and other emergencies. At the age of 13, Steve, who was not allowed to have a dog when growing up, volunteered at the Manawatu SPCA during weekends and school holidays. There he most enjoyed walking and playing with the unwanted dogs. He became New Zealand's youngest warranted SPCA inspector five years later when working for Wellington SPCA. 'They didn't know if there was a legal minimum age for inspectors back then,' Steve admits, 'so they took advice that it should be the same as [for] a police constable'. As a teenage inspector, having to inform older adults that dogs they had neglected or hurt were to be removed into care, was in Steve's words, 'a character-building experience'. Despite his young inauguration to animal welfare inspection work, he says with a smile that he was never assaulted.

Steve has also worked for a range of other organisations, including St John ambulance, the Ministry of Civil Defence, and the Ministry of Social Development chairing the national welfare coordination group. He has also worked overseas for the United Nations' World Food Programme. In 2008 Steve completed a Masters degree at Charles Sturt University in Australia, specialising in the management of animal welfare during emergencies. Along with Ritchie Dawson (see chapter 1) and others, Steve helped set up Wellington SPCA's Animal Rescue Unit, and he was also a member of the National Animal Welfare Emergency Management advisory group. More recently he has been involved in aid agency work in the Philippines following the devastation wrought by Cyclone Haiyan/Yolanda. In 2013 Steve took up employment as the Associate Director of the University of Canterbury's Centre for Risk, Resilience and Renewal (UCR3), which promotes research and teaching in the area of disaster management.

When the February earthquake struck Christchurch, Steve, who was then working at Massey University in Palmerston North, came south with a graduate student, Todd Balogh, who had also worked with the Animal Rescue Unit (see chapter 1). Steve was assigned to the University of Canterbury's Rescue Team, which he led into the city to conduct house-to-house checks. He also ended up working with the Taiwan search and rescue taskforce, which arrived on 24 February 2011.

Steve advises that there are two key lenses though which to view

Opposite page: New Zealand expert on animal welfare in emergencies, Steve Glassey, with his German Shepherd Diesel.

animal emergency management. 'Disasters can strike developed and less-developed countries,' he explains. 'In a less-developed country, the focus is on survivability, on keeping livestock safe and healthy because these animals are essentially bank accounts on four legs for the people of poorer communities. In developed countries, the focus tends to be on companion animals. In either case, protecting animals actually protects the people – you save animals, you save people.' Steve provides an example that demonstrates the different priorities of developed and less-developed countries following natural catastrophes, as well as the need to take both human and animal welfare into account when disasters strike. After one event in Myanmar, an important goal was to prevent famine and economic devastation by quickly re-establishing the rice fields that had been flooded. Normally, oxen were used to sow rice, but they had perished. One aid agency focusing on human welfare brought in seeding machines to help sow the rice, but these required maintenance and petrol and eventually stopped functioning. Another agency brought in more oxen from a different region, but within a year they had all died because they were the wrong breed of animal for this type of work and had not been vaccinated against diseases in that area. 'There were important veterinary issues that hadn't been considered ahead of these decisions,' Steve explains. 'This is where an organisation with knowledge on how animals and humans connect can offer vital assistance. For instance, WSPA (World Society for the Protection of Animals) would be able to come into this situation with qualified veterinarians who would determine the appropriate breed of oxen and whether or not to introduce a rebreeding programme. It's important to understand veterinary science, too, when providing effective interventions for people and animals in need after disasters.'

When it comes to a developed nation like New Zealand, Steve says the focus of emergency management has been more on companion animals. 'It is vital to realise that pets are part of the family here and they shouldn't be left behind when people are evacuating. I think there is still a mind-set that prejudices animals – you know, it's that "people first!" mentality that disaster and action movies often show – but by excluding animals you actually put people in harm's way.' Steve's thesis research demonstrated that 99% of pet owners in New Zealand identified animals as part of their family, while nearly 60% stated that they would refuse to leave in an emergency unless their pets could go with them. A further 63% of pet owners reported that their pets were important in helping them to cope in times of stress and distress. Steve also cites the high rate of animal deaths following Hurricane Katrina in New Orleans – while more than 15,000 pets were rescued during the largest animal rescue operation in United States history, 80–90% of the pets in that city were left behind. The majority of these abandoned animals perished (Glassey, 2010).

Another real-life case study, Steve reports, involved a small town in Wisconsin affected by the derailment of a 'dangerous goods' train carrying propane. The volunteer fire brigade ordered the evacuation of the entire town but required its residents to leave pets behind. 'After two days 50% of pet owners in this town had tried to breach the cordons to retrieve their animals,' Steve says. Out of frustration, on the fourth day following the derailment, one pet owner rang up the emergency operations centre with a bomb threat. 'This got into the news, the governor got involved and ended up deploying the National Guard to go around the town and collect all the pets!'

Closer to home Steve recalls how, during the Napier siege of May 2009, residents of the street under guard were evacuated with instructions to abandon their animals. 'Then because everyone was worried and complaining, the armed offenders squad had to organise food drops for the animals left behind. This put people at risk. It's actually safer for everyone if animals are evacuated with people.' Steve is also quick to point out that this does not indicate pet owners are eccentric, irresponsible or unreasonably demanding. He recounts how police officers involved in the same siege also re-entered a risky area in order to retrieve a police dog stuck in the back of a utility vehicle outside the offender's residence. 'Police officers know when a dog starts training that she or he will be put in harm's way – that this dog is not a pet – but they still develop a special bond. It always comes back to that bond.'

Speaking of the bond between human and canine – after decades of waiting, Steve is finally able to have his own dog. He has now settled in Christchurch with his wife Lisa, and the couple adopted a one-year-old German Shepherd called Diesel in January 2014. 'He's an absolute little character,' Steve declares. 'He's very much part of the family and constantly fooling me with his cuteness.'

While drawing upon accounts of the 4th of September 2010 event, this book concentrates predominantly on the devastating earthquake of Tuesday 22 February 2011. This magnitude 6.3 tremor, which struck the Canterbury region at 12.51pm (a busy lunchtime in the city), was centred 10 kilometres southeast of Christchurch (2 kilometres west of the port town of Lyttelton) at a depth of 5 kilometres. Tragically 185 people were killed, most of these fatalities occurring in the CBD where buildings collapsed, in some cases because infrastructure had been weakened during the September shakes. The government declared a National State of Emergency, which stayed in effect until the end

of April 2011. The worst-affected areas of the city were central and eastern suburbs, as well as Lyttelton and surrounding environs on Banks Peninsula. Substantial liquefaction occurred, in eastern areas in particular, producing 400,000 tonnes of silt. Christchurch residents' lives – both human and non-human – were immediately and extensively affected. Two further significant quakes measuring 5.6 and 6.3 struck within two hours of each other in the early afternoon on Monday 13 June 2011; and on Friday 23 December 2011 a series of large aftershocks measuring 5.8, 5.3 and 6.0 on the Richter scale once again disrupted life in New Zealand's second largest city.

In the following chapters we examine how different species living in Canterbury were affected by the region's seismic activity. Part One concentrates on the experiences of professionals and volunteers associated with animal rescue, shelter and advocacy, including local veterinarians, Christchurch City Council's Animal Control unit, SPCA Canterbury, Wellington SPCA's Animal Rescue Unit, Massey University's Veterinary Emergency Response Team, Dogwatch, Wellington's HUHA (Helping You Help Animals) Sanctuary, Cat Rescue Christchurch, Cat Help, Cats' Protection League Canterbury and Save Animals From Exploitation (SAFE). We also present the accounts of a local veterinarian, Debbie Yates, who witnessed and helped to treat the immediate and long-term health effects of the quakes on her animal patients, and the story of local hero, Paul Dahl, who took responsibility for ensuring the animals of Lyttelton were cared for after the February 2011 disaster. Part Two focuses on the personal tales of human guardians and their companion animals in the aftermath of the earthquakes. Chapters 3 and 4 feature feline and canine earthquake stories respectively, while in chapter 5 we report on the experiences of other companion species living in the city (turtles, rats, horses, cockatiels and chickens), as well as those of urban wildlife (hedgehogs and seabirds), the exotic and native species inhabiting Orana Wildlife Park, and the people who helped these animals during the turmoil in Christchurch. Chapter 6 examines the impact of natural or human-induced catastrophes on our most vulnerable animals, those living in confinement in laboratories or on factory farms.

In the conclusion to this book we revisit New Zealand's current situation regarding the management of animal welfare during emergencies, and, with advice from the country's experts, recommend ways to enhance the protection, safety and welfare of animals caught in disasters.

Opposite page: A refugee in safe hands with HUHA (see chapter 2).

Jo Moore

Part One
Rescue, Shelter and Advocacy

Opposite page:
Wellington SPCA's Animal Rescue Unit in the CBD red zone.

Blair Hilyard/ARU

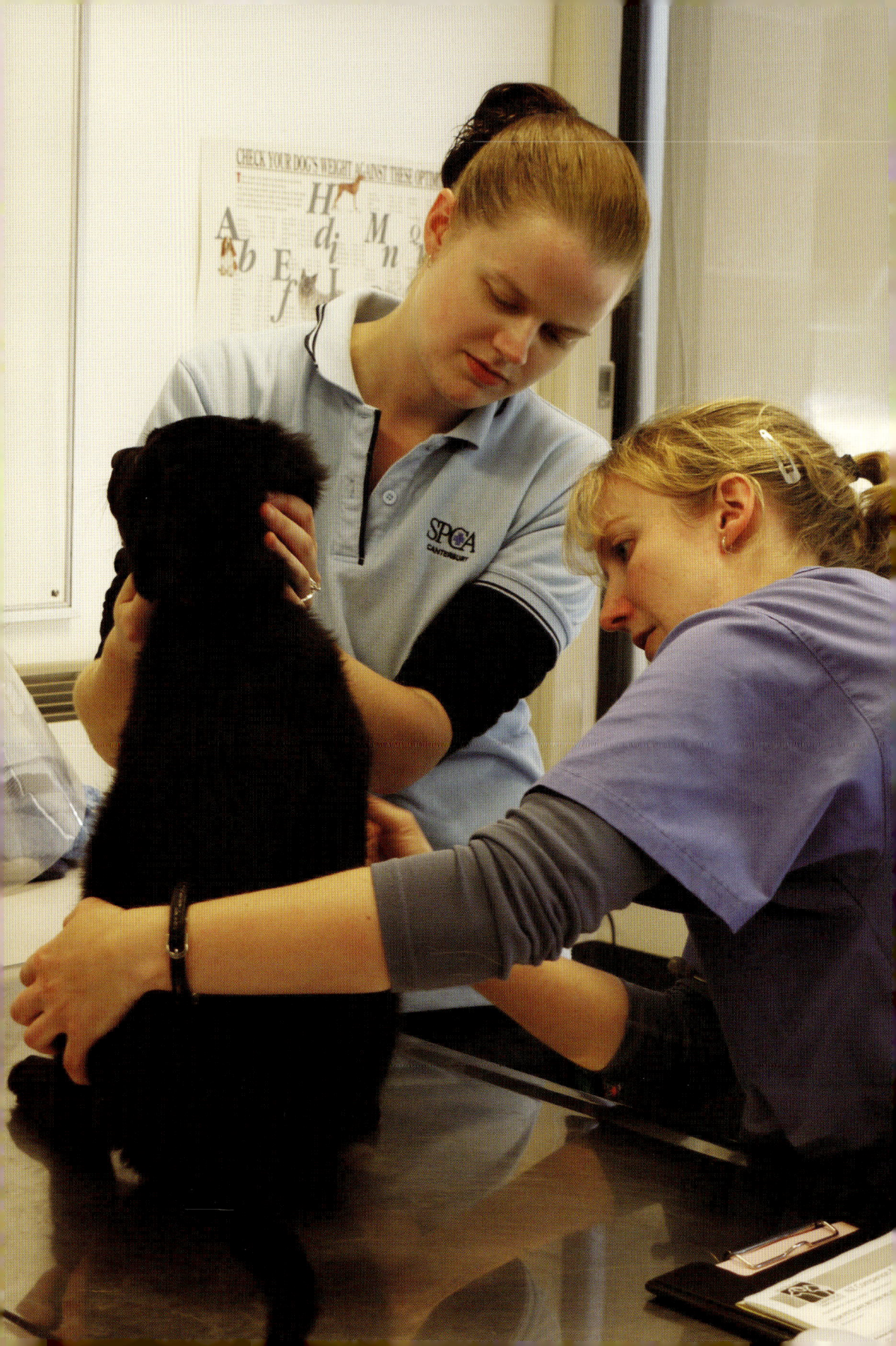

Chapter 1
Front-line responders

In this chapter we focus on the expertise of those national and local agencies involved in planning for and managing the welfare of companion animals when disasters strike. We include the accounts of professionals at the Society for the Protection of Animals (SPCA) in Canterbury, Christchurch City Council's Animal Control unit, Wellington SPCA's Animal Rescue Unit (ARU) and Massey University's Veterinary Emergency Response Team (VERT). We also report on the physical traumas and medical issues that affected animals immediately after the earthquakes – and which continue to upset them now – as relayed by veterinarian Debbie Yates, who works at a clinic in one of the more damaged suburbs of Christchurch. New Zealand is fortunate to have a group of dedicated experts who offer guidance on, and lobby for, more effective planning and management of animal welfare matters in emergencies. This chapter therefore also introduces the National Animal Welfare Emergency Management (NAWEM) advisory group and its achievements to date.

SPCA Canterbury

SPCA Canterbury, whose administrative centre and animal shelter is based in Hornby, west Christchurch, would play a pivotal role in maintaining the welfare and safety of companion animals following the earthquake of 22 February 2011. While the city had experienced a substantial magnitude 7.1 tremor on 4 September 2010, in the words of Geoff Sutton, central manager of SPCA Canterbury at the time: 'that experience became but a dress rehearsal for February 22nd'. The SPCA had looked after the animals of evacuees following the September earthquake, but it had not been tested by serious animal injuries or a

Opposite page: SPCA staff checking a puppy for injuries after the 22 February 2011 quake.

SPCA Canterbury

need for rescues. However, the earlier earthquake did result in far greater awareness of the need to have effective management plans in place.

When the magnitude 6.3 quake struck Christchurch at lunchtime on 22 February, staff members were all together at the SPCA complex. The quake could be felt there, but its devastating impact was not immediately apparent to them as the greatest damage occurred in the east. Geoff Sutton recalls it felt like 'another big aftershock'; even those animals residing at the SPCA at the time were not overly concerned. Education Officer Jasmine Lewis remembers: 'I was walking past the cat adoption area and looking in the window, and there was a cat sitting on the very top of the shelf. When the earthquake happened I went back in to check the cat, and she was still asleep on the top shelf!'

They realised the gravity of this event when a woman visiting the Centre to adopt a kitten answered a cellphone call from her husband advising her to come straight home as the city was in chaos. They turned on the television (the SPCA facility retained power) and the enormity of the disaster became evident. 'As part of our normal response, we met as a team and divided the responsibilities of building, property and animal inspection,' Geoff recalls. 'Within half an hour we reported back together that all was good on site; however news of the devastation in the city was filtering in and we knew from September that we had to prepare for a major undertaking. We worked to the plan that there would be three distinct phases to this disaster: reaction, response and recovery.'

In anticipation of incoming animals, the team hurried to feed and water those animals already on site and secure all housing areas. Staff members whose homes were located in what were presumed to be the worst-affected areas were sent home. 'For those who remained, it was all about preparing the Centre for the influx of animals from owners made homeless.' Within two hours, procedures had been put in place that would identify earthquake-related arrivals from other animals at the Centre. Geoff explains: 'All our normal paperwork, which was on black and white, was pulled out of everywhere and replaced with pink paper so we could identify what we called the "EQ animals". Pink was the colour for anything related to the earthquake.' A special separate register for 'EQ animals' was also set up. In preparation for an influx of quake victims, staff cleared out one complete dog unit and a complete cat unit.

The first EQ animals began arriving around 3.30pm, approximately two and a half hours after the earthquake had struck. While the majority of pets dropped off by distressed people leaving the city were dogs, SPCA Inspector Alex Walker recalls that the first official EQ animal to reach the SPCA's Hornby shelter was actually a cat called Brownie. 'Unfortunately, he did not return to his original owners,' Alex says. 'Some people just couldn't take their animals back. But he did eventually find a new home.' Luckily, the percentage of animals left in the care of the SPCA by distressed people and never reclaimed was low. Geoff believes more than 95% of animals who arrived at the SPCA following the February quake were beloved pets whose owners had brought them there to be cared for because they just needed to flee the city for a while. 'It might have taken two to three months, but these animals went back to those people,' Geoff confirms. 'I can still remember quite vividly the passion, the huge responsibility of dealing with distraught people and trying to give them confidence that their animals were going to be fine with us. We needed to let them know they could trust us.'

Staff started work early the following day. Not only had a disaster struck, profoundly affecting the lives of the city's people and animals, but it was also a typical kitten season, and pre-quake feline numbers at the Centre were already higher than usual (prior to the influx of EQ animals, 170 animals were already being sheltered at the complex). 'Communal cat living was a going to be a reality,' Geoff explains, 'so we had to introduce some non-negotiable rules to enable us to accept more cats'. One rule required owners of entire (non-castrated) male cats to agree to the neutering of their cats within 12 hours of drop-off. Another rule required that anyone dropping off kittens surrender them to the SPCA so that new homes could promptly be found for them: 'While we would take care of adult animals for an unspecified time, kittens needed to be adopted without delay.'

The decision was made to contact South Canterbury SPCA, four hours' drive south in Timaru, to ascertain whether this agency could help out with the growing numbers of 'owned' animals being received as people left the city. Two days post-quake, and being increasingly called upon to help displaced companion animals, SPCA Canterbury moved 9 owned dogs and 23 owned cats to its off-site boarding facility. But as Jasmine explains:

> At the same time we knew that over the coming weeks and months we would have even more general SPCA animals coming in too – more strays and lost animals. That's when we contacted other SPCAs around the country and asked them to help out by taking some of the cats we already had up for adoption. They were cats who had been living here long before the earthquake even happened. We sent them to Auckland, Gisborne, Hokitika, Greymouth, Otago and Southland.

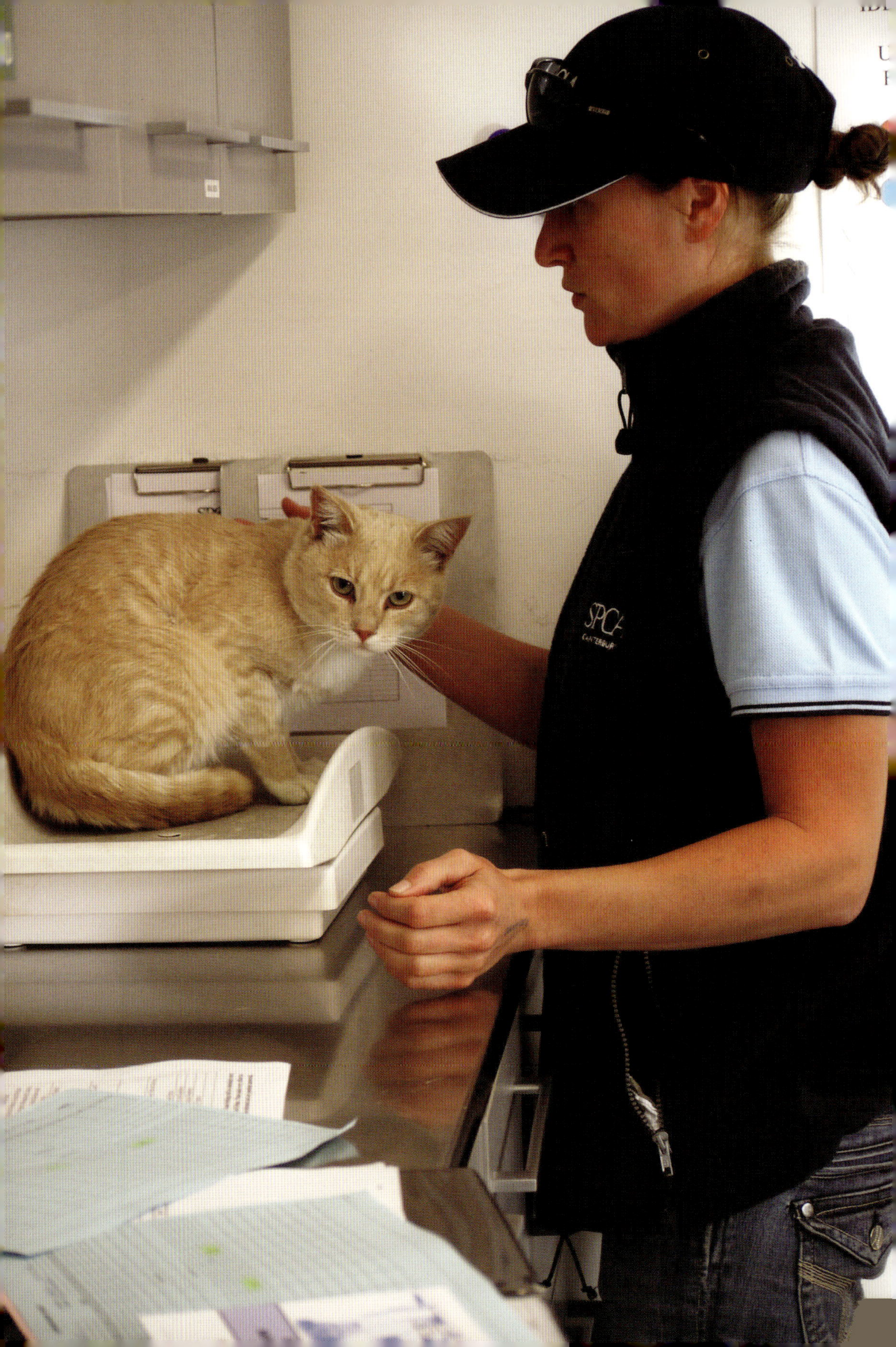

By day two the SPCA was also responding to animal rescue calls associated with injured and exhausted cats and dogs found on the streets. One cat was found on the SPCA doorstep with internal injuries – she had apparently crawled there herself. 'And we had some stressed dogs who'd been running the streets and had suffered abrasions and injuries to their pads,' Auxiliary Officer Ingrid Morris recalls. 'We also had animals showing massive signs of stress and feeding off their owner's stress as well.' As Geoff explains:

> Animals are so much like children. If the people who care for those animals or children are upset, then they will be too. If everything is calm around them, they think it's OK and that they don't need to be worried. We can also generate a lot of fear in animals by our own anxious behaviour.

By day four the SPCA was receiving 150–200 calls per day (this continued until mid-March 2011), and a database was established to enlist offers of help from the public. It became apparent that animals living in some of the worst-affected areas were getting hungry. In response, two tonnes of pet food were picked up from the SPCA's Centre and delivered by helicopter to Sumner, a seaside suburb that had become inaccessible by road, as the causeway linking it to the city had been ripped up in the shaking. In all, between 15 and 20 tonnes of food and bedding were distributed to collection points in the most damaged parts of the city.

'We also set up food and water stations for cats,' Field Officer Vanessa Hampton remembers. 'We were knocking on doors to ask about cats we found, and sticking notes on cats asking "Do you own this cat?" There were two Burmese cats we called "the lions", they were lovely, and they'd come waltzing out of the bushes when we called them. They were owned by a vet who had set them up with access to their abandoned home via a cat door and he left them lots of food, too. They were well fed!' Geoff comments: 'We'd been around long enough to know the last thing we wanted to do was prematurely remove a lot of animals from where they lived. It was better, unless they were unwell, to let them stay there to calm down, and we'd feed them and give them water, until their owners could come back.'

In situations where human lives have been profoundly affected by a natural disaster, it is often several days before animal welfare agencies feel it is appropriate to draw attention to the fate of animals. This has been the case in disasters occurring in New Zealand and overseas. However, the lack of publicity about animal welfare post-earthquakes

Opposite page: SPCA Field Officer Vanessa Hampton recording details of a cat whose family had to vacate their home after the 22 February 2011 earthquake.

SPCA Canterbury

in the first few days after the February event obviously did not reflect what was actually happening on the ground during this time. As Geoff Sutton points out:

> There was a lot of coordination in the first four or five days following February 22nd, even though it was day three or four before we got media attention and were able to talk about the plight of the city's animals. You've got to remember that whilst animals mattered to us and they mattered to the public, there was so much tragedy happening to humans; we had to wait until a lot of the rescue work was done and that took a few days before media was starting to widen the sphere of interest.

By 26 February the media were relaying in earnest the SPCA's advice for pet owners to act responsibly and care for affected animals, and imparting information from the SPCA about where advice or help could be obtained.

The records of the SPCA over this time report that within the first three weeks following the earthquake, staff worked 12-hour days, seven days a week, the Centre taking in more than 200 abandoned or stray animals – 182 were cats, 7 were dogs and 11 were a mixture of farm animals, small mammals, fish and birds. A veterinarian was on site most days so that incoming EQ animals could be immediately assessed, de-fleaed, vaccinated and micro-chipped. Additionally, 97 animals were left there in temporary care by owners forced to evacuate their homes or otherwise needing time to cope with the aftermath of the earthquake. Sixty of these owned animals (43 cats and 17 dogs) were temporarily transferred to South Canterbury SPCA in Timaru, in order to free up space for more arrivals in Christchurch. All animals temporarily relinquished like this were allocated an EQ number and cared for separately from the centre's other animals (57 EQ animals were cats, 35 were dogs).

More than 120 animals were adopted directly from SPCA Canterbury, 23 cats were transferred to other South Island branches of the SPCA for adoption, and 21 were returned to owners from the stray animal category during this period. As well as the more typical companion dogs and cats, SPCA staff remember being asked about found rabbits, fish in tanks, displaced chickens and goats. Budgies and other birds caught outside – having flown from their cages when they tipped over – were also brought to the SPCA by concerned people. Not all these species were housed at the Hornby Centre, as more appropriate temporary shelter could be found for them elsewhere.

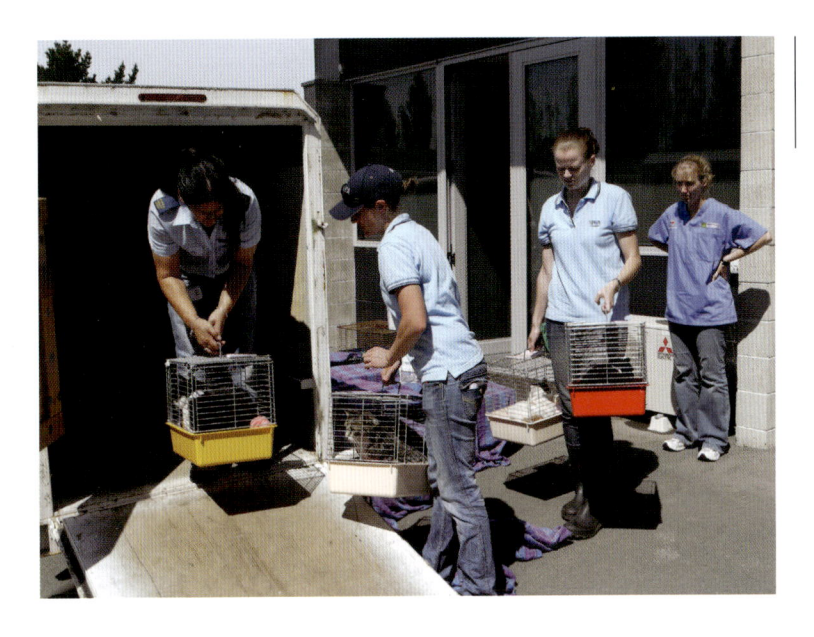

SPCA staff and volunteers preparing 'owned' cats for their journey to Timaru.

SPCA Canterbury

Because of the sheer numbers of animals being processed by the Centre following the earthquake, the normal Track A Pet service offered by SPCA Canterbury was not in operation; instead the public was asked to assist by reuniting lost animals with their owners via the online agencies Trade Me and Pets on the Net. These domains (as well as one called Animal Aid, set up by SAFE and discussed in chapter 2) were posting 'Lost and Found' notices on special webpages dedicated to the Canterbury earthquakes.

Unfortunately, SPCA inspectors also encountered the sadder side of animal abandonment and neglect after the quakes. 'People would take everything and go – just leaving the dog behind at home,' Geoff recounts. While this behaviour may be considered an extreme response in the face of unparalleled trauma, it is also the case that such occurrences are routinely handled by SPCA staff on typical work days. Disregard for and abuse of animals is a reality for those who work or volunteer for the SPCA. 'That's a difference we live with every day,' Geoff says. 'We deal with people who love their animals beyond belief and they are their life, and we also deal with the ones who couldn't care less. This difference was there before, it was there during the earthquakes, and it is there after them. It's the way people see animals in their lives and their families.'

While many people simply abandoned their pets, others showed extraordinary kindness. Ingrid recalls hearing of an elderly man whose wife was incapacitated, and their house severely damaged: 'They had no power and had to leave, and he was standing on the edge of the

SPCA staff member Maria Petrova rescuing a dog abandoned after the February quake.

SPCA Canterbury

road after the quake, with his wife in the wheelchair and his dog beside them. Then a complete stranger pulled up and said, "You've got plenty enough to worry about, let me help by taking your dog", and so this person took the dog and drove straight to the vet, who then figured out this dog was diabetic and needed insulin. The stranger paid the bill and rang us to arrange temporary accommodation for this dog.'

Similarly, Jasmine recounts:

> We also had a lot of people in the community just getting on with what needed to be done. I took a call from someone who lived in a cul-de-sac in a badly affected suburb, and everyone from that cul-de-sac had fled, leaving their animals behind, but she stayed and fed those animals for two or more weeks. She called us because she had run out of money to buy them more food and all she wanted from us was help with food.

Cats tend to stay within their home territories and, even if they initially run away in fear, are more likely return to their homes when things settle than to go somewhere else. It is for this reason that the SPCA advised people who were displaced from their homes and could not find their cats, or were not permitted to take them to their temporary accommodation, to ask neighbours to look out for their cats and feed them. But this woman's compassion towards both the people and the animals in her deserted neighbourhood seems exceptional.

Jasmine also remembers more instances of the kindness of strangers: 'We had a massive truck pull up one day with eight pallets of food for us, and we don't have a forklift so we rang Meadow Mushrooms next door and they sent a man in a forklift who loaded all this food for us. It was really cool.' Another way the public helped was by matching found animals to those listed as lost. 'People everywhere would help us. They were sitting there on Trade Me on the lost-and-found pages. People in Australia were trying to find matches!'

The phrase 'tale of two cities' has become widely used in Christchurch since 22 February 2011. It seemed to many that the city was divided into those areas, generally west or north, that had been largely unaffected by the devastating summer earthquake and were able to carry on as normal, versus the eastern districts where homes, businesses, roads and shops had been ruined. 'Half the city was just absolutely shattered and the other half of the city had water and power,' Geoff says. 'I remember being amazed by the number of people from less-affected parts of Christchurch who, two or three days after the big quake, came in to adopt animals.'

Unpacking veterinary supplies at SPCA Canterbury, February 2011.

SPCA Canterbury

While staff members at the SPCA spend their working lives helping traumatised animals, after the quakes some of them were returning home to look after their own feline or canine companions who had been affected by the city's seismic activity. Even now Jasmine's dog, Sasha, is terrified by the world shaking around her. 'Sasha hides between my legs, to the point that if a truck drives past our house she thinks it's another earthquake,' she explains. 'Even in the backseat of the car, when the car is moving, she thinks it's an earthquake.' Post-earthquakes, Jasmine is involved in humane education (the teaching of compassion and respect in human–animal relationships) in schools:

> When I tell a story to the children about my dog and how she is with aftershocks, I start by asking who has animals at home freaked out by the quakes, and at least two-thirds to three-quarters of the kids in the room put their hands up. I guess if I asked how many of them have been freaked out by the quakes too, the answer would probably be the same. All the stressors people are going through, their pets are going through as well.

Geoff agrees: 'Without a doubt people's lives are more up in the air now … people have lost their jobs, their homes, so there is additional stress out there we wouldn't have seen prior to the earthquakes. But I think it's really that this is the new normal for Christchurch. We're still adjusting.'

SPCA staff also experienced the same kinds of worries and personal reactions to the devastation of Christchurch that affected other residents of the city. The disaster had a profound impact on Jasmine at the time:

> My house wasn't damaged, my family and I were lucky. But I've lived in Christchurch my whole life and I couldn't get my head around the fact that everything I'd known had changed forever. I struggled with that for a good week after the quake, and I was really only capable of coming in and cleaning out cat litter trays because I couldn't cope with much more than that. I was involved in helping out the EQ animals who had been moved off-site, so there was a big responsibility there and I got chosen to do that because I'm pedantic. An owner could ring up and ask how their cat was, and I could give them a rundown of what they ate that morning and how they were feeling, what patch of sunshine they were sitting in that day!

In the middle of such environmental and personal chaos, the staff at SPCA Canterbury managed to remain steadfast professionals. One EQ animal was to provide a constant ray of sunshine for them throughout the bleak days and weeks of late summer in 2011. This creature was not a dog or a cat, but a humble wild pigeon who was given the name of Barney Rubble because he had been rescued from the debris of the collapsed Christ Church Cathedral. Vanessa recounts:

> I was on call the day Barney arrived. We heard from a rescuer who had been searching for people trapped in the fallen Cathedral and had instead found this bird. When I picked the bird up I saw he was the most dusty, lethargic little pigeon. The rescuer had obviously seen some horrible tragic things and was determined not to leave this bird behind so he called us. We helped the pigeon recover by feeding and caring for him.

Barney Rubble at a television news interview. He is being held by Ross Blanks, SPCA veterinarian and board chairperson at the time.

SPCA Canterbury

The city was to shut down as a mark of respect at 12.51pm on Tuesday 1 March, a week after the disaster; Barney seemed well enough to return to the wild and the staff planned to release him, at the same time, in their own special memorial gesture. 'We did attempt to release him in this memorable way the week after the quake. At that time there was still the firm belief that half a dozen people had been trapped when the Cathedral collapsed – they were still desperately trying to find these people,' Vanessa explains. 'Barney was so symbolic to us – we thought he might have been the only survivor, the only one who got out of the Cathedral. It was very emotional. And we thought he was ready … but he wasn't. He landed unceremoniously after we let him go that time, and so we had to look after him for another three weeks until he could leave. Now we think Barney's probably back in the Cathedral because he flew off that way.'

In autumn 2011, the SPCA launched a couple of important campaigns. One in March 2011 focused on micro-chipping and was organised in conjunction with local Canterbury veterinarians, the New Zealand Companion Animal Register (NZCAR) and the New Zealand Companion Animal Council (NZCAC). 'All the animals we adopt out are micro-chipped for good reason,' SPCA Inspector Alex Walker explains. 'A lot of the animals we received after the quakes were not micro-chipped, which meant tracing these animals back to owners was very slow. Being able to reunite owners with pets within a short time would have been really helpful to us. So on the back of this knowledge we ran a "Chip Your Pet for Free" campaign where we distributed free micro-chips throughout Christchurch – 10,000 animals got micro-chipped during that campaign, which was funded by the SPCA.' It is a sobering fact that 85% of micro-chipped animals were reunited with owners post-quakes, compared with a rate of just 15% reunion for non-micro-chipped animals and their owners (New Zealand Press Association, 2011). The second major campaign undertaken by the SPCA that year involved desexing companion animals, as many of the animals received by the SPCA following the February event had not already been desexed when they were surrendered.

Now, more than three years later, the SPCA front-line team members reflect on what they learnt through their professional experiences at the forefront of animal welfare in the wake of the city's crisis. At the time, the constant review of operations was essential in order to quickly address any issues and ensure the best outcomes for animals. For those organisations facing similar events in the future, Geoff advises:

> Insisting on owner responsibility in the first instance is a must, and this needs to be supported by access to useful advice on how they can achieve this. Also, during what we called the 'Reaction Phase' – the first three to four days – a sound level of preparedness is vital because outside help is not likely during this time. We learnt that at least two separate systems of operational communications are necessary. We now also realise how important it is to keep our vehicles topped up. We got caught out, with three of our response vehicles running out of fuel in a city with minimal petrol stations open and queues at the pumps. Luckily, we found a station catering just for emergency vehicles, but this taught us that you never know when disaster will strike so keep the tank topped up!

Christchurch City Council's Animal Control unit

Mark Vincent has worked for the Christchurch City Council for nearly 40 years; 30 of these have been as Team Leader of Animal Control. He is passionate about his ability to help dogs and humans. 'I have a huge emotional and professional investment in this city, one I cherish and take seriously, in particular when helping the animals that live here,' Mark says. 'The animals don't have a voice and we have to act for them. I remind my field officers: "If you walk onto a property and the dog doesn't have shelter, food or water, then that's your one chance to make a difference to that dog's life." If they turn their back on that dog, there may never be another chance.'

Christchurch City Council's Animal Control unit operates in a uniquely progressive way that is not always fully understood or appreciated. Specifically, Mark and his team are keen to support people to live safely and happily with dogs, as a valued part of the community. To this end, the Council's Animal Control unit offers educational assistance to dog owners. 'We want dogs and the community to safely cohabit and for dog owners to understand the potential risks dogs can pose to other people,' Mark explains. 'Not everyone likes dogs so we need to be aware of that. Our "dog safe" school education programme targeting children promotes the "dos and don'ts" of keeping safe around dogs.' Animal Control also encourages people to keep dogs safely contained on their properties so as to ensure they do not create a nuisance. When a dog is found roaming at large, the unit's policy is to return the dog to his or her owner as quickly as possible, without penalty. 'There are significant benefits to the dog, the owner, the Council and the wider community for taking the dog home,' Mark points out. 'We'd rather teach people how their dog is escaping and change that situation than punish them with fines.'

Another key initiative of Mark's team – thankfully undertaken prior to the devastating earthquakes – focused on preparation for animal welfare and care during unforeseen emergencies. 'I was watching the news about Hurricane Katrina in 2005, and I saw people trying to save their animals who had perched on roofs,' Mark recalls. 'Rescuers told one woman she had to leave, but she couldn't take her dog with her. She refused to go without her dog though. I remember thinking at the time that I didn't want a similar situation occurring in Christchurch in the future.' Consequently, Mark and others established the Animal Welfare Emergency Response Team (AWERT). Mark outlines how this was instigated:

> I talked to Civil Defence and the Council and explained we needed to get ourselves organised and be prepared for any emergency. We all agreed that the Council's Animal Control unit, the SPCA and other agencies in the field of law enforcement and animal welfare should be involved. We had a number of meetings as a big group and each year from 2007 we also conducted simulated training exercises relating to emergency management of animals. Staff members broke into groups and had specific jobs or roles.

This resulted in the development of streamlined operations in the event of any natural disaster striking the city. Should a disaster occur, Mark and his second-in-command would take on the role of chief coordinator, splitting 12-hour shifts between them each day. Animal Control staff would separate into three key domains: extraction and evacuation, identification and communications, operations and welfare. Mark explains:

> These main areas had their own leaders and on the trial runs we conducted – which were like games because all sorts of situations and scenarios were thrown at us so we could strengthen our responses as a team – we found out what worked and what didn't. We ran one at Hagley Community College, where we set up kennels that the operations division looked after. We had people coming in with their dogs – it was like a mock-up – and we acted as we would have in an actual event. We explained the process to them, registered the dogs, and then put identification tags on them so we knew which

> dogs were there and who they belonged to. We then took care of them and when the people returned it was easy to reunite them with their own dogs.

The training paid off. Mark laughs: 'We thought at the time "that's a bit of fun!" and then a couple of years after we'd begun these trial situations it actually happened. And when the first earthquake struck on September 4th 2010 we all arrived at work as soon as daylight came and were immediately back into the roles we'd rehearsed – we were able to coordinate things and know how to manage the situation effectively from the start.'

After the September event, welfare centres at Burnside High School, Linwood College and Addington Raceway – established for people living in areas without water, power or sewerage – were also equipped with facilities to care for companion animals. In each of those compounds, AWERT had a person in charge of receiving dogs and cats, putting identity tags on them, placing them in kennels on site, and ensuring they were fed, watered, exercised and looked after, while their owners were accommodated inside the centre. Mark clarifies how it all worked:

Christchurch City Council's Animal Control unit Team Leader Mark Vincent with his companion dogs Max and Teddi.

Mark Vincent

> When there is an emergency the public are asked to go to a designated high school – we call them 'sectors' – and if you arrive at one of these centres you would find Civil Defence and Red Cross there. If you have animals with you, we would stop you at the gate, receive your pets and care for them outside the centre. Red Cross and Civil Defence ensure you have food and water and a place to sleep. They also attend to any human health needs. The beauty of setting up animal welfare centres alongside the places where people go is that you can see that your animals are OK, and that they are cared for, so you have peace of mind. If you're at one of these centres, you probably have enough to worry about – at least you can be reassured that your pet is well looked after.

Mark also believes the availability of such facilities, which cater for both animal and human welfare needs together, is essential for the safe evacuation of people and their pets when emergencies strike. 'It's actually dangerous to leave animals behind,' he points out. 'There's a risk to the rescuers, to the person being rescued and to the animals forced to stay.'

Animal Control's response to the major quake of 22 February 2011 was, according to Mark, a replay of September's exercise. However, this time there were larger numbers of frightened stray dogs found on the city's streets. 'We had a lot of kind people bringing dogs they'd found to our Bromley shelter. People also brought their own pets to us and they didn't always return for them. Sometimes they were just too traumatised by the whole event, they never came back to reclaim a dog.' Despite the tragedy for these dogs of having been moved from their family homes, Mark proudly recalls that not one dog who arrived at the shelter as a consequence of the earthquakes had to be destroyed. He praises his staff and the shelter's Bromley neighbours Dogwatch (see chapter 2) for helping scores of dogs to find new homes. As Mark explains:

> The dogs people relinquished to us weren't bad dogs. They were frightened, though – it was a very traumatic time for them, too. But it wasn't so much the earthquakes that affected these dogs as the upheaval that happened in people's lives and homes afterwards. Life couldn't go on as before, and the routine they were used to was suddenly gone. They got confused and ran away.

Other organisations and charities across the country also helped the lost and abandoned dogs of Christchurch by donating money and practical items such as blankets, bedding and food to the shelter.

Mark is quick to point out how professionally the staff at Animal Control handled these unprecedented events. The shelter lost power and water after the quakes in both September 2010 and February 2011. This meant that kennels could not be easily cleaned and drinking water was not readily available for the canine residents. 'An amazing woman called Clare in our communications centre did everything she could to find us water and to have food delivered here on a regular basis, despite the chaos in the city,' he recalls. 'We got big tanks of water and we went to food companies and asked for dog roll. We didn't experience any health problems with our dogs despite the lack of water for regular cleaning. We had the gates open 24/7 and staff working around the clock. We had rotational shifts because people were also finding dogs out on the streets at night and bringing them here.'

Animal Control was also inundated with people offering practical help. 'We had volunteers coming out of the woodwork,' Mark exclaims. In particular, one person stands out in his mind:

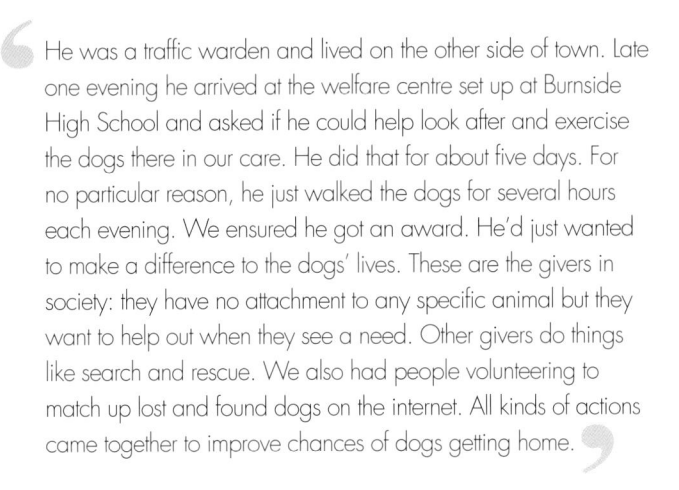

> He was a traffic warden and lived on the other side of town. Late one evening he arrived at the welfare centre set up at Burnside High School and asked if he could help look after and exercise the dogs there in our care. He did that for about five days. For no particular reason, he just walked the dogs for several hours each evening. We ensured he got an award. He'd just wanted to make a difference to the dogs' lives. These are the givers in society: they have no attachment to any specific animal but they want to help out when they see a need. Other givers do things like search and rescue. We also had people volunteering to match up lost and found dogs on the internet. All kinds of actions came together to improve chances of dogs getting home.

There is one important measure that Mark cannot emphasise enough when it comes to ensuring frightened canine escapees can be returned home quickly and easily after disasters strike: micro-chipping. This is why Christchurch City Council's Animal Control unit provides free micro-chipping for dogs every Wednesday morning at its Bromley animal shelter. As Mark points out:

> The micro-chipped dogs were able to be reunited with their owners straight away because we knew who they belonged to. If an owner was in a welfare centre when we called them to say their dog had been found on the streets, then we could reassure them we would take care of the dog. There were never

any charges imposed on these people. When something like this occurs, then it's covered by Civil Defence.'

There are around 35,000 dogs in Christchurch city, the highest number of dogs in a single city in New Zealand aside from the greater Auckland area. From his vast experience of managing Animal Control services for the city, Mark believes 98 per cent of dog owners are good people and want to be responsible dog owners.

'We take a different approach to animal control here – we're trying to help people, to educate them about how to care for their animals themselves, because we care about their animals too. I don't like dogs being in the shelter here. If that shelter was empty every day I'd be happy. And if the dogs aren't micro-chipped and no one claims them then we have to put them down. No dog deserves to be in there.'

This progressive, canine-focused perspective of Christchurch City Council's Animal Control staff affected how this unit dealt with animals displaced by the earthquakes. As we have seen, Animal Control worked with other agencies to ensure the short- and long-term well-being of individual dogs, rather than merely 'policing' local communities and incarcerating canine refugees.

On a more personal note, Mark describes the emotional impact the earthquakes and their repercussions had on him:

'I can remember being at home on June 13th 2011 and another big earthquake started. I grabbed all five of our dogs because my wife Kim and I were fearful for them. I took them outside and I started crying as they panicked, and one of neighbours asked me if I was OK because I was as white as a ghost. Sometimes those quakes were really frightening – I was afraid for the animals. And then you see your house shaking – having the living soul shaken out of it. I'd experienced earthquakes before in Christchurch, they were little ones, and I used to think they were quite cool actually, but these ones were something else. They change your life. You get a different perspective on things. All of a sudden you don't care so much about your home and possessions – what's important is the safety of my wife Kim and our dogs.'

Ritchie Dawson – the all-important middle man

When the February earthquakes struck, a four-person Christchurch Disaster Management Team focused on animal rescue was established, comprising Ross Blanks (SPCA Canterbury president and veterinarian), Geoff Sutton (SPCA Canterbury chief manager at the time), Stephanie Saunders from Dunedin (SPCA Southern Regional chief inspector) and Ritchie Dawson (chief inspector of Wellington SPCA). This team apportioned roles, responsibilities and reporting lines – vital aspects in ensuring an efficient and smooth-running operation not just of animal rescues but also of animal fostering and rehoming post-earthquakes. Ritchie Dawson was a founding member of Wellington SPCA's ARU, the first group of its kind in the country comprising experts in animal rescue and care in emergencies. Ritchie trained at national and international disaster management courses run by the World Society for the Protection of Animals (WSPA), and has had experience working as part of WSPA's

Wellington SPCA Chief Inspector Ritchie Dawson with a foster kitten he had rescued from an abandoned garden where she had got entangled in netting.

Ritchie Dawson

Disaster Animal Rescue Team in Samoa following the 2009 tsunami and in Fiji after Cyclone Thomas. He is also a long-term member of NAWEM (see pages 58–60).

After assessing the situation on his arrival in Christchurch, Ritchie quickly deployed Wellington SPCA's ARU and became SPCA Canterbury's liaison person between this unit, NAWEM and Civil Defence. He also acted as triage assessor of all animal-assistance requests received by the SPCA from the public. 'I was in the bunker,' he says. 'Calls would come into reception, they were taken down in note form and then brought to me. My job was to prioritise these in terms of urgency, and then we would get staff to respond. We were also shipping food out to local vets. There was a lot of food being given to the SPCA by the public and also by companies to be distributed to others in need.'

Ritchie recalls being overwhelmed by the generosity and selflessness of people in the face of such an immense crisis:

> I spoke to one man who had arrived home in Christchurch after driving for 12 hours and he'd found everything upside down in his house. He looked for and found his cats, checked his neighbours were alright too, and then he came all the way over to the SPCA from the other side of town where he lived, with several huge bags of cat food and a $100 donation for us. He was exhausted – mentally, physically and emotionally – and he just asked me if there was anything he could do for *us*!

Ritchie suggests that for some people, helping others is an important way of coping with devastation. 'When your place is wrecked, your life is upside down, and there's nothing you can do, then you want to go out and help someone else.' He recalls some people who drove down from the North Island in a 4-wheel drive with a horse float full of all kinds of animal supplies: 'They drove all the way from Taupo, went across Cook Strait, and kept collecting food from people wherever they went.' Ritchie helped arrange for this group to be led by the ARU through the Lyttelton tunnel, which had been closed to the public after the quakes, in order to deliver the food to the animals in the cut-off port town.

Ritchie's role involved organising animal rescues within restricted areas and arranging the return of animals uplifted from the red-zoned central business district (CBD) to their owners waiting outside the Civil Defence cordons. He also received calls concerning the animals used in teaching by Christchurch Polytechnic Institute of Technology's (CPIT's) veterinary nursing school, and the elderly cats stuck in an inner city apartment building. Both rescues were undertaken by the ARU and filmed for the first episode of *SPCA Rescue*'s sixth season on television. However, as Ritchie points out: 'You see these things on TV but you don't really realise the enormity of it. The rescuers have to carry lanyards around their necks and tags with their personal details available, and when they go into a building they leave these outside so we will know who's in there if the building collapses. These people are putting themselves at huge risk to help dogs and cats and other animals.'

Ritchie also ensured that staff from the SPCA or ARU checked out properties reported to contain abandoned animals. In such cases, a notice was left on the door stating that the home had been visited by animal welfare officials and asking the home-owner either to remove the notice from the door if the animals were being looked after, or to contact the SPCA Centre if they needed help taking care of them. 'We actually had a lot of people returning to their homes to care for animals – they just couldn't physically live there. Other times when neighbours rang up because they were concerned animals weren't being fed, we asked them to help look after the animals in the meantime. Most were very willing to help. The community really pulled together – it was terrific to see.'

Shamus Jackson from ARU attaching an SPCA notice to a resident's door.

Blair Hillyard/ARU

One of the biggest lessons Ritchie feels people should learn from this disaster regards fish (see Conclusion). Essentially, the fish in Christchurch city were casualties of a lack of preparation. 'We were finding them in homes. But the teams in the red zone were locating fish all the time because of all the shops and restaurants in there.' Local pet shops were generous in providing tanks, filters and food for fish rescued from the CBD red zone and deserted houses in the suburbs. Although human–fish relationships are likely to be trivialised or dismissed in an anthropocentric society, it is important to realise that fish are treasured by some as a companion species. Ritchie recalls one fish tale with a happy ending: 'One of my jobs was to liaise with agencies like Housing New Zealand and council housing. If we found animals in state or council properties and we didn't know who they belonged to, we could send these agencies a list. Their night teams would go through our records and then let me know the details of owners and we would try to locate where these people had gone. Through this process we found the owner of five goldfish we'd rescued and they were really happy to get the goldfish back for their children. It made all the difference to them.'

During his time in animal rescue triage and liaison post-quakes, Ritchie witnessed both the wonder of human–animal companionship and its downside. 'Disasters like this bring out the best in people, and also the worst. It's all about communities being ready. If you have cats and dogs you have a responsibility. It doesn't matter whether it's a Civil Defence emergency or some other type of incident. You've still got responsibility. You can't leave your animal behind and think someone else will deal with it.' He stresses that the Animal Welfare Act does not just cease to apply during disasters. 'Then there are those people who really shine. Being in Christchurch was an awesome experience for me, quite humbling. The people at the SPCA had all been affected, either personally or through family and friends, and yet every day they soldiered in there. They were coming in tirelessly – on their days off too. I walked in fresh – I had my family to think about in Wellington but didn't have any family connection in Christchurch. But the people there soon became family.'

The Animal Rescue Unit (ARU)

Wellington SPCA's Animal Rescue Unit (ARU) is unique in New Zealand as it provides a highly skilled, technical rescue service for trapped animals. Its members have all completed first-aid, health and safety, and specialist rope-rescue training, as well as instruction in high-angle rescue so they can assist with retrieving animals from cliffs, trees, small spaces (such as under houses) and holes in the ground (see http://www.wellingtonspca.org.nz/aru.htm). Blair Hillyard, the Rescue Manager of ARU when the team was deployed to Canterbury, has 25 years of experience of volunteer fire-fighting, Civil Defence and SPCA work. 'We're all competent at abseiling – we actually qualified

Wellington SPCA's Animal Rescue Unit (ARU).
From left: Kelly Adams, Shamus Jackson, Blair Hillyard, Olena Khytko, Jill Brakensiek, Samantha Hughes, Emily Meilink. Absent: Alicia Sloan.

Blair Hillyard/ARU

with certification to rescue people and basically adjusted that to fit animals,' Blair explains. While Urban Search and Rescue (USAR) teams focus on the rescue and recovery of humans, the ARU attends to the humane rescue of animals. Blair says that, having been called out to many regional incidents, the ARU's deployment to Christchurch was the first time the team had assisted at a national disaster.

On their way to Christchurch from Wellington, ARU travelled in convoy with Massey University's Veterinary Emergency Response Team (VERT) (see pages 52–57). Blair recalls: 'Every place we stopped on that trip south we were greeted by applause. At Kaikoura we bought food and fuel and met many people who had just left Christchurch – it was very humbling to speak with them – our eyes were opened to what really lay ahead of us when we got there.'

Arriving in the devastated city at midday on Sunday 27 February, Blair went directly to the SPCA Centre in Hornby where he met with Geoff Sutton and Ritchie Dawson to devise a plan forward. It was decided that ARU would lead the rescue and recovery of any animals still trapped inside the red-zoned CBD (as well as respond to situations requiring their unique skills in the wider Christchurch area), while SPCA Canterbury would concentrate on those abandoned, displaced and lost animals outside the red zone.

An ARU van navigates its way through the CBD red zone.

Blair Hillyard/ARU

Chapter 1 : Front-line responders | 45

While USAR teams searched for human victims in apartments and houses in the CBD, the ARU worked alongside them, managing any shaken or aggressive animals who were trying to protect buildings and potentially injured people. 'Because every property, every room, was being systematically checked, we were being called in whenever USAR found an animal,' Blair explains. ARU was split into two key groups that often converged to enter some of the more high-risk buildings in order to carry out a rescue operation. One group had high-angle gear, and was focused on access to higher structures, while the other group worked with heavier tools. The individual physical capability, skills and experience of the team members were also factored into tasks. When asked how the team coped with fear of the unknown, and the potential risk involved with entering unstable buildings when aftershocks were occurring regularly, Blair replies:

> It's all about accepting risk. We make calculated risk assessments of any buildings we're going into. Every member has to set some rules about how far they are willing to go. We always note where the closest window or the nearest door is to get out. Then we can't really worry about it further because we have a job to do.

Although the team entered buildings only after engineers had first checked them, there were still many scary moments. Blair recalls how just being in the red zone was challenging to the senses and nerves: 'There was always an intense smell of rotting food – that's the first thing that would hit you. A lot of the time, in order to get into certain buildings to retrieve animals, we had to go through holes the USAR task forces had cut, then work our way down and across several buildings, sometimes through a restaurant or a shop to get in, as some buildings didn't have any front or back doors any longer.'

A usual day for members of the ARU commenced at 5am with a team briefing. 'We had to make the most of every sunlight hour because the dangers of the red zone tripled at night with there being no lights there,' Blair recalls. 'It was very eerie in there after dark. Apart from a few of the large task force teams working around the clock on certain buildings, and police patrols, the red zone was effectively empty at night.' The early morning meeting was followed by team briefings inside the red zone and then the day's tasks were carried out. Operations usually wound up around dusk and the team would dine with others at the rescue base in Latimer Square before returning to their accommodation at the Royal New Zealand Air Force base in Wigram, where a final team debrief would be completed.

ARU in the city.
Blair Hillyard/ARU

One incident to which the ARU were called out involved elderly cats trapped inside apartments in the CBD (the rescue of these two cats was filmed for *SPCA Rescue*; see also Ritchie Dawson's story above). Blair recounts how precarious this operation was: 'The building we'd arrived at had another building leaning on it that had tipped over in the big quake.' An engineer passing by agreed to conduct a quick examination of this property for ARU. When he signalled that it was safe to proceed, they entered through the ground floor. 'It's hard to describe – it was dark and full of the smells from broken sewerage pipes and decaying food,' Blair says. 'The engineer had us go up one person at a time so we weren't overloading stairwells. It was a slow progression and on each floor the engineer would do another series of checks. When we got to the floor the cats were on he said, "It's looking OK", so we forced the door on the first address, got in and found the cat. She was just asleep on the couch in the sun and quite happy! She'd been feeding off food from the fridge that had tipped over.'

Suddenly the situation became more urgent. 'We were about to search for the next cat when the engineer came running back and said, "We need to get out of here! Make this one real fast!" He didn't tell me why, but his face had gone completely white!' Despite the imminent danger, the ARU team forced open the door to the second apartment to find the second cat. 'Even the engineer was rushing around trying to find the cat – he wanted out! It was so hot too – we were wearing helmets, dust masks and gloves for protection.' This cat proved to be more timid than the first. 'She was very scared and had made her way to the back of a cupboard and was nestled in amongst the towels. It was a big search in a big hurry!'

Thirty-five minutes had passed by the time they all re-emerged to the safety of the street, both cats secure in carriers and ready to be handed over to their owners who were waiting at the 'animal transfer point' on Moorhouse Avenue, in the car park of the Countdown supermarket which had been closed due to quake damage. 'It was a fantastic feeling,' Blair says. 'We were reuniting family. These people were so relieved to have their cats back.' On the episode of *SPCA Rescue* that documented this rescue, the owners of these cats speak of their delight in having their elderly feline companions returned seven days after the February event. 'Chloe is nearly 19,' remarks Eleanor Davis. 'I thought she'd cope but wasn't sure she could last for a week.' Glenis Fisher tells the camera: 'Last time I saw my cat was nine o'clock on the morning of the 22nd and we hadn't seen her since. She only had enough food for two days.'

ARU encountered a range of domesticated species during their rescue operations – from cats, dogs, hamsters and rabbits in the CBD to chickens, goats and pigs in more rural areas that had been evacuated due to rock falls or power and sewerage outages. They also recovered fish that had survived in tanks in commercial buildings in the CBD.[1] One of the more unusual species rescued by ARU was a tropical shark living in premises associated with the sex industry. 'One of the Australian USAR team members found a tiny red shark and radioed us about it,' Blair says. 'We knew it was a shark from the position of the fins – but it wasn't going to eat anybody – it was too small!' (The shark was eventually rehomed after attempts to locate the building's owner were unsuccessful.)

Another ARU call-out, which has become a Christchurch urban legend, involves the rescue of a parrot from a building in the CBD red zone. In one version of this story, the parrot is called Dimitri and was never found. In another rendition, the parrot was rescued. Blair is able to

---

[1] One story of extreme survival following the February earthquake involves two goldfish in a display tank in the reception area of Quantum Chartered Accountants in Christchurch's restricted downtown area. They endured 134 days without food or electricity to power their tank filter, apparently living off algae and possibly the remains of four other goldfish who perished during those months. The fish have since gone to live in the home of the firm's company director (*NZ Herald*, 27 July 2011).

confirm the correct details of 'the parrot rescue story', and it is perhaps even stranger than fiction. 'About our third night in Christchurch, a USAR task force was inside a building on Colombo Street where they'd made access to a superette on the ground floor,' he explains. 'They'd conducted a search with cameras and found an open cage with no parrot inside it, so they wondered if they might come across the missing parrot when they kept cutting through this building.' Consequently, ARU was contacted to help locate the bird. 'It was pitch dark and they were using the snap chemical lights, while we were searching for the parrot,' Blair recounts. He continues:

> We heard a big bang, which is not a good thing to hear under those circumstances, and a fireman comes crashing through the door yelling "I've got the parrot! I've got the parrot!" We were all there in the dark as every torch went onto him, and he was actually just holding a teddy bear parrot! He was even giving it CPR! It was one of those funny moments that occur when you're operating on only three hours' sleep. We still don't know what happened to the *real* parrot, but we did manage to rescue three fish!

To complete this tale, the guardians of these fish were eventually traced and the reunion of these aquatic companions with the children was no less joyful than if the fish had been treasured cats or dogs: 'The kids had been petrified their goldfish had died,' Blair recalls. 'They meant everything to them – they'd raised these fish from when they were small and they were now *really huge!*'

One of ARU's more intense jobs involved retrieving around 20 animals used for teaching purposes by CPIT's veterinary nursing school. The multi-species group, including one terrapin, two chinchilla, two rabbits, cockatiels, budgies, canaries and rats, were located on the third floor of a red-stickered building considered unstable. In the *SPCA Rescue* episode covering the earthquakes, Stephanie Ballantine, head carer for these animals, waited anxiously to be reunited with her wards. She told the reporter: 'I know animals are pretty much down the ladder in terms of priority, but to me they're the most important. They're my babies. I mean, I've got three children, too, but these guys are part of my family as well, so it's been hard knowing they've been up there without food or water for six days.' Stephanie was particularly concerned about Boomer, an elderly rabbit, but he was retrieved, safe and well. The fish kept in this facility had all perished.

Another situation attended by ARU involved the rescue of 40

Emily Meilink cares for a rabbit living on an evacuated property.

Blair Hillyard/ARU

chickens from Avoca Valley, near the city side of the Lyttelton tunnel (and therefore very close to the epicentre of the February 2011 earthquake). All the residents of Avoca Valley with houses under the hill were required to evacuate due to the risk of rock falls being triggered by aftershocks. A police guard was preventing people from returning to feed their animals. The scenario facing ARU in Avoca Valley demonstrates how important it is to recognise and validate that a diversity of species are considered close companions of humans. The guardian of these hens refused to leave her home until the chickens were also safe and being cared for. 'They were her birds and she wasn't leaving the property,' Blair explains. 'Other people might feel that's quite irrational but she cared very much for these chickens. If she was forced to leave then, no matter what, she would want to return to look after the hens.' Ritchie Dawson (see page 41) located a rural property where the flock could go, and the woman expertly gathered her chickens together. ARU was then able to collect and transport these birds to their new safer location, thus preventing a police confrontation and forced evacuation. 'It made this person's life easier and helped the lives of her chickens too,' Blair says.

By 10 March 2011, when ARU's deployment in Christchurch finished, the team had retrieved 90 animals from dangerous situations, and

Shamus Jackson feeding chickens on Bridle Path Road, Heathcote Valley.

Blair Hillyard/ARU

helped reunite many pets with their worried guardians. 'The complete and utter relief was obvious on people's faces when we returned their loved ones,' Blair recalls. ARU also received positive feedback from American and Australian USAR teams which had not encountered a systematic and highly trained animal rescue team during their previous deployments. 'They thought it was fantastic that New Zealand has got animal rescue organised like this. Even during Hurricane Katrina these USAR teams hadn't seen dedicated animal rescue squads that could come into a building behind them and help out with any animals.'

Just as their arrival in the damaged city of Christchurch took some adjustment, returning to their routine lives in Wellington also produced a shift in perspective for ARU members. Blair admits:

> It was really strange going back home. It's very mentally draining and so intense for that period of deployment. And everywhere you go from then, you are assessing things like where is safe to park your car. You're looking at the height of buildings. We were always looking upwards! And wishing we didn't live in brick houses!

Massey University's Veterinary Emergency Response Team (VERT)

> For me, when I went into the red zone, I just felt complete numbness. I don't think you could ever be prepared to walk into that. It was so quiet in there, even though there were armoured vehicles everywhere. It literally looked like a warzone, unbelievable and very surreal. But when we began working with the USAR dogs we were so focused on them that I forgot what was around me.
>
> The reality hit me on the week anniversary of the February quake. We were all taken to the CTV building site for the minute of silence, and it was an extremely emotional time for everyone. We all stopped and thought about why we were there. We saw family members of the victims holding up photos and a boy playing the bagpipes.

— Hayley Squance, VERT team leader

The next story in this chapter is told by Massey University's recently established Veterinary Emergency Response Team (VERT), led by veterinary technologist, NAWEM member and animal emergency management expert, Hayley Squance. VERT is based at the Institute of Veterinary, Animal and Biomedical Sciences at the Palmerston North campus, and comprises 12 members with proficiency in small-animal and equine surgery, veterinary nursing and technology, epidemiology and animal behaviour. VERT was the first such group of its kind in Australasia, and its members were initially trained by Steve Glassey (see pages 14–17). The team is skilled at conducting technical rescues and performing disaster assessment and veterinary treatment in the field. 'We adapt human rescue operations – such as those involving high rescue or water – to situations involving animals,' explains VERT's animal behaviourist, Rachael Stratton. 'We volunteer our time, and fortunately our employer Massey University allows us to attend emergencies and helps us by providing a vehicle and other equipment.'

VERT is associated with WSPA's disaster management division and is able to be deployed both nationally and internationally if required. As Hayley explains:

> We work with local authorities and other agencies such as the fire service and the SPCA in a support role in response to

> emergencies or disasters involving animals. Such a response is important because natural disasters in New Zealand and around the world have highlighted the need for animal care in times of crisis. Many owners have risked and lost their lives for their animals, and thousands more have felt long-term emotional and financial impacts of animal loss.

As soon as the February earthquake occurred in Christchurch, the team went on standby; those available for deployment – veterinarians Fred Pauwels and Rachael Stratton and veterinary nurse Jenny Nixey, led by Hayley Squance – were called south three days later by Ritchie Dawson (on behalf of NAWEM and the SPCA Canterbury). The VERT team travelled to Christchurch on Sunday 27 February in convoy with the ARU, and stayed with their Wellington counterparts at the Wigram air force base.

Like the ARU, this was the first time VERT had been able to use its specialised training in an extreme national emergency. Post-quake reports of animal injuries were few, so by the time the team arrived in the damaged city it had been decided that its most useful contribution would involve clinical assessments of the 28 police and service dogs assisting the USAR crews in the CBD red zone. Rachael, who had previously worked with guide dogs, had already been contacted while in transit to Christchurch about one of the USAR dogs (Sacha) who had become depressed and was refusing to eat or drink. They arranged for Sacha to go to the After Hours clinic (see page 61) and be looked after there. Hayley recalls:

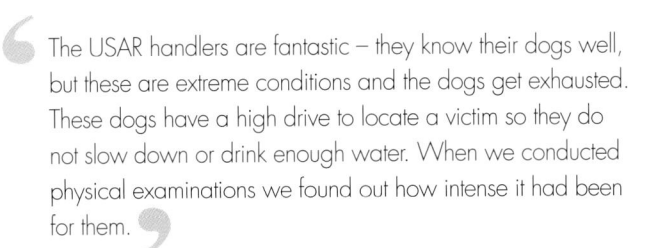

> The USAR handlers are fantastic – they know their dogs well, but these are extreme conditions and the dogs get exhausted. These dogs have a high drive to locate a victim so they do not slow down or drink enough water. When we conducted physical examinations we found out how intense it had been for them.

When assessing dogs returning from a shift, the veterinary team looked for problems associated with cut pads or legs, dust in their eyes and noses, and checked levels of hydration, and fatigue. They also noted any issues with toileting, and whether or not dogs were coughing or sneezing. 'We were correcting dehydration, and also giving prophylactic fluids to prevent dehydration occurring,' Jenny says. 'We were flushing out eyes and noses. The dogs all had their own diets, which their teams brought along, and you don't change what they're eating in case this upsets their stomachs.' VERT members also provided physiotherapy for cramped muscles, took blood, urine and hair samples from dogs to check for exposure to toxins such as lead, and set up a decontamination unit for the USAR dogs within the cordon area. While the local rescue dogs could be brought out of the cordoned-off zone for more intense treatment, quarantine regulations did not permit those dogs who had arrived with the Australian, Japanese and Singaporean crews to leave the restricted areas. 'We had to stand down one of the dogs on the Australian team, but he went into a quarantine area to be rested and treated,' Hayley recounts.

Rachael, Hayley and Jenny all recall special bonds they formed with the service dogs they helped. They agree that treating service or working dogs is very different from caring for companion dogs. 'The dog is an extension of the handler and the rest of the rescue team as well,' Hayley explains, 'so you're not only treating the dog'. The canine handlers of USAR teams worked long shifts of 12 hours or more, which explains why VERT members were also working such extreme hours, with a usual day starting at 6am and finishing after 11pm. 'The New Zealand and Singaporean handlers and their dogs had day and night shifts, while the Queensland crews initially worked around the clock,' Hayley says. 'Different teams had different ways of managing their dogs, too.'

Jenny recalls one experience early on that brought home to her the precariousness of the environment they were working in: 'I had a needle in a dog rehydrating her and we had an *almighty thumper* of an earthquake … I couldn't believe Christchurch people put up with those on a daily basis! It was something like 5.6 on the Richter scale – they called it an aftershock, I called it an earthquake!' However, she remembers how quickly those on the front line adjusted to the frequently shaking ground beneath them. 'We were at the Japanese

Massey University's Veterinary Emergency Response Team (VERT) assesses the health and well-being of Singaporean USAR dogs, February 2011.

Hayley Squance

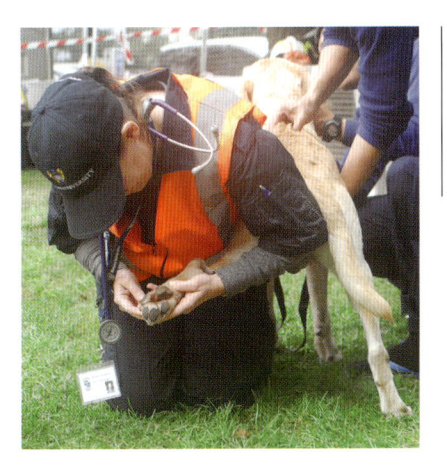

VERT Team Leader Hayley Squance checks one of the Singaporean USAR dog's gums (left) and paws (right).

Hayley Squance

USAR camp later, under the trees treating the dogs, and then there was a *huge* jolt! We all just stood there, nobody spoke, there was complete silence, and then when the tremor stopped we all just kept going on with what we were doing.'

Unlike the other agencies discussed so far, VERT had explicit responsibility for evaluating the capabilities of Christchurch's veterinary clinics post-quake, in order to ensure that the health requirements of the city's animals could continue to be met. 'There were quite a few clinics that were unable to operate or sustained significant damage,' Hayley says. 'I remember one vet whose practice had been badly damaged and who had converted his own house into a makeshift clinic. Vets were mostly doing pro bono work, too, because they knew that animals were important. They still had drugs they could use but were limited in what they could do. The worst affected areas were like that – regardless of the situation their own homes and families were in, vets and nurses would be still trying to help out and keep clinics operating.'

Hayley also reports cases of people, in post-quake panic, relinquishing animals and later regretting this:

> Animals were moved out of Christchurch because shelters were over capacity and owners felt like they had nowhere to take their pets. But people need their animals close by as they are known to be important during times of stress to help them cope, particularly for older adults as the pet may be their only companion. Some people thought they would be able to see their pets again but they were adopted out and did not return. It's easy to see how things could have been improved with hindsight, but at the time it was an urgent and difficult situation to manage.

In 2011 the VERT team faced specific challenges associated with being a newly established voluntary group of veterinary professionals focused on the clinical treatment of animals in emergencies. 'Because it's a team dedicated to helping animals, we don't receive financial assistance,' Rachael says. 'Animal rescue isn't viewed as significant or necessary in the same way human rescue is. If we had been deployed by Civil Defence we would be able to claim expenses, but because at that time there was no animal welfare component to the legislation, animals were not on the radar, so to speak, and we were not entitled to any compensation.' This observation was repeated by people from across all of the other animal emergency response teams, from the SPCA to ARU. As Hayley, whose 2012 Master's thesis explored educational needs in animal welfare emergency management, points out:

> From an emergency management perspective, animals haven't mattered as much even though there is no doubt that animal welfare improves human welfare during crises. Unfortunately, we sometimes have to step away from the fact we are focused on helping animals – we've had to redirect this focus in order for authorities to listen to us – it is a human issue. The research is there that shows what happens to animals impacts on humans, and it's just slowly filtering into emergency management now. Also, it's just so important for the animal suffering too – but with so many people hurt, it's difficult to say "What about the animals?" It's a sensitive issue. We were warned that if we went into areas that hadn't seen any form of help, we might experience some resentment that we were there to evaluate the animal welfare needs. In fact it was the opposite, people were thrilled that we were there to ensure the animal members of their family were thought of and there would be care available if they needed it.

This situation reflects the lower status attributed to animals in Western culture, but Jenny draws attention to how such indifference can go a step further, with companion animals mattering more than 'financial animals'. Hayley agrees: 'Production animals are the most vulnerable. During the September earthquake over 3000 chickens were killed on a battery farm. In the February 2011 event, cattle and sheep were killed on hills due to crush injuries from falling boulders and rocks.' The other side of this paradox is that statistics are kept on those animal victims whose deaths affect human businesses or profits (that is, farmed animals), whereas records of other animal fatalities that occurred following the quakes have not been kept or are very difficult to find. Hayley knows of one dog crushed to death alongside his owner when parts of a building fell on a parked car in the February 2011 earthquake, but says this animal's death has not been reported anywhere. 'There was no one collating information – who would this even be reported to?' she asks.

After their intense ordeal of working with the USAR dogs in the red-zoned CBD, Rachael and Hayley voiced unexpected regrets on the journey home. 'I felt kind of guilty that we were in the lucky position to help out but then able to leave,' Rachael admits. 'In Christchurch there were people and animals who would have to keep enduring that awful situation long after we were safe back home'. Hayley also recalls 'the very sombre drive back' to Palmerston North:

> I missed my family but what I felt that I most wanted to do was go home, pick up my dog and drive back down there. I wanted to take my dog there for people to pat – a dog who wasn't a working dog, but a companion dog. I thought this could help the rescuers cope, as well as others within the red zone, and Christchurch residents too – just to have some normality in the midst of everything they were enduring. I had that feeling for almost a year afterwards.

If there is one thing Rachael, Jenny and Hayley want to emphasise after their experiences in Christchurch it is the need for national emergency management policy and national, regional and local plans to factor in protection and care of animals following unforeseen disasters. 'The nation has to acknowledge there is an urgent role for animal welfare in emergency management and this must be written into the Civil Defence Emergency Management Plan,' Hayley stresses. 'After the February quake, VERT was a small cog in a very large wheel. I felt privileged to be in Christchurch then. But it was also really important that we were there to ensure the animal welfare component was recognised'.[1]

Hayley Squance with her dog Zia.

Hayley Squance

---

1 VERT's role with USAR dogs did not end with the team's departure from Christchurch. They were also involved in follow-up research led by Kate Hill and undertaken at Massey University's Centre for Service and Working Dog Health. This required the monitoring of those dogs who had worked in Christchurch's CBD for any after-effects and evidence of exposure to toxic substances. VERT members took blood and urine samples, and also questioned dog handlers about the canines' working hours, diets, and possible exposure to contaminants. The results of this study showed there were no abnormalities or physical ill-effects following the dogs' involvement in USAR searches post-quakes (Rachael Stratton, personal communication, 30 May 2012).

National Animal Welfare Emergency Management (NAWEM) advisory group

National Animal Welfare Emergency Management (NAWEM) advisory group, March 2014. *From left*: Wayne Ricketts (NZVA), Roger Poland (MPI), Hayley Squance (Massey University), Leonie Waayer (MCDEM), Bridget Vercoe (WSPA), Mark Ross (Federated Farmers), Ritchie Dawson (SPCA), Paul Molloy (Department of Internal Affairs). Absent: Les Dalton (Animal Control group), Annie Potts (NZCAC).

At the time the Canterbury earthquakes occurred, the New Zealand Civil Defence Emergency Management Act did not provide for a coordinated approach to the evacuation, rescue and assistance of animals affected by natural or human-induced disasters, nor did it detail effective planning or procedures for them. The SPCA has always played an important role in caring for displaced and abandoned animals, but this is problematic when faced with a large influx of animals as the result of a disaster, in part because the SPCA is a registered charitable trust relying on donations. While ratified human welfare agencies are compensated under existing legislation, animal welfare organisations assisting during emergencies are not, because until now they have not been officially called upon to assist by Civil Defence Controllers.[1]

In 2006, in the aftermath of flooding in the lower North Island and a major snow storm in Canterbury, a group was formed in New Zealand to represent agencies concerned about improving animal emergency management and planning. The National Animal Welfare Emergency Management (NAWEM) advisory group, as its name suggests, provides advice on matters pertaining to animal welfare during emergencies. Members of NAWEM are appointed by various professional bodies,

---

[1] The Civil Defence Emergency Management Act (2002) identifies clear and specific organisational arrangements in disasters, including the appointment of group and local controllers. Specifically, group controllers coordinate, and local controllers manage, accessibility to available resources during an emergency.

including the SPCA, WSPA, New Zealand Veterinary Association (NZVA), Massey University and NZCAC. NAWEM also includes representatives from Federated Farmers of New Zealand and the Ministry for Primary Industries (MPI, formerly the Ministry of Agriculture and Forestry), attesting to the prominence of farming in New Zealand, with farmed animals 'occupying close to 50% of our land mass and therefore particularly at risk in major adverse events' (MPI, 2007). The Ministry of Civil Defence and Emergency Management (MCDEM) also appoints a member to NAWEM. Thus, the varied expertise of those contributing to this group ensures all species in New Zealand are represented in the development and promotion of information, advice and policy aimed at improving disaster management for animals.

NAWEM supports the notion that animal welfare is first and foremost the responsibility of individual animal guardians (or owners), but also recognises that in times of crisis people may be so overwhelmed by circumstances that their capacity to act on behalf of their animals can be severely compromised – for instance, they may have sustained injuries themselves and/or suffered loss of loved ones and property, or they may no longer have adequate access to resources. Sometimes, the sheer scale of a disaster necessitates the intervention of skilled agencies, despite the best intentions and actions of animal guardians. NAWEM therefore stresses the importance of professional planning and training in animal welfare management in order to ensure the most effective local and national responses in the event of human-induced or natural disasters. NAWEM also has a role in assisting with the coordination of any animal-focused response following disaster, channeling its advice through MCDEM's infrastructure (MPI, 2007).

Led by Co-Chairs Bridget Vercoe (also WSPA New Zealand's country director) and Wayne Ricketts (until recently the veterinary resources manager for the NZVA), NAWEM has worked hard to factor lessons learnt in the Canterbury quakes into its recommended amendments to current Animal Welfare and Civil Defence Emergency Management (CDEM) legislation. Significantly, one of NAWEM's key objectives is soon to be realised: the National CDEM plan is in the process of being revised to include in its Welfare Services section significant advances for animal welfare in this country. The new National CDEM plan is likely to come into force in 2015 following a period of public consultation mid-2014; in large part due to NAWEM's concerted foregrounding of and professional instruction on animal welfare issues in emergencies, it will include for the first time the legal requirement for emergency planning to take into account all animals including companion, farmed and wild animals, and those used in entertainment, research and testing. Under the draft Revised National CDEM plan, one agency – MPI – will take responsibility for coordinating animal welfare needs in times of crisis. The fact that the animals of New Zealand will be protected in emergencies under law is a breakthrough. Only a few other countries or states have similar strategies: Costa Rica has had a government-sponsored Animal Welfare Emergency Management programme for many years, while the Australian State of Victoria's Department of Primary Industries has recently taken a lead role in animal welfare emergency management (NAWEM member Roger Poland, personal communication, April 2014).

NAWEM is also helping to draft MCDEM's new Welfare in Emergencies Director's Guidelines, which will shortly include animal welfare alongside human-directed welfare services. The guidelines also provide templates for Companion Animal Welfare Assessment Forms and Animal Registration Forms for use at evacuation centres in New Zealand, as well as information forms for Civil Defence planners on how to provide for companion animals in case of emergency. NAWEM has also assisted in changing policy relating to Disability Assist Dogs (canines who work to protect and guide people diagnosed as epileptic or living with impaired vision, hearing and mobility): this policy ensures that these dogs now wear official Civil Defence tags so they can be easily identifiable as service dogs who must stay with their humans at all times and, vitally, during emergency situations. Co-Chair Bridget Vercoe is pleased with this progress:

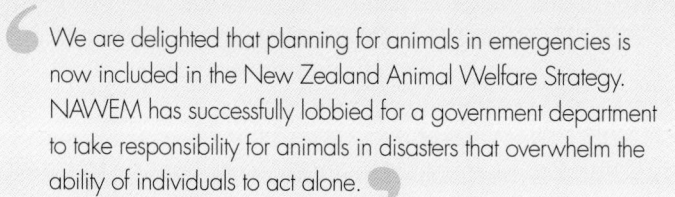

> We are delighted that planning for animals in emergencies is now included in the New Zealand Animal Welfare Strategy. NAWEM has successfully lobbied for a government department to take responsibility for animals in disasters that overwhelm the ability of individuals to act alone.

Veterinary tales

Christchurch is home to more than 30 veterinary clinics. One of these, the Christchurch After Hours Veterinary Clinic, caters for emergencies that arise when the city's daytime practices are closed. When the earthquake struck at lunchtime on 22 February 2011, this facility was not in service, nor could it immediately reopen its Addington premises to receive animals injured by the tremor, as water and power supplies had been disrupted. In an article published in the *Press* on 7 April 2011, Christchurch After Hours Clinic veterinarian Ian Ross tells reporter Keith Lynch: 'We grabbed as much equipment and drugs as we could. We had a full staff. Even though we couldn't contact them, staff members came straight in. Nobody was sure what was going to happen or where we'd work from.' In the same article Clinical Director Andrew Hay describes how, having worked the previous night shift, he was woken by the quake and immediately started searching for an alternative location for urgent over-night consultations. This turned out to be Halswell Veterinary Clinic in the west of the city, which had survived the quake relatively unscathed. The following night the emergency services relocated to Hornby Veterinary Centre, where they stayed for a week (Lynch, 2011).

The emergency veterinarians looked after the police dogs who required more intensive care than VERT could give them in the field. They also looked after Sacha, the USAR dog who became dehydrated on duty. One of the most common injuries seen in dogs entering the clinic was cut paws, typically incurred while dogs were running panicked after the tremors. Cats were being seen with fight wounds after having fled into other cats' territories. However, the worst health problems encountered by the veterinarians involved cats with urinary tract infections or inflammation, potentially life-threatening conditions which may be caused or exacerbated by stress. 'Male cats can become plugged from the illness and they go into kidney failure,' Ian Ross told Keith Lynch.

Ross's experiences of the Christchurch earthquakes led him to think more about the crucial role veterinarians play in times of disaster. At the New Zealand Veterinary Association's conference in 2012 he recommended several ways in which the nation's clinics could prepare for future crises, including the following provisions: ensuring clean water stores and back-up power arrangements exist; designing clear evacuation plans and guidelines regarding the safe and quick transfer of patients to designated alternative venues; and holding files and records (particularly of complicated cases) in more than one place in case a clinic becomes inaccessible post-emergency. Ross also believes that it is important for veterinary staff to learn effective ways of communicating with and helping clients who come to clinics with animal patients and who may themselves be traumatised in the aftermath of a shocking event (Ross, 2012).

While the after-hours veterinary clinic had to shift for a while from its usual location in the central city, there were other clinics – particularly in the eastern areas of the city – that were even more severely affected. Some closed permanently. Others were able to soldier on, despite lack of usual power and water supplies. Veterinarian Debbie Yates works at the Animal and Bird Hospital in Woolston and lives on a farm at Waimakariri with her husband, Tim, their two daughters, Aine and

Roisin, special-breed large black and saddleback pigs, dogs, cats and free-ranging hens. Debbie recalls being woken when the 4 September 2010 earthquake struck at 4.35 in the morning:

> We were probably about 15 kilometres from the epicentre. Our house just sits on a concrete pad, which seemed to be swimming around like a boat on a rough sea. My primary thought was getting to the children. The dogs were asleep in the living room and once the children were OK we opened the door for them to come through to us. At the time we had about 300 hens sleeping in mobile sheds outside in the paddocks but there was no risk of trees coming down on them or anything like that. It ended up with the four of us on the bed surrounded by four dogs and three cats, basically we all sat on the bed together and there were lots and lots of aftershocks. When it was daylight and we could check the hens, they were all running around outside as normal. The quake didn't interrupt their laying – they kept on going as they had before.

Debbie wonders whether the unfazed attitudes of her hens might suggest that birds do not have a fear of objects falling on them. 'I think a lot of our human fears come from thinking things will fall on us or break. Presumably, hens don't have those kinds of fears.' In fact, the stoic chooks were able to help those people less fortunate. 'At the time, we were absolutely over-run with eggs,' Debbie explains. 'This was because the cafes we supplied eggs to had been damaged and were closed. We had vast numbers of eggs that we took instead to the welfare centres. They all got used.'

When the February 2011 earthquake occurred, Debbie was at work. No one at the clinic was hurt, but the quake caused moderate damage and cut off power and water supply to the facility. 'Luckily there wasn't any surgery underway at that time,' Debbie remembers:

> There were in-patients, and some of these had just had surgery. Our priority at that time was to move all animals that could be caged into portable carriers, so if we needed to evacuate the building we could do so instantly. All of the patients were caged and gathered by the front door. Larger dogs who couldn't be caged were put on leads and tethered by the door, so if we had to dash they were right there ready to come with us. Because the phones were down, we couldn't contact any of the animals' owners.

Despite the state of the clinic, it was not yet apparent just how severely the inner city had been affected. Debbie's husband Tim worked on the ninth floor of a building next to the Cathedral, which was all but destroyed. Fortuitously, by the time she became aware of the devastation in Cathedral Square, Debbie already knew her husband was safe:

> It wasn't until the first client arrived to collect his pet that I found out how bad things were in the central city. This was hours after the quake struck. This particular client had actually been in the Cathedral and run out. He'd managed to get home and then had cycled to the clinic – traffic was too dense to get through with a vehicle – so he came to collect his guinea pig who was here for X-rays that day. It was only when he told us the Cathedral had collapsed and people had been killed that we became aware of how terrible things were. By that time, most of us had managed to contact family. We had been so focused on the immediate – caging the animals, sweeping up glass and ensuring the clinic was safe – that it was some time before we wondered what had happened elsewhere.

One of the surprising aspects of that afternoon of 22 February was that, despite the chaos in the city, clients continued to show up for scheduled appointments as if nothing had happened. Debbie remembers: 'Someone came in for flea treatment, just carrying on with their day. Even though there were sirens going, power poles were down, and there were sink holes in the roads.' Later in the afternoon, dogs who had fled their homes started being brought to the clinic. Debbie recalls:

> Because fences and gates were down, people were finding animals on the streets and then bringing them into us. It was frustrating because, even though some were micro-chipped, if they only had council registration (and not NZCAR registration) then we couldn't contact the Council because the local phone lines were down, and so we had to take them directly to the pound or to Dogwatch. These dogs had cuts and bruises where furniture had fallen on them. One had a broken bone from a television tumbling onto him. That was one of the worst injuries I saw caused by the quake.

Debbie stayed home on her farm for the next two days, returning to the clinic on Friday 25 February, but, as she explains, at that stage they were not able to carry out surgical procedures as power and water were still unavailable:

> We were really just doing first aid and medical management of any conditions. We were very limited because the sterilisation of instruments for surgery relied on electricity. Once we got power back we were still limited as we didn't have water. Even when the main water supply came back we couldn't use that for surgical cleaning because of the potential for contamination. So for weeks we were using bottled water for all our surgical scrubbing and preparation.

Debbie had a well at home, so she was able to regularly fill up water carriers and take them into the clinic. 'I was also taking all surgical washing home. And everyone's laundry at the clinic as well!'

Since the February event, the clinic has impressed upon clients the importance of transporting animals in carriers and on leads. 'This was always a necessity for their pets' safety anyway,' says Debbie, 'but we've had to reinforce it even further because if we have to evacuate the premises we need cages and leads at the ready.' The clinic already had emergency procedures in place but had anticipated these might be used in the event of fire or of flooding, which had once seemed more likely than a serious earthquake! Following February 2011, emergency plans were fine-tuned to maximise the safety of patients undergoing surgery during tremors. Debbie explains:

> For the first few months after the big quake, we spent every surgery with a skin stapler on the table, thinking that if the worst happened, we could at least staple the wound closed and move the patient out. Of course there are limitations and restrictions because if you have to evacuate an animal who is undergoing surgery, then that animal will wake up because a state of unconsciousness can only be maintained if it's on the gas. So we have to consider things like: is it better for the animal to wake up in the middle of surgery or should we ensure it remains oblivious on the table? It would always depend on the moment. But as far as welfare is concerned, it's a constant dilemma.

In the immediate weeks following February 2011, patients presented at the clinic with a number of similar, earthquake-related health concerns. 'We saw a lot of injuries in caged birds, sadly,' Debbie recalls. 'Mostly

Christchurch veterinarian Debbie Yates with her three-legged companion cat, Pod (short for Tripod).

Debbie Yates

they damaged their wings from flapping in fright. Sometimes cages fell over or other things fell on them. Mainly we saw injuries to the leading edge of wings where they flap and flap and flap and bleed a lot. We also saw some broken wings.' (See also Lyane Scarlett's discussion on the impact of earthquakes on parrots in chapter 5.)

Most of the initial injuries incurred by cats and dogs were cuts and bruises, the consequence of animals running off during aftershocks. 'These injuries were themselves quite problematic,' Debbie says. 'Where we might usually have applied dressings and put bandages on, a lot of people weren't able to keep dressings on their pets clean and dry because houses and gardens were full of liquefaction. There were clients whose gardens had liquefaction to knee-height. The family dog couldn't even get outside to pee properly, let alone keep a bandage clean while an injury healed.' In these cases, plastic bags were supplied to cover bandages when dogs or cats went outside.

There were also gastroenterological problems occurring in dogs and cats, which Debbie suspects were related to contaminated water around the city. Unfortunately, there were no quick-fix solutions in the worst-affected suburbs of Christchurch. As Debbie explains:

> Normally speaking, we would advise people on the diet of their sick pets, tell them to give an animal cooked rice and potato and a bland meat diet, but owners couldn't do any shopping because there weren't any grocery stores open around here. Sometimes they didn't even have anything in the pantry for themselves, let alone any special kind of diet for the dog. In some cases, the best we could do was send clients home with clean water. There was one case I recall where the only thing I could do was give them a bottle of clean water to take home. They didn't have any food of their own and were relying on meals provided by the emergency agencies. All our normal modes of treatment were hopeless because people could barely look after themselves, let alone look after a pet in the way they usually would. That was the most horrible thing really.

Because people were also financially affected, with banks closed and money machines out of order, much of the clinic's treatment and care of animals was provided on trust of future payment for the first few days post-quake. 'We also had a lot of food delivered by the SPCA and other welfare organisations that we could offer to pet owners in need, which was really excellent.'

For weeks after February's event, Debbie's animal patients presented with a variety of quake-related physical and emotional issues:

> There were clouds of liquefaction dust everywhere around here, causing eye, skin and respiratory irritations. There was also a huge increase in the number of fleas. People weren't keeping up with their normal flea control because they had other things to worry about, but we also wondered if the actual physical vibration of the aftershocks was a factor because the flea pupae are stimulated to hatch out by vibration. Also dogs weren't getting their usual exercise because people couldn't get out and use the footpaths or parks.

Debbie also noticed that the kinds of procedures carried out by the clinic changed after February 2011. 'The quakes affected people financially, so in the immediate aftermath we were performing a lot fewer elective procedures and prophylactic treatments. Dental work was reduced, so were diagnostic investigations. A lot of people moved away and we were instead busy with preparing animals for exportation overseas. This involves lots of paperwork, export certificates, as well as pre-travel examinations.'

Clinic staff also helped animals who were distressed. 'We still see a lot of anxiety issues,' says Debbie:

> Dogs have become phobic about loud noises, but this is pretty easy to address. A lot of the anxiety felt by an animal can be related to an owner's level of anxiety, particularly in smaller breeds of dog because they are generally handled more, so if a person is anxious and their reaction is to pick up and cuddle a dog, the anxiety of the owner is easily transferred to the dog. But we can help dogs through a combination of retraining, medications and reacclimatising them to certain noises.

It was from the worst-affected, eastern suburbs that the saddest tales were emerging. Not only were people facing the reality of unliveable homes, displacement from communities, and uncertainty about employment, but they were also confronted with the hardest choices regarding companion animals. 'There were those cases where animals were older and frail or ill. They were pets already on the brink, already deteriorating before the first earthquake, and then following February's quake, people's abilities to look after these animals was greatly reduced due to their changed circumstances. So some animals were euthanased earlier than they would normally be,' Debbie recounts. 'There were some people whose own enormous anxieties and worries meant that looking after a dependent pet was just too much for them. And there were practicalities: homes had been destroyed and some people had to move suddenly – they couldn't take pets with them, so some of those animals were euthanased.' Euthanising an otherwise healthy animal due to restricted options for on-going guardianship was perhaps one of the greatest challenges the clinic's staff faced. Whenever possible, the choice to rehome rather than destroy was discussed with clients, but, as Debbie laments, 'the welfare rehoming agencies were also full to the gills – so it was very difficult'.

Even when new homes could be found for animals who had been displaced, or whose owners could no longer care for them, this was not always the option taken by a client/owner. 'Some people still want and prefer to go down the route of euthanasia so they know exactly what has happened to their pet,' Debbie explains. 'They have been responsible for and cared for that animal, and if they euthanase it, then they don't have to worry about it being rehomed and what that might entail.' Debbie remembers one particularly tragic case of a young dog who was suitable for rehoming but whose traumatised owner refused to relinquish him to a new home and insisted he was euthanised:

> *That was the most difficult case we had to deal with. It was a huge dilemma, but if we hadn't done this, then the owner said they would have gone elsewhere. Euthanasia was probably a stress-related decision due to very difficult personal circumstances.*

The decision to euthanise this healthy dog was made by a person under extreme pressure and it is possible that they may have come to regret it; however, because (as explained in the introduction to this book) companion animals are regarded as 'property' under the law, it was within this client's rights to end the life of their dog. This incident was profoundly distressing for clinic staff, and they were concerned to see requests for euthanasia of pets double after the February quake.

Although this tale reveals the sobering fate of some companion animals whose families and homes in Christchurch were profoundly affected in February 2011, Debbie is also keen to draw attention to the other side of the story – where the on-going companionship of humans and their beloved animals has been a blessing following the city's upheaval. Furthermore, she knows of many happier outcomes where displaced animals were fostered, adopted and rehomed by caring clients of the clinic.

Postscript

Almost two years after the February earthquake, VERT Team Leader Hayley Squance and her colleagues undertook a study to evaluate post-quake morbidity and mortality of animals in Christchurch. The researchers asked veterinarians in the worst-affected areas of the city to supply information about patient visits from nine months prior to 4 September 2010 up until December 2012, one year after the last major quake. They found that after each large earthquake, there was at first an instant decrease and then a rapid increase in the number of patients presenting with gastrointestinal problems; animals living in areas most impacted by liquefaction were affected more than others. It was noted that cases of both acute and chronic feline urinary tract disorders and cystitis increased after each major quake. The number of deaths and euthanasia procedures also spiked after earthquakes and after related events such as relocation required by the Earthquake Commission (Squance et al., 2013).

In summary

Several themes emerge in the stories shared in this chapter by those at the front-line of animal rescue and welfare following the Canterbury earthquakes. One recurring sentiment expressed by these professionals and specialised volunteers is how special it was to help the animals (and humans) in the wake of this disaster, and also how humbling it was to witness the strong sense of solidarity and community spirit evident in the damaged city. The experiences of informants also indicate how their interactions with quake-affected animals were deeply rewarding but at times also disheartening. They speak of the extraordinarily selfless actions of many ordinary Christchurch residents especially those whose own lives had been severely affected by the quakes. On a sadder note, they also highlight how some people facing sudden extreme pressure and radical change in their lives may abandon or destroy animals who have been loyal companions, possibly regretting such decisions at a later time.

From the accounts of these professionals it is clear that one simple measure can help us be better prepared to protect our companion animals should disasters strike: micro-chipping. Dogs and cats who were micro-chipped prior to the quakes in Canterbury were easily identified and quickly returned to homes from which they had fled in panic when the tremors occurred.

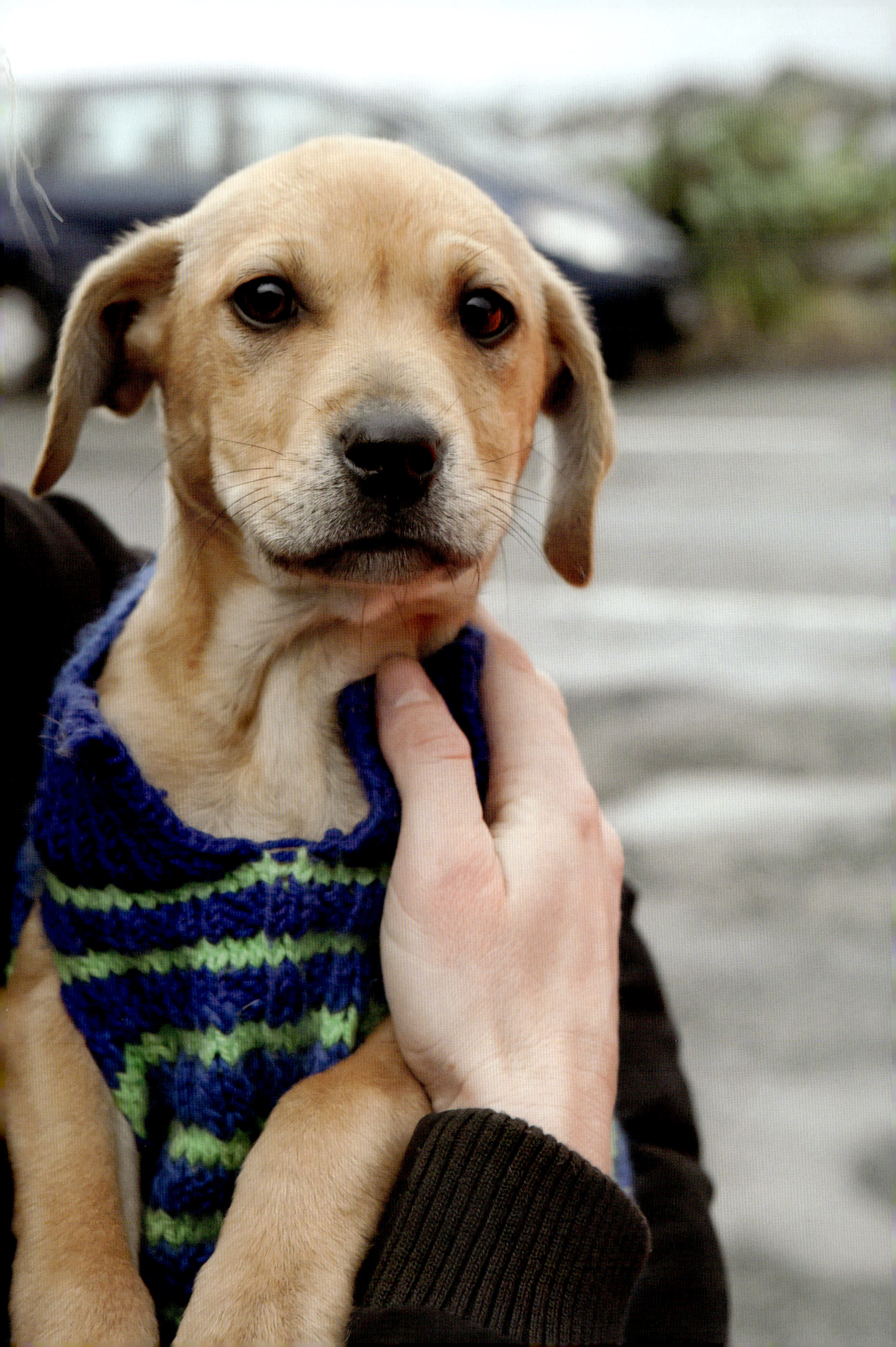

Chapter 2
Shelter and advocacy

The previous chapter focused on the accounts of professionals and volunteers from agencies responsible for the immediate rescue and emergency care of animals following the Canterbury earthquakes. This chapter records the experiences and perspectives of those organisations and individuals involved in providing short or longer term safe shelter for animal earthquake refugees, as well as securing new homes for the abandoned and rejected. It includes accounts of those who advocated on behalf of animals in the devastated city. Organisations represented here include Dogwatch, Wellington's HUHA (Helping You Help Animals) Sanctuary, Save Animals from Exploitation (SAFE), Cat Rescue Christchurch, Cat Help and Canterbury Cats' Protection League. This chapter also pays tribute to local hero Paul Dahl and his efforts to care for Lyttelton's animals after the February 2011 earthquake.

Dogwatch

One agency repeatedly praised by other professionals and volunteers at the forefront of animal rescue and shelter in Christchurch post-quakes is Dogwatch, a charitable trust that, in normal times, rescues and rehomes dogs and puppies from the Christchurch City, Selwyn and Waimakariri pounds. Under local law, when a dog is impounded there is a seven-day holding period during which guardians can locate and uplift an animal. After this time, if a dog is not reclaimed, the City Council becomes his or her legal owner and can, at its discretion, have the animal destroyed. However, pound staff do everything in their power to avoid this outcome for individual dogs. One such measure involves moving 'death row' dogs to Dogwatch kennels, located in Dyers Road in Bromley. Dogwatch will also organise for dogs with special needs,

Opposite page: An earthquake refugee arrives in Wellington with HUHA.

Jo Moore

including extremely young puppies, to go into foster homes until they are ready for permanent adoption.

When dogs arrive at Dogwatch they are placed in the care of manager Pam Howard and the Dogwatch team, which at the time of the quakes included Charmaine McLaren (known as Charlie) and other devoted volunteers from the public, who help clean kennels, feed, water and walk the dogs. The adoption centre ensures all dogs are vaccinated, micro-chipped, desexed, wormed and socialised with other dogs, puppies and people before leaving for permanent homes. Dogwatch also provides education about responsible dog guardianship (www.dogwatch.co.nz).

When the 2010 and 2011 earthquakes struck Christchurch, Dogwatch was operating with eight kennels which, in theory, can cater for 16 resident dogs (if two dogs can be housed together). Sometimes a litter of puppies would fill up one kennel and the number of dogs housed at the facility would be higher. However, following the February quake, Pam recalls the centre stretching at one time to accommodate 43 dogs. 'We had dogs everywhere! They were in foster homes, doubled up in the kennels. Some were in crates in the office. It's not the ideal way to run a facility like this but these were exceptional circumstances.' In fact, Dogwatch's annual statistics for 2011 showed that the organisation cared for 100 more dogs that year than the year before.

Luckily, although the suburb of Bromley was badly affected by the February event, Dogwatch's administrative buildings and kennels were not damaged, nor were the spacious exercise yards. The complex is situated on land with artesian wells, so water was readily available. However, sewerage, power and telephone services were disrupted. Charlie recalls that 'the dogs were pretty shaken'. She remembers how the volunteers rallied around to calm them down, even as multiple aftershocks continued. 'Some of the really scared dogs were trying to leap over eight-foot fences. One named Nova actually did! One of the volunteers here at the time took this distressed dog home to personally foster her, and she ended up keeping her, so that was a happy ending for an upset dog!'

Immediately after the February earthquake, once the dogs on site had been checked for injuries, staff and volunteers cleaned up spillages and breakages around the complex. They were unaware of the severity of the tremor until a few hours later when news of human deaths in the central business district surfaced. At this time they contacted Animal Control to put in place a management plan for all the dogs who had fled their homes and were running around the streets, parks and beaches. Charlie recalls:

> Immediately after the lunchtime earthquake, and for a few hours, it was very quiet here. We had time to settle all the dogs and clean things up. Then all of a sudden, it got really busy. People were turning up with dogs they'd found on the streets, which was fantastic, but they had to take them to the pound first because that is the official holding facility. We had about 20 dogs arrive that day, and there was also a steady flow of people looking for dogs too. When Pam and I visited the pound to discuss a plan forward, we saw some happy reunions. It was frantic there, they bore the brunt of it – everyone had gone there to drop off dogs or to look for them.

While Dogwatch was managing many more canine residents post-22 February 2011, it was also inundated with assistance – both practical and financial. 'Lots of people offered to help – from all over the country, but mainly the South Island. I couldn't get over it,' Charlie says:

> We were able to transfer many more dogs into foster care in the community. There were donations coming in – pet food was given to us too. And people were bringing us baking and sandwiches to keep up going! Because our power was down, we even had one of our volunteers, Charlotte, who was in Australia at the time, take on the management of our website from over there – so she kept updating it and explaining our day-to-day situation to the public.

Dogwatch had two old-fashioned phones connected to functioning landlines, and dog owners had begun ringing them to ask for help with finding alternative homes for their pets because they were no longer able to look after them. Dogwatch passed these details on to Anthony Terry from SAFE, who loaded information onto the Animal Aid Facebook site about individual dogs who urgently required new homes (see pages 85–88). 'What happened that was really surprising is that we were actually adopting [dogs] out

Dogwatch Manager Pam Howard welcomes an earthquake refugee on 23 February 2011.

The first dog brought to Dogwatch on 22 February, having already spent eight days impounded in the city's Animal Control shelter, was named Shake after the quakes. She was adopted by Lisa Duff, who has another five dogs and is an agility competitor. 'As it happens,' Dogwatch's Charlie McLaren says, 'Shake has turned into a fantastic agility dog and she's even been profiled in *Fetch* magazine!'

Lisa Duff

after the quake,' Charlie exclaims. 'We didn't expect this, but we had people offering to take the dogs we already had up for adoption prior to the earthquake, and this made way, of course, for other dogs at the pound to come here.'

Dogwatch insists on thorough screening of and education for potential guardians prior to dog adoption or foster care; the earthquakes made such a rigorous system even more important.

Runaway finds a home

The saying that it is an ill wind that blows nobody any good was borne out for Yoda, one of the death-row pound dogs rescued by Dogwatch: the February earthquake brought him the chance to find a new, loving home with Harry Kerr and Jill Vosper in Dunedin. A short while before the Canterbury earthquakes, Harry and Jill had moved to a lifestyle block near the Brighton coast, 18 kilometres south of Dunedin. With them went Button the cat and dalmations Briar, Dougal and Bridie. The family was soon joined by six alpacas and a horse named Zeke. Sadly, Briar and Dougal succumbed to age-related illnessses shortly after the shift to the country, and Bridie was left alone. 'Initially, our prime motivation was to find a companion for Bridie, although gradually the idea of providing a home for an abandoned or ill-treated dog began to influence our search,' Harry recalls. 'We had heard of Dogwatch and knew that they were at pains to match their available dogs with prospective adopters and ensure that specific problems were resolved before the dogs were rehomed.'

Perusing the Dogwatch adoption site Jill spotted Yoda, a labrador/boxer cross. He had been fostered twice, once with his sister who, like Yoda, had a talent for leaping over fences and escaping. Tragically, this shared skill for escaping had led to her being killed by a car, and to Yoda being returned from the foster home to Dogwatch. After the February earthquake, in order to clear some room for the incoming canine casualties, Yoda was fostered out again, this time to a family in Rangiora. However, he was unable to be contained on their property and ended up back at Dogwatch once more. Harry recalls: 'When we asked about him, we were told that as long as his carers were on the property he never wandered away and kept them firmly in his line of sight. He was great with stock. He was caring and gentle. We made up our mind to bring him into our home.'

On a sunny day in March 2011, Jill and Harry travelled up the South Island and eight-month-old Yoda met his new family. Harry recalls driving back to Dunedin with Yoda stretched out quite comfortably and relaxed in the back seat of the car, ready to start his new life. 'But a new home and a new life required a new name,' Harry explains. 'This dog was an escapist, but we didn't learn of his jumping ability until we introduced him to Bridie and our garden with its boundary cyclone fence, which he cleared effortlessly! He was ginger-haired. As a Scot I knew that Rob Roy MacGregor had red hair and had made some great leaps to escape his British pursuers in his day.' Thus, Yoda became Robbie.

Harry points out that they soon noticed a couple of differences between Robbie and the other dogs with whom Jill and he had shared their lives. 'Dalmatians seldom bark. Robbie made sure that anyone who came into view within about 200 metres was made to realise there was a new sheriff in town. His bark was a deep, assertive warning, until he neared the visitor or passer-by, or they approached him. Then his tail began to swing and they were greeted enthusiastically.' To start with, Robbie was also very vigilant. 'We wondered if we should have called him "Sting". Inside, no matter where he lies or sits, his eyes are on us and follow every movement. Outside, he appears within seconds and follows, casually watchful, or finds a position a few metres away and watches from there.' Harry recalls that if he and Jill were working in different parts of the property Robbie would be bemused; he was faced with a big dilemma: 'Then he had to decide that keeping an eye on one out of the two would have to do.' Eventually, they were able to convince him that he needed to accept the boundaries set for him. 'It took time, of course, and he made sure by his swaggering return from those areas when called that it was *his* decision to do so.'

Former Dogwatch resident Yoda, now Robbie, lives at Brighton, Dunedin, with his new companions Harry Kerr and Jill Vosper.

Stories of dogs being left behind by their guardians were deeply troubling to Dogwatch staff and volunteers. 'One of the worst things was when they started evacuating the suburbs of Redcliffs and Sumner,' Charlie says. 'People were told to leave their pets behind because the welfare centres they were being taken to wouldn't allow pets; some did and some didn't. From where Dogwatch is you could see in the darkness all the cars leaving the hills, and the lights in houses going out one by one, and you knew there would be some animals up there left behind.' Along with other agencies like SAFE, which was circulating information about animals post-quakes via social media (see pages 85–88), Dogwatch was urgently helping to update lists of dogs requiring new homes, whether because their owners had left the city or because they were unable to take them to new accommodation in Christchurch. 'We were getting calls from desperate people considering putting dogs down because they had nowhere for them,' she recalls:

> It was heart-breaking. These people would say their dogs were friendly and loving but they couldn't find them new homes. One man rang me back the day after we'd listed his dog on SAFE's Animal Aid site, and said, "Don't worry about advertising my dog now. I've had him put down." When I asked why, he said, "Because we're leaving Saturday and have too much to do before then." I rang all the vets and they said they usually don't like euthanising healthy dogs but they were making some allowances due to people's emotional states and changed circumstances.

A week or so after the February event, a woman came to Dogwatch wanting to adopt a puppy. As Charlie recounts:

> When we asked if she'd had a dog before – which is one of our standard questions so we have some idea of a potential adopter's experience and knowledge of dogs – she said, "Yes, we had one but we had to leave the city after the quake and when we came back home he was gone, so I'd like to get another." It turns out the family had left the city for over 10 days without arranging care for their dog. A neighbour alerted the SPCA, who rescued this dog. But of course we wouldn't rehome a dog to this person, not after she abandoned her other pet for so long. I can't understand how anyone could do that.

One story with an even sadder outcome involved a young dog whom Dogwatch staff named Chance, as they wanted him to have a second opportunity to have a good life after his first six years of neglect and abuse. On 22 February 2011 his owners had left their property in Aranui, abandoning him there, along with a black dog. Neighbours were aware of the black dog as he was kept as a guard-dog, always tied to a tree in the front yard; they realised something was amiss when the dog's lead grew shorter and shorter in the following days, as he twisted himself around the tree in an effort to get away. When they gave him some food and water they noticed there was a thin dog living behind the gate at the same property. They had not been aware of this other dog's existence, despite having lived next to the home for several years. The well-meaning neighbours opened the gate to enable both dogs to eat together. Unfortunately, having led separate lives, the two dogs were not familiar pack-mates and began fighting, resulting in Chance's face being badly torn.

Pam picks up the story from here:

> We were called as the neighbours didn't know what to do at that time of night. So we took him to the After Hours emergency vet. The dog was emaciated, dehydrated and injured. He had puncture wounds and tears down his face. At the vet's clinic there was some discussion about whether it might be kinder to euthanise him but he perked up after 24 hours and eventually he came to Dogwatch for rehoming. We had him here for several months and the difference at the end was amazing, but unfortunately he had been neglected for so long that his behaviour deteriorated and he started guarding in an extreme way. We asked a behaviourist to help but were told he was an unstable dog who believed he had to guard all the time and this made him a threat to people.

Pam fostered Chance at her home, where there were no such issues and he enjoyed the company of her other dogs. She continues:

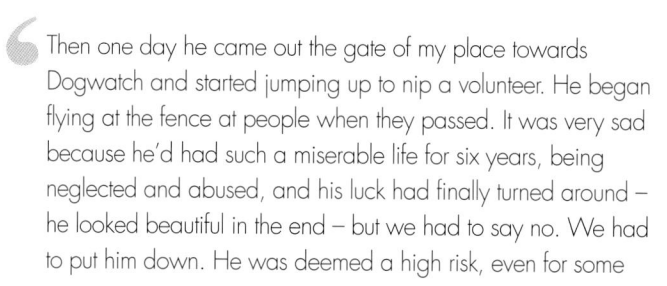

> Then one day he came out the gate of my place towards Dogwatch and started jumping up to nip a volunteer. He began flying at the fence at people when they passed. It was very sad because he'd had such a miserable life for six years, being neglected and abused, and his luck had finally turned around – he looked beautiful in the end – but we had to say no. We had to put him down. He was deemed a high risk, even for some

Chance during his happier days at Dogwatch.

Dogwatch

of the handlers. He had a happy story for a while though – several months where he enjoyed good food and exercise, the company of other dogs – he loved playing with puppies. But when his confidence to guard grew, I couldn't control him and that was a big problem. He had such hope in his face._

One consequence of the earthquakes, which could easily have been prevented through responsible desexing of companion animals, was an increase in litters of puppies several months after major shakes. 'We had people coming here with puppies saying that their bitch in heat had got pregnant when the fence collapsed at their home and she ran away for a while,' says Charlie.

A few years on from the February 2011 earthquake and the numbers at Dogwatch remain high. 'They have never really gone down', says Pam. 'I think the lowest we got to at one stage was 16 dogs in our care, and that lasted a few days only.' 2013 was another difficult year for Dogwatch, as many more litters of puppies were abandoned or dumped. 'Sadly,' Pam says, 'the reality is that Christchurch has far more dogs than it has good homes for, so that for many dogs and puppies there is little hope of them having their "forever family" and home to grow old in.'

Pam also feels that the swelling numbers of dogs needing foster care and new homes can be attributed to the challenges of life in a damaged and struggling city:

> Christchurch is still in crisis. There are so many issues out there – unemployment, businesses and homes lost, land damaged. There is a long-term recovery ahead. People elsewhere think it's already fixed or will be soon, but the fall-out will go on for a long time yet. We're still hearing of homes that have just been red-stickered, this long after the quake, and some of these homes will have animals in them. People can't find affordable rental homes in Christchurch easily any more, let alone rental properties that allow animals too.

In addition, the effects of the relentless uncertainty experienced by humans after the earthquakes have consequences for the city's dogs. 'If people are emotionally affected by the quakes, this impacts on how they interact with their pets as well,' Pam comments. 'So we are seeing dogs who are stressed all the time because their owners are stressed.'

Pam is realistic about the extent of problems actually caused by the earthquakes. She's careful to distinguish between problems involving displaced, abandoned and lost dogs post-quakes, and situations that Dogwatch already encountered on a regular basis before the disaster:

> We have to stop blaming the earthquakes for people's neglect and irresponsible care of animals. People keep letting their dogs breed; then when they have a litter of 13 puppies and they don't want them anymore, or can't afford them, they dump them. They won't desex. And they won't micro-chip. Micro-chipping is good because it also prevents owners absconding from their responsibilities towards dogs. But the breeding is so frustrating. If you go on Trade Me you will see litter after litter, and designer breeds as well. These people need to take a step back and realise that Christchurch doesn't

> need this at the moment. We don't need all these puppies. Sure the quakes exacerbated the usual issues we have, but people need to think.

Pam looks back on 2011 as a 'real learning curve'. Dogwatch has since fine-tuned its emergency strategies in order to ensure the safety and well-being of volunteers and dogs in the event of further earthquakes. 'We have an emergency drum that contains torches and batteries, blankets, dehydrated and tinned food. Anything perishable in the freezers we feed the dogs first, if the power should go out again. We have the artesian wells here so water isn't an issue, though we still have to boil it,' she says. Charlie adds: 'We also have emergency procedures written up for volunteers. If you're out walking the dogs and an earthquake happens, calmly bring the dog back to the yard, or, if they're panicking, just let them go, because we are fully fenced and they won't be able to get out onto the road.'

This Dogwatch story finishes with Christchurch citizens showing their appreciation of the charity's dedication to the city's dogs and people in the wake of the region's earthquakes. In 2012 when they reopened having been closed for major earthquake repairs, The Palms shopping mall in Shirley celebrated with a competition offering Christchurch residents the chance to vote for the charity that they felt had helped the community the most after the earthquakes. There was strong competition from other worthy nominees like the Student Volunteer Army, but Dogwatch won the vote and the prize of $50,000. How to use this money was not a hard decision, says Pam: 'What became obvious after the quakes was that we needed to expand. We aim to start building new kennels here before the end of 2014.'

HUHA animal sanctuary

Experienced surgical veterinary nurse Carolyn Press-McKenzie and her husband Jim established their 13-acre property outside Wellington as a sanctuary for abused and unwanted animals. HUHA (Helping You Help Animals) is both the name of this sanctuary and the charitable trust that supports it. With the help of 20 or so dedicated volunteers, HUHA's objectives are to rescue and rehabilitate wildlife or domesticated animals in trouble, as well as educate the community about responsible guardianship of all animal species.

When the February 2011 quake struck, Carolyn, who also sits on the Board of Trustees for the Wellington SPCA, immediately began collecting collapsible cages and blankets for the Animal Rescue Unit (ARU) to take south to Christchurch (see chapter 1). She also sourced bottles and

Right: Dogwatch resident on the way with HUHA to a new home in the North Island.

Jo Moore

Far right: HUHA's Carolyn Press-McKenzie and other volunteers arrive in Christchurch to help the city's animals, February 2011.

Jo Moore

ingredients for a natural anti-anxiety remedy, which a local pharmacy was able to prepare for traumatised animals. Carolyn recounts:

> After a few days, we knew from the ARU that many pets had been left behind in the red zone and that the shelters in Christchurch were all full. We decided the best way for HUHA to help was to go down there ourselves and retrieve some of the animals who had been in shelters before the quake, and were therefore more likely to be permanently homeless. We could bring them back to Wellington, find new homes for them here, and free up the shelters for incoming earthquake refugees.

HUHA's rescue truck left the capital with a tankful of gifted diesel and loaded up with donated pet food and carriers, cat litter and even hand sanitisers; free ferry passage was granted across Cook Strait. Hans and Nichola Kriek from SAFE had offered the HUHA crew beds for the night, despite their own home in St Albans having been severely damaged. 'I realised that there really was no limit to what could be done if you just picked up the phone and asked,' Carolyn says. 'Everybody felt affected. People were stepping up all over the country.'

On their arrival in Christchurch, HUHA volunteers delivered all the donated goods they had brought with them. The next morning they collected dogs, cats, turtles and even a large group of unwanted roosters and hens who had been dumped at the side of Ruru Road in Bromley and rescued by Dogwatch volunteer Charmaine McLaren. All these new multi-species 'guests' of HUHA sanctuary then travelled straight back to Wellington. Carolyn says:

Charmaine McLaren (right) from Dogwatch, with fellow advocate Erika Costello (left) and the rescued chickens.

Charmaine McLaren

> We went down again after the June 13th quakes in 2011. This time we travelled all night, drove all day, picked unwanted dogs up from Dogwatch, turned around and came right back because we already had over 50 new homes in Wellington and elsewhere ready to accept these animals. We had people wanting dogs for the first time and also those who already had one or two dogs asking for another.

After this winter reconnaissance trip, Carolyn enlisted the aid of an animal behaviourist to explain to new guardians some of the anxious and unusual behaviours they might expect from the traumatised dogs they had adopted from Christchurch. 'The reality was these dogs were shaken, they were in turmoil,' she says. 'The June trip was about bringing back dogs found in the red zone who hadn't had homes for weeks, so they needed a lot of special care.'

The June 2011 collection of dogs was also gruelling for HUHA staff because this time they were witnessing people having to part with their much-loved dogs. For instance, one anxious German Shepherd-cross, who lost clumps of hair every time there was an aftershock, was reluctantly relinquished by his owner. 'It was extremely hard for families to give up their pets, even though we were able to reassure them we would find them loving homes and they could ring us to know where their dogs had gone,' Carolyn says. 'We also offered to foster dogs for a month or two until their guardians were more settled, but only one person took us up on that offer.' HUHA has a policy that all animals processed through the sanctuary receive care for the rest of their lives. 'We could honestly look these people in the eye and say that no matter what happens in the future, HUHA will be there for your pet.'

Such a conscientious system is both reassuring and warranted, as the story of Asher story bears out. Carolyn remembers:

> Asher was an eight-year-old schnauzer and so fearful when she arrived here in Wellington after the June 13th quakes. When we opened the truck for all the dogs to come out, she just cowered in the corner and wouldn't leave. She withdrew and was very despondent and afraid. It was distressing because she had really loved her family in Christchurch but they'd had to give her up because she was so upset living with all the tremors.

Asher.

Jo Moore

Asher was fostered for a while, but she continued to be deeply traumatised: 'She was very clingy and urinating all the time,' Carolyn says. Despite these anxious behaviours, Asher displayed great affection for children. 'Whenever she saw a child her tail started to wag. For her, children were comforting.' The family with whom she was eventually rehomed in the North Island included a child, but unfortunately the parents in this family parted ways, so Asher was returned to HUHA. 'From the moment we picked her up in Christchurch after the quakes, she was family to us,' Carolyn says.

> Asher's back with us now and she is the most bouncy bundle of fun these days. She's so cuddly and full of love, and so *full* of life! I can't believe she's the same dog we picked up after the June quakes three years ago – she's so adjusted and happy.'

Asher now lives permanently at HUHA sanctuary where she is 'Queen of the Castle'. 'We have 30 dogs here and she loves charging around and playing with them, being part of a pack,' Carolyn says.

When she reflects on how disaster response could have been improved post-quakes, particularly with her own hometown of Wellington now in mind, Carolyn stresses the importance of effective emergency preparation for animals. She advises guardians of animals to store food and water for their pets in case of disaster. 'When you make up your emergency kit for the family, make one for your animals too. And make it extra big because animals eat a lot!'

By the end of 2011, HUHA volunteers around the North Island had rehomed 120 earthquake refugees. 'We are still continuing to bring dogs up via the pet taxi – problems are on-going in Christchurch,' Carolyn concedes.

Save Animals from Exploitation (SAFE) and Animal Aid

For more than 80 years the non-profit charitable organisation Save Animals From Exploitation (SAFE) has been campaigning on behalf of New Zealand's animals. As well as combating abuse, neglect and exploitation of animals, SAFE's staff and volunteers work hard to change attitudes that devalue other species. This influential and reputable animal advocacy agency has more than 10,000 members and 200 active volunteers nationwide (www.safe.org.nz).

Auckland-based Anthony Terry, executive director of SAFE at the time, leapt into action as soon as he heard the news of the destructive February earthquake and realised what its likely impact

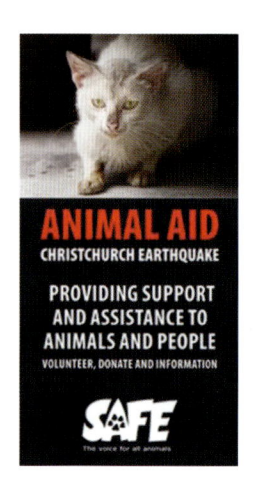

Animal Aid posters appeared all around Christchurch after the February 2011 earthquake.

SAFE

would be on his Christchurch colleagues and the animals of the city. Immediately, he contacted all animal welfare groups in the region to ascertain what assistance they required in order to cope with the impending deluge of earthquake victims needing protection and care. He then rang around pet food companies for donations. Within a week Anthony had established Animal Aid on Facebook, initially as a go-between site where welfare organisations such as HUHA, Cat Rescue and Dogwatch could post their requirements and where volunteers could help address these deficits. However, Animal Aid's patronage grew rapidly to over 3000 supporters, many of them concerned members of the public also wanting to assist. One of the most poignant messages posted on SAFE's Animal Aid site related to the canine companion of one of the victims killed when the Canterbury Television (CTV) Building collapsed. Concerned that the dog was trapped alone in this person's home in the red zone, Animal Aid was able to ensure the animal's safe rescue within hours.

An important notice was posted on 15 June 2011, a couple of days after two major aftershocks had rocked the city and just when its residents were hoping seismic activity was settling. It read:

> We are hearing reports of animals becoming unwell or showing signs of allergic reactions, believed to be from the dust and liquefaction. We recommend, where possible, to bathe, rinse, wash or simply comb (if on restricted water) your animals' coats to reduce their level of exposure and ingestion of this muck. If you're feeling alone, know that New Zealand is thinking of you.

While Anthony managed the Animal Aid Facebook site from Auckland, his Christchurch-based colleagues in SAFE were active on the ground: Nichola and Hans Kriek (at the time education officer and campaign director, respectively) dealt with practical and administrative matters from their severely damaged home in St Albans, and Sacha Dowell (then national volunteer coordinator) organised respite for displaced animals found in the community. Sacha was also in charge of Cat Rescue Christchurch when the earthquakes occurred (see pages 90–93). SAFE's office in the central city was inaccessible following the February quake and staff who had fled the building that lunchtime were unable to return to retrieve computers and files. Fortunately Wellington SPCA's Animal Rescue Unit effected a 'rescue' of SAFE's computers and brought them out of the restricted red zone.

Incoming calls to SAFE were divided into two categories: those offering help with animal issues and those voicing concerns about particular animals in the community. Nichola explains:

> We set up an operation where people could contact us if they were worried about possible abandoned animals. We also put posters up around the city advertising what we did. Our volunteers went to homes where it was suspected animals had been left behind and posted a notice on the door, basically stating we'd been there and to contact us about the animals within 24 hours or we'd assume no one was looking after them. It was a similar system to the SPCA's, but we first talked to them and made sure we weren't encroaching. Our system was intended to assist what they were doing – we weren't investigating complaints as such, but the SPCA was swamped with animals arriving at the Hornby Centre so we were able to check the validity of some of the calls about suspected abandoned animals before they went to uplift them. A lot of people volunteered to put up our Animal Aid posters around the city. And our volunteers often worked on the assumption people weren't around to look after animals and left them food and water. It was the safest thing to do for the animals.

SAFE also helped organise more than 20 skilled veterinary nurses, some from outside Christchurch, to assist in the care of injured and dehydrated animals rescued in the community, as well as to provide professional support to fosterers dealing with sick animals and to assist with micro-chipping. In the months following the major earthquakes, local SAFE volunteers took food to people who were feeding neighbourhood pets in areas without water, power, public transport or functioning supermarkets, helped to arrange water for the Heathcote Riding School

SAFE's Sacha Dowell organising animal advocacy volunteers, February 2011.

SAFE

horses (see chapter 5) and delivered water containers (and port-a-loos for volunteers) to the Cats' Protection League facilities. SAFE helpers around the country, and even volunteers in Australia, worked to match 'lost and found' animals posted on internet sites such as Pets on the Net (run by Kim Buchanan based in Thames) and Trade Me. SAFE also raised thousands of dollars for animal earthquake casualties through the Give a Little website.

'Another great thing we noticed was the level of cooperation across animal advocacy and welfare groups. We were all helping each other,' Sacha says. 'There were many agencies here looking after humans, but it was great to see how all the animal groups pulled together too in an emergency situation.' Some examples of this cooperation included: SAFE helping the SPCA by vetting the validity of calls about abandoned or neglected animals; HUHA delivering food and supplies to animal shelters, then uplifting long-term animal residents to Wellington in order to clear space for incoming earthquake refugees; Paw Justice volunteers setting up stalls at the side of roads to distribute free animal food to those who were unable to travel to obtain it, or who could not easily afford it; and Pets on the Net matching posts advertising lost animals with posts listing found ones.

When asked whether they feel that the city was prepared in February 2011 for such a catastrophe affecting its animal (and human) residents, SAFE staff members express doubts. However, they do believe that important lessons have been learnt and experiences gained. 'I think the difference between intellectually thinking about the possibility of natural disaster and what you might do if it happens, and then actually responding in the face of an event is huge,' Sacha explains. 'Once something happens there are so many logistical issues. Communication may not be possible. You may not be able to get anywhere, or else travel times will be much, much longer. It may not be easy to access the things you really need.'

Ultimately Hans is positive about the response of Christchurch citizens to the plight of the city's animals. 'I was actually impressed with the fact that, despite how traumatic things were for people, most of them took their animals into account when deciding what to do. Some people fled but then came back a couple of days later in order to arrange something more long-term for their animals.'

Earthquake refugees

While caring for animals (and their people) in the wider community through their work for SAFE, Nichola and Hans Kriek were also affected significantly on a personal level by the disaster, and by the February quake in particular. Their villa, which Hans had spent many years restoring to its original splendour before the earthquakes, was severely damaged (although it was not until the 13 June 2011 aftershocks that their chimney collapsed), and for a week they lost water and power. 'We had plaster from the ceiling everywhere – it took us a week to be able to deal with anything beyond our own plight, and our elderly cat Presto was really traumatised,' Nichola recalls. Initially unable to sleep in their home, the family pitched a tent in the yard and camped there for a week. Seventeen-year-old Presto, who fled when the February quake occurred, showed up hours later worse for wear. 'He was soaking wet,' Hans explains. 'The bottom half of him was grey and his top half was orange, so he'd obviously got stuck somewhere with liquefaction. He wouldn't come inside the house at first, or eat, and he was losing weight fast, which was a worry for us when he was already so old.' When Presto eventually re-entered the Kriek's damaged home over a week later, he was kept inside for five weeks, during which he remained under the bed, venturing out only at night to sleep beside Hans and Nichola. 'We had to feed and give him water under the bed, and put his litter box in the bedroom – he was too upset to go anywhere else.'

Nichola also found and cared for two panicking dogs immediately after

Presto.

Nichola Kriek waits outside the Kriek's severely damaged home with Jake, the elderly dog she rescued off the street on 22 February 2011.

the February event. One of the dogs she recognised as her neighbour's – he had broken out of their property in fright. The other dog was old and limping past on the street. 'I just grabbed him. I made a lead out of a bit of cabbage tree and tied it to his collar. Then I stood around with our neighbours because none of us could get into our houses as we'd all had to leave our work offices in the city with our bags and keys in them. My keys were still in SAFE's office.' This dog, whose name turned out to be Jake, stayed with Hans, Nichola and Presto for four days in their tent. 'Although he had a collar and tag, it was almost impossible for us to get through to anyone official in those first few days,' Hans explains. 'We didn't have a phone, so we had to ask Anthony Terry to ring the Christchurch City Council from Auckland – and then eventually Anthony managed to locate Jake's owners. It turned out they lived around the corner on Manchester Street, their house was destroyed and the family picked up their kids, put them in the car, and were looking everywhere for Jake but couldn't find him.'

Hans and Nichola also cared for a feline earthquake refugee who turned up after the February quake. 'We noticed him hanging around our garden and he was very, very scared and very, very thin,' Nichola reports. 'He hid under our house for around three months,' Hans adds. 'It was getting wintery and we started putting food in our workroom at home for him. He would come in and gobble it up like crazy. He was absolutely terrified of people. We managed to take a photo of him and posted it on Pets on the Net and Trade Me.' Over time this stray cat grew less wary, and Nichola was able to entice him in from the cold at night by placing in the workroom a basket containing a warm water bottle. Eventually, they were contacted by a family who confirmed that this cat was their lost companion Ginger. 'We still call his family from time to time to see how he is,' says Nichola. 'Apparently he's doing better, but still won't go outside.'

Community cat rescuers
Cat Rescue Christchurch

Of the scores of cats that reacted to the sudden impact of the earthquakes by fleeing their homes, some found their way back home. Sadly, others became earthquake refugees and were never seen by their original carers again, although the lucky ones found themselves in the care of organisations like Cat Rescue Christchurch, Cat Help, Cats Unloved and Cats' Protection League. The volunteers from these agencies have numerous stories about the cats they helped to rescue and, in many cases, rehome. While these stories touch on the heartbreak experienced by the families who lost cats, they also reflect the warmth and generosity of people who, at a difficult time, welcomed feline earthquake refugees into their lives and homes.

Sacha Dowell founded Cat Rescue Christchurch Charitable Trust in 2006 when she saw a need to help unsocialised cats in the community. Dissatisfied with the catch-and-kill system of managing stray cat populations, Cat Rescue Christchurch adopted a no-kill policy, along with the trap–neuter–return (TNR) method of controlling free-roaming cats. Before 22 February 2011 the organisation had about 12 people volunteering daily in an administrative capacity, and many more involved in the fostering of 50–60 cats around the city. In the aftermath of the quake, many of these cats had to be returned to Cat Rescue Christchurch because fosterers' homes were so badly damaged that they had to leave the city or relocate to alternative accommodation.

Sacha's house in Woolston became the focal point for the charity's operations.

> I was driving around the city a lot, picking up cats and bringing them back to my place while people were also arriving at my home to collect food and cats. I had liquefaction in the conservatory as you walk in the front door. I had to put down a plank for everyone to walk over!

At one stage Sacha had 40 cats and kittens contained in her house awaiting new foster carers or homes. 'There were earthquakes throughout the night, but I tried to continue sleeping because when I woke up it was constantly go, go, go!'

As well as providing ongoing care to cats already in their possession and awaiting permanent homes, Cat Rescue Christchurch was involved with retrieving abandoned felines from vacated properties. 'One house in Linwood came to our attention through Animal Aid,' recalls Sacha.

> People had deserted the property and left behind 12 neglected cats. The place was completely damaged. Windows were broken and there was rubbish and cat poo everywhere. It was so sad because none of the cats were desexed, they were all flea-ridden, and their kittens were actually anaemic because of the fleas.

One young cat rescued from this situation was so traumatised by his ordeal that he had developed a compulsive disorder, pulling out his own fur. Initially, he went to a home in Wellington, but was returned to Cat Rescue Christchurch when his relentless self-harming was too

Charlie (right) is one of the older ex-feral cats rescued and rehomed by Cat Rescue immediately after the February 2011 earthquake. He is sitting with another former feral cat, Lupe, also rescued post-quakes.

Annie Potts

distressing for the adopter to manage. Despite the tragic state of these cats and kittens, patient volunteers nursed them all back to health. Cat Rescue Christchurch also ensured each cat was desexed, vaccinated and micro-chipped. 'They're all still scaredy cats and it took a while, but eventually we found them all homes,' Sacha says.

Sacha feels that clear communication and collaboration with other welfare agencies played a key part in successfully managing the demand for assisting unsocialised cats after the earthquakes. As the numbers of foster carers decreased and the capacity to foster cats diminished, it was necessary to share resources with other cat rescue organisations. Part of the stray cat management process lay in counselling those people who could no longer keep their cats about how to secure a new home for them, rather than leaving the cats to fend for themselves. People who were feeding a stray cat were encouraged to exhaust all avenues to find the cat's original owner, such as reviewing lost-and-found forums on the internet.

Cat Rescue Christchurch was stretched to capacity before the earthquakes, so it came as a surprise and relief to them that cat adoptions remained steady in the weeks after the February 2011 earthquake. Sacha recalls the positive response to the call-out for volunteers which they had posted via Animal Aid on Facebook. New and previously 'retired' foster carers from Dunedin, Timaru, Ashburton and Nelson stepped up to care for the cats until permanent homes could be found. Two kittens who had arrived at Cat Rescue Christchurch with severe conjunctivitis, and who subsequently each lost an eye, were flown to Tauranga for adoption; the flight fee was waived by the airline.

Sacha was grateful for citizens collecting much-needed cash donations from friends, family and neighbours. 'It was amazing how much people wanted to help. HUHA and Paw Justice also delivered food donations, kitty litter, and TNR equipment to us.' Just as Dogwatch reported an increase in litters of puppies being born post-quake, the city's cat rescuers also noticed rising numbers of kittens, particularly out of season. Sacha explains:

> When the February quake hit, kitten season was slowing down. You tend to notice a drop-off after April but it just kept going! We were busy all year with kittens coming in. One of our vets hypothesised that stress from the earthquakes may have caused a disruption in hormonal systems, which led to the cats continuing to breed.

Cat Help

Cat Help is another charitable organisation that was involved in assisting feline casualties of the Canterbury earthquakes. With a focus on trapping urban strays living in industrial areas (such as saw mills) in order to rehabilitate, sterilise, micro-chip and rehome them, Cat Help also extends its service to helping with feline matters affecting the city's elderly and disabled citizens. Volunteer Janis Richards explains how they operate:

The Cat Help crew, Janis, Karena and Jo, with feline friend Miss Lili.

Annie Potts

> We foster in our homes, we don't have an established cattery. Although on a practical level this limits how many cats we can take at a given time, it does mean that the cats get used to living in a house with humans, and this makes them more likely to adjust to a new home when adopted.

After the February earthquake, Janis and fellow volunteers Karena Brown and Jo Nicol found that Cat Help's 24-hour rescue hotline became increasingly busy. At its peak, the charity was caring for 23 kittens and an untold number of cats, and fielding a constant flow of calls about additional cats requiring refuge. As well as fostering and rehoming earthquake refugees, the organisation assisted with front-line rescue: one case required them to climb into a roof cavity in order to set a humane cat trap so that a number of feral cats living in an elderly woman's home could be retrieved. 'EQC rang us about this issue,' explains Janis. 'They wanted to work on the house and seal the roof, but they couldn't get the cats to come out. They were feral and traumatised but this woman wanted to keep them. It's sad, but extreme hunger makes them take the risk to enter the trap,' Jo adds. In a similar case after the September 2010 earthquake, a roof cavity had already been sealed and a mother cat could not get back in to her kittens. 'We were told to come and retrieve one kitten but it turned out to be three,' Janis recalls. 'The house was lived in, and the tenants had seen the mother on the roof crying and heard kittens calling back. Once we got up into the roof and shone the torch around, there were all these little eyes. We had to hand-feed those kittens because they were so weak and dehydrated.' Unfortunately, the mother cat disappeared during the rescue of her kittens, and was not seen again.

The need to rescue deliberately abandoned cats was particularly upsetting. Janis remembers one distressing case of neglect:

> A man rang up and left a message saying "We're flying to Australia today, can you look after our 11-year-old cat?" He gave us no description of the cat, just told us where she was and to go and get her. I couldn't even ring him back as he wasn't able to be contacted. We went around to this property and it was completely trashed. They'd obviously left in a hurry because there were piles of cat food everywhere and most of it was flyblown. But we couldn't find this poor cat.

Jo adds: 'We get despondent about people's failure to realise or care that when you have a pet it's a commitment, like a child is. An animal is not an object or thing.'

Cat Help volunteers have noticed more cats being reported as strays post-quakes, and believe this increase is largely due to cats being abandoned. Jo points out:

> People who leave pet cats behind need to know that we often find their cats crying. It makes me tearful to think about it. They'd be there waiting for their owners to come back. So to all those people who think the cat will be all right, that it will survive — well, it won't survive. It's a domestic cat, not a wild one.

Janis, Jo and Karena also urge members of the public who took in stray cats post-quakes to have these animals checked for micro-chips. 'It's possible that there are people out there who haven't given up hope that their lost cats will be found, even now,' Karena explains, 'and so we ask those people who are still finding or feeding stray cats to ring our hotline so we can come around with our micro-chip scanner and check if the stray actually belongs to someone.'

Like Cat Rescue, the volunteers at Cat Help acknowledge the collaborative nature of the feline rescue effort in Christchurch. While they

One memorable Cat Help rescue story involved Chippy, who was only five months old when he was discovered in late March 2011 at the Wainoni Fish and Chips shop, where he had been surviving on cooking fat. 'He was a mess when we got him,' Jo remembers. 'We had to bathe him regularly for a few days because his digestive system was suffering from his diet on the fat.' Chippy found a loving home with Inez and her family.

lost the ability to fundraise for a few months, as their usual Saturday stall at New Brighton mall was no longer possible, SAFE and the Humane Society donated funds to Cat Help to assist them with their ever-increasing veterinary bills.

Cats' Protection League (CPL)

More stories about feline shelter and advocacy come from a well-known Christchurch institution, the Cats' Protection League (CPL), set up during the early 1970s by the late Ruby Austin. In 1997 Ruby's house in Woolston was sold to the League for the purpose of carrying on the charity's work, but the home, which now serves as a cattery for up to 40 cats at a time, was severely damaged in the February 2011 event. Secretary/Treasurer of CPL Sandra Leys explains:

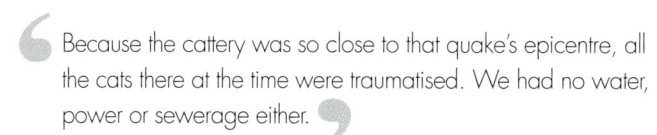

> Because the cattery was so close to that quake's epicentre, all the cats there at the time were traumatised. We had no water, power or sewerage either.

The destruction to the premises made maintaining services in the weeks and months following the earthquake stressful. Moreover, the land was zoned TC3 (indicating significant land damage from liquefaction is possible in future large earthquakes), forcing the organisation to consider permanent relocation.

While CPL's property was in upheaval, the lives of its volunteers were also turned upside down. CPL President Robin Thomson remembers that when the February quake struck she not only had to worry about her elderly mother's welfare, but was also concerned about the fate of her own cat, 'Stevie Wonder', blind from birth, who had gone missing (although he returned the following day). Added to which, she was caring for kittens in her garage who had been traumatised by objects falling on their cage during the shakes. Robin says:

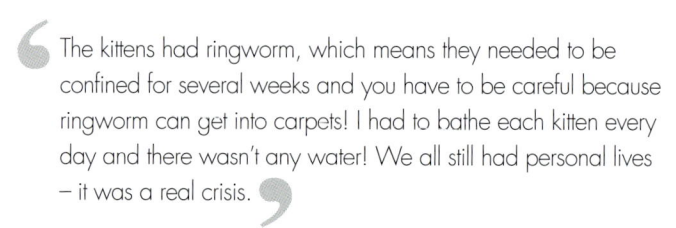

> The kittens had ringworm, which means they needed to be confined for several weeks and you have to be careful because ringworm can get into carpets! I had to bathe each kitten every day and there wasn't any water! We all still had personal lives – it was a real crisis.

Sandra tells the story of her own cat Nellie, whose reaction to the quakes seemed somewhat perverse:

> Nellie spent the first 14 years of her life under the bed – she used to hide all the time. Then suddenly after the earthquakes she was fine! What she dreaded would happen, happened! So she was finally OK and she became a lot more confident.

There were many obstacles to overcome in order to keep the organisation functioning post-quakes. Feeding the cats that were in their care was one issue. Luckily, a pallet of cat food had been delivered the day before the February earthquake, so the shed was full of food. CPL did, however, get down to one bag of kitty litter. Sandra praises SAFE's Animal Aid social media page for uniting groups and individuals so that issues such as a need for essential supplies for the cats could be broadcast and quickly resolved. Since the house-cattery was badly impaired and had lost its water supply, SAFE also set up a makeshift water tank and a port-a-loo for the volunteers. Fortunately, in the weeks after the earthquake, the rate of adoptions picked up, although it was thought best at that time to rehome cats and kittens only to families living outside Christchurch or to homes in relatively undamaged parts of the city.

Sandra, Judith Shakespeare (a CPL volunteer) and Robin remember several of CPL's post-quake success stories. One involves a cat named Boy, characterised as a 'real rogue', whose ordeal was the subject of a TV3 news clip and an article in the Christchurch *Press*. On 22 February 2011, when the magnitude 6.3 earthquake struck, Boy ran away from his Sumner home of 16 months. His then owner, Bev Harris, launched an exhaustive search for him, placing posters around the neighbourhood and listing him as lost on Trade Me. Boy had been missing for almost a year and a half, and Bev had lost all hope of finding him again, when she

Cats' Protection League's Robin Thomson and Sandra Leys (with Perfect Boy) and Judith Shakespeare (with Clover). Both cats became refugees after the February quake destroyed Sandra's brother's home. Since this image was taken in March 2013, Clover has returned to Sandra's brother, whose house was rebuilt in June 2013, while Perfect Boy remains with Sandra.

Annie Potts

Boy.

received a call to inform her that, having been found in Mt Pleasant, he had been taken in by CPL in July 2012. Although he had been micro-chipped, this had proved a dead-end as the registration details had not been updated. Unknown to the CPL and Bev Harris, Boy had also changed hands a few times since being micro-chipped. Judith explains:

> Everybody had been trying to trace where this cat belonged, then one of our CPL volunteers recognised his face from posters she'd seen put up in Sumner after the February quake. Although Boy had been living in the interim with someone else, he'd obviously taken off again. Some cats are like that, attached to places.

After his reunion with Bev, Boy continued to make his way back up the hill (depending on which way he went, this would have been a 4–10 kilometre trek), even after being kept inside for almost three months. 'Whenever he disappeared, Bev would go looking for him and he would be hanging around Summit Road waiting for her to take him back home!' Sandra laughs. When CPL last had contact with Bev, they heard the family was moving to a house in Waimate where they had been taking Boy with them on holidays for the last couple of years. 'He apparently loves it there and doesn't wander off, so it's a great move for him as well,' Sandra says.

It is usually more difficult to find new homes for mature cats, as they are not as 'cute' or playful as kittens and may already be burdened by some age-related health issues. Judith says the increased number of elderly cats requiring new homes post-quakes was at first a cause for concern, but 'in fact people have responded very positively and our worries that they would be "left on the shelf" have proved unfounded'. One mature cat whose life was saved by the CPL is Darfield. An earthquake refugee, he arrived at the cattery in poor health and CPL volunteers did not realise just how old he was at first. Sandra remembers:

> When he was surrendered to us, after being found as a stray who had either been abandoned or displaced following the

> February quake, he was very run down. A vet told us he was about 10 years old and that he'd suffered a brain injury at one time as his pupils were different sizes. His kidneys were tiny and painful, and he had a rotten tooth. He also has an allergy to fleas!

Ziggy (Darfield).

Darfield – renamed Ziggy – has continued to be bothered by stress-related health issues, but some of his anxiety responses have begun to disappear the longer he is with his new family, a young couple who live on a busy road so wanted an older cat who wouldn't wander. The couple posted this message on social media a few days after adopting the cat: 'Ziggy has spent the morning racing up and down the hallway, at one point crashing into the bathroom door while chasing his own tail! He then spent the afternoon sleeping on the bed recovering from the morning's antics'. Sandra is delighted that 'he is now very loved and spoilt rotten – and all his human grandparents look upon him as the only grandchild in the family!' Unfortunately, Darfield/Ziggy has now developed back problems too, but as Sandra points out, 'he has battled the odds and is a true survivor'.

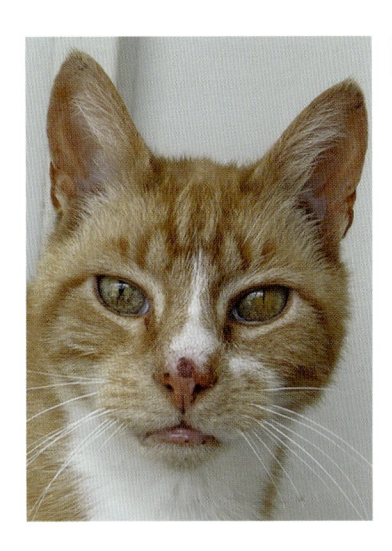

Canterbury's earthquakes also brought an abrupt end to the long-term companionship that many elderly humans and their cats had enjoyed until then. One story that demonstrates this is that of a 17-year-old feline earthquake victim called Bailey, whose guardian, a life member of CPL, had to move into a rest-home (where she later died) after her house on St Andrews Hill was destroyed in the February tremor. Sandra recounts:

> Bailey lived alone on the property for about two years after her human friend left, although the family ensured she was fed. Then she ended up coming to CPL after requiring teeth extractions and other vet treatment. We just couldn't put her to sleep after the poor cat had been alone for two years and then had her teeth out.

Bailey led a happier life with the CPL volunteers for a few more months after this ordeal, before being euthanised when her health deteriorated further.

One feline earthquake story with a happy ending involved a tiny kitten, later named Brittany, who was found in the X-ray room of Vets for Pets, the clinic used by CPL. Robin recalls:

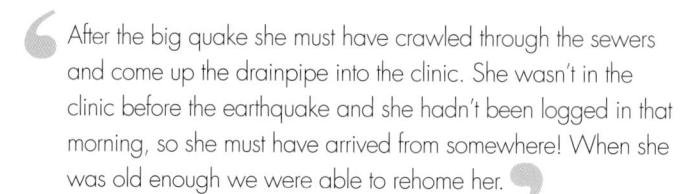

> After the big quake she must have crawled through the sewers and come up the drainpipe into the clinic. She wasn't in the clinic before the earthquake and she hadn't been logged in that morning, so she must have arrived from somewhere! When she was old enough we were able to rehome her.

Few stories in this book relate to the 13 June 2011 lunchtime earthquakes (two within an hour of each other, measuring 5.6 and 6.3 on the Richter scale). However, these events, once again centred close to Woolston, are remembered vividly by Judith and Sandra, who were both at the cattery on that day. 'We were still boiling water at that point and I had two big urns on the boil,' Judith recalls. 'I put my hands on the tops of them to keep them still!' Meanwhile, Sandra was just pulling up the drive in her car. She recalls:

> I saw all the liquefaction coming up from the ground. There were two cat-runs under liquefaction almost immediately – and the cats prefer to hide on the bottom of pens when they're frightened. We couldn't get one of the cats, Gregory, safely inside from on top of the in-built shelter in the adjoining outside enclosure – he didn't like to be handled or picked up. There was a seat, so I stood on that, grabbed him and stuck him under my arm! He wasn't grateful at all!

Gregory was a character – 'a grumpy little stray who didn't like being fussed over' – who was brought to CPL after the death of the woman who had originally found and adopted him as a stray. Later revealed to be a 'she' and renamed Gigi, this cat (whose grumpiness turned out to be due to chronic pain from an old injury) was rehomed by a woman whose previous feline companion had died on the day she moved to a new house from the residential red zone. 'She tells us that Gigi has been a great source of strength for her,' Sandra reports. 'The cat is never far away and she can't sit down without Gigi plonking herself next to her or climbing on her for a snooze.'

CPL says that even now, in 2014, they are receiving feline casualties, indirectly caused by the seismic events of 2010 and 2011. This is largely due to a shortage of sympathetic landlords in the city, as many rental properties will not permit pets. There are also signs that more

Gigi (Gregory).

and more cats continue to be neglected and abandoned as Cat Help and Cat Rescue are capturing numerous kittens growing up as strays around the city.

Paul Dahl – local hero

A name mentioned frequently during discussions with residents of Lyttelton is former ambulance officer and search and rescue volunteer Paul Dahl: with no previous experience of supporting animals in emergencies but plenty assisting humans, he stepped up to ensure that the animals in the port town were well cared for after the February 2011 earthquake. When the massive tremor occurred, Paul was underneath his house, about to leave on his motorbike for Manawatu where he was to referee an international push-bike race. 'I ran outside with my bike and all my gear! It was very confusing. From the middle of the road I was watching boulders falling from the hills above Lyttelton, and rocks coming down on Quail Island across the harbour. I knew it was very serious.'

At the time Paul was working for the QEII fitness complex (irreparably damaged on 22 February 2011), but, having learnt first aid as an ambulance officer, he quickly changed out of his riding gear and into more suitable clothes for helping anyone in the town who was injured or distressed. 'That first day I just went around the streets on my scooter, talking with people and checking they were alright.' Displaced Lyttelton residents were being looked after at the town's Recreation Centre, while the local Volunteer Fire Brigade was attending to serious infrastructure and housing issues. 'I was trying to find what I'd be most useful at. I wanted to keep busy and contribute,' Paul says.

It was the next day that he realised where he could best help out.

> In my contact with people, the issue that kept popping up most was the well-being of animals. People were telling me about animals they were concerned about – like a goat tied to a post on the hill who had fallen down the bank. They were also asking me to keep an eye on their cats when they had to evacuate their homes. So I started off feeding the cats of friends and then found out there were more and more animals around needing help.

Paul is quick to point out that the main reason animals were left at home alone in Lyttelton was because their guardians could not easily get back into the town, as both the coastal Evans Pass road to Sumner and the tunnel connecting Lyttelton to Christchurch city were closed. 'People were so worried about their pets, so I'd tell them I would go to their homes twice a day to feed and check on them. Initially, I was looking after cats, then a few goldfish, some sheep, and one woman had 25 hens whose food was trapped underneath a building and too dangerous to get to.'

Paul kept a log of addresses where animals had been left and of incidents that he attended. At the end of February 2011, a vehicle was given dispensation to travel through the tunnel from Christchurch so that it could bring hay, rabbit food and other supplies that Paul needed to look after Lyttelton's animals. 'Paw Justice volunteers dropped off some stock donated by Aucklanders. They'd also collected animal food donated by suppliers. We ended up with two to three truckloads that we shared with another woman from Paw Justice who stockpiled at her place. I'd just go there, fill up my van, and head off to feed animals.' Lyttelton's animals came to know Paul's generosity very well. He laughs as he recalls:

> There's one dog who still comes back to my house! He lives way up the hill but he remembers I had all the food back then! And the cat next door knows where the food came from too – if the dog arrives down from the hill, she also goes on patrol, and they both come upstairs to the kitchen to check if anything exciting is happening.

Paul's voluntary work on behalf of animals took him beyond Lyttelton, to Aranui and New Brighton, two of the worst-affected eastern suburbs. 'Many elderly people were struggling during this time,' he recalls. 'When I found them, they were reluctant to take food from me, but since there were no supermarkets open around these areas they'd resign themselves to my getting some things for them. Whatever they asked for, I'd double it in quantity. They were special because, even under those awful circumstances, these older people were so selfless. They would tell me to first look after others worse off than them.' Paul remembers delivering animal food to centres that were caring for the needs of senior citizens. 'We wouldn't ask if the people wanted or needed the pet food. We'd just ask if they had a pet, and if they said yes, we gave it to them without any further questions.'

Paul also teamed up with veterinarians following the February disaster. Although he did not see any physical injuries, he did observe great distress amongst the animals he looked after in some of the worst-affected areas. He also witnessed the darker side of human relationships with animals:

> I saw animals abused by their people. When we heard about possible instances of animal abuse, we'd go to that property with donations of pet food as a way to assess the situation, and sometimes we'd leave with dogs having to be carried out. I could tell they were in bad shape. There was one place where the backyard contained 50 hens. The owners had deserted this home and were no longer living there. There were cats and geese and chickens – it was filthy and stinking – they'd been neglected for a while. Paw Justice acted as a conduit for getting animals like this out, and into the care of welfare agencies.

In summary

A number of organisations and individuals were committed to helping animals in the aftermath of the Canterbury earthqakes, providing temporary shelter, securing permanent new homes, and advocating for their welfare. The stories in this chapter demonstrate the extraordinary energy that these compassionate people invested in improving the outcomes for the region's animals. Significantly, the safety and well-being of *individual animals* matters to them, whether these animals are loved companions or are categorised as stray or feral. The accounts show the high degree of generosity and solidarity demonstrated across agencies, and reveals how they shared resources and pooled their respective areas of expertise in order to achieve the common goal of saving the city's non-human residents from dire circumstances, and even death.

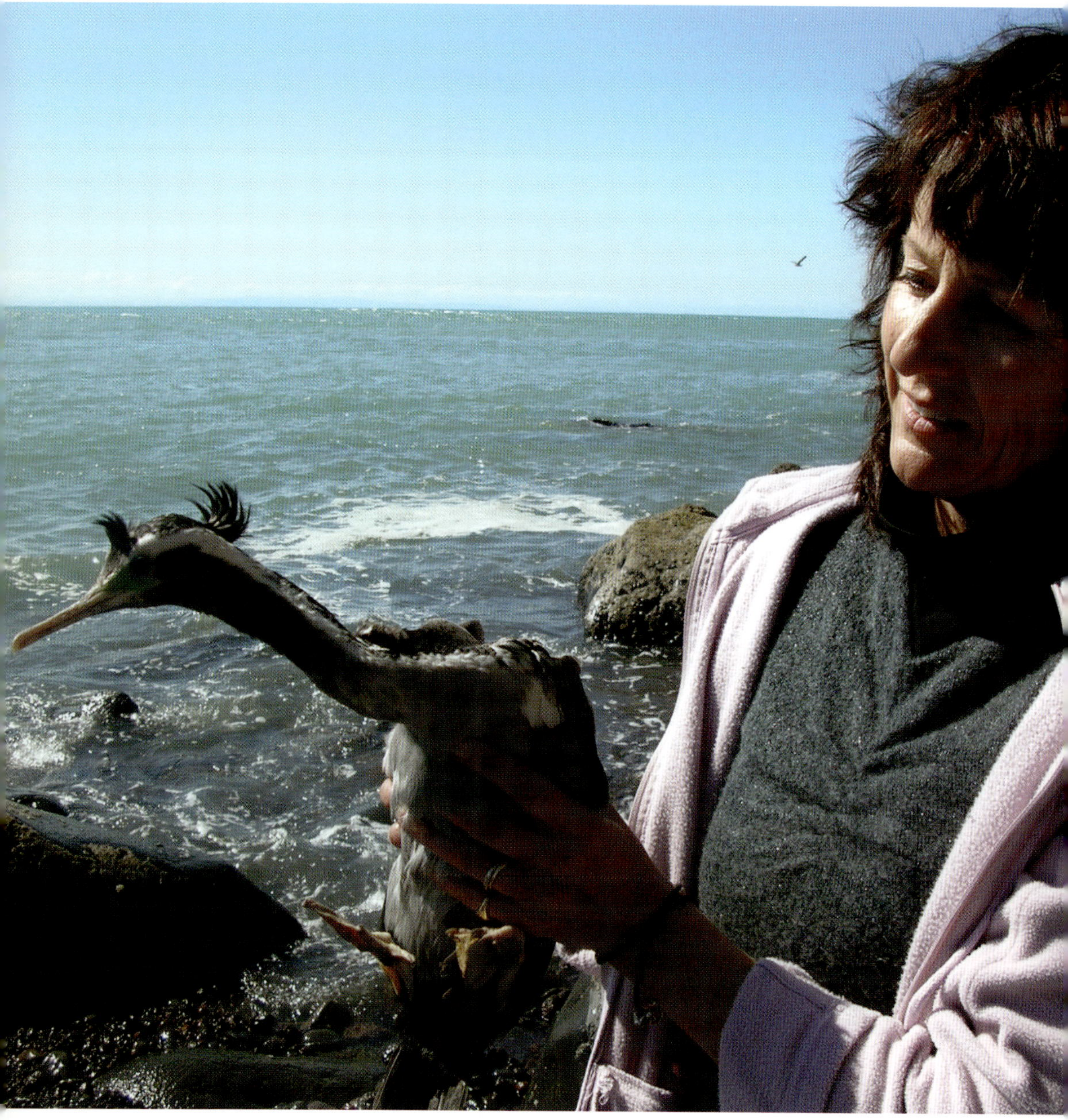

Part Two
Animal Earthquake Stories

Opposite page: Urban wildlife rescuer Janetta Stead about to release a shag displaced by the earthquakes from the Scarborough cliffs nesting ground (story page 210).

Janetta Stead

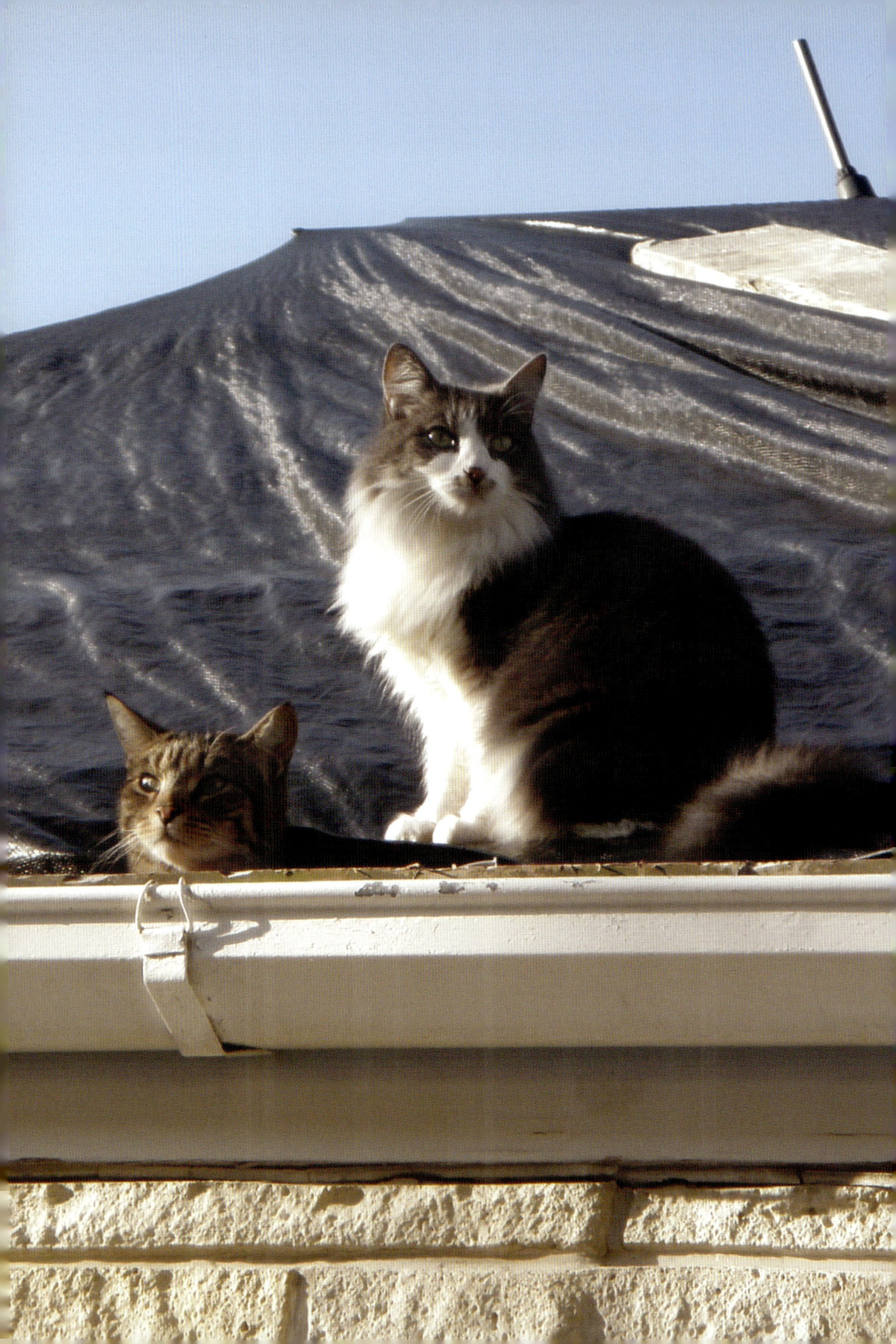

Chapter 3
Feline tales

The cat is a species that has adapted well to living alongside human beings. This mutually beneficial relationship between felines and humans has seen cats forge a prolific presence in urban landscapes as they share these built-up spaces alongside their human guardians as part of our families. Cats are independent, yet most are also affectionate, and it is this combination of characteristics that makes this species a popular choice of companion animal, especially in New Zealand, which boasts the highest rate of feline guardianship in the world, with more than half our homes housing at least one cat and more than a quarter housing more than one (New Zealand Companion Animal Council, 2011).

The proverbial 'nine lives' attributed to cats reflects the uncanny ability of this species to survive in extreme circumstances, to prevail against the odds and overcome adversity; however, it also risks misrepresenting them as being far less susceptible to harm and trauma than they are. As a result of joining our human families, cats are in a situation where they are exposed to traumas such as earthquakes in much the same way as we are. They are sensitive creatures, and equally vulnerable in emergency situations. Cats tend to develop strong territorial bonds with their built environment – the homes they share with human beings – and they grow deeply attached to those who care for them. Just as humans may be physically injured and psychologically traumatised, and can be forced to leave their homes after major earthquakes, cats may also suffer injury, stress and displacement. Displacement occurs when cats run away in fright; or they may be abandoned by their guardians and left behind to fend for themselves.

Beginning with accounts of cats who seemed to predict seismic activity, this chapter then moves through a collection of stories from

Opposite page: Stella and housemate Echo survey the damage from the roof of their house in Heathcote Valley, spring 2011 (story on page 120).

people whose lives intersected with the feline casualties of the Canterbury earthquakes. They involve cats who were physically injured and/or psychologically traumatised by the quakes, those who fled their homes during tremors and were lost permanently, and others who ran away but were reunited with their guardians or found new homes with different families. This small sample of stories offers a snapshot of the myriad ways in which earthquakes have affected Canterbury's cats.

Sensing seismic shifts

While it has proved difficult for geologists, physicists and seismologists to develop a system capable of predicting tectonic jolts, there is some consensus that many animal species possess the ability to sense the geological activity leading up to an earthquake before the quake strikes (see pages 111–113). Cats are one such species.

In his blog *Four Legs Good* Nick Barnett posted an article 'Pets and the Quake' about the reactions of cats to the 4 September 2010 earthquake; he drew on Kirsty Johnston's interviews with people who reported that their cats seemed to sense impending seismic activity, which they appeared to communicate via their agitated behaviour. Lea Hullet of Timaru, for example, stated that just before the tremor at 4.35am that morning, her Siamese cat Moses became restless and tried to wake her by touching her face with his paw. Similarly, Penny McMurtrie of Ashburton says that she was woken just before the quake by her cat's persistent meowing (Barnett, 2011).

Residents in Ashburton, a town about an hour's drive south of Christchurch, were affected by the region's tremors, and particularly by the September event. Rae Magson is another Ashburton resident who can recount her personal experience of cats predicting earthquakes. Since 2001, she and her and husband had been sharing their home with two Burmese cats, Celcee and Chelcee:

> In the early hours of that morning on September 4th 2010, I was woken by Chelcee frantically trying to crawl up my body underneath my nightgown, which she had never done before. Believe me, it was not pleasant! She seemed to be in a real panic. Then the earthquake started and she was terrified. She had obviously known something was wrong. I clutched her as we stood under the doorway. Our other cat, Celcee, disappeared for several hours.

Rae Magson's granddaughter Danielle McNab with one of the Burmese cats, Chelcee.

Smudge

One feline who seemed to sense impending seismic activity consistently was Di Barritt's 12-year-old tortoiseshell and white cat, Smudge. In September 2010 Di and Smudge were living in a council flat with a private courtyard in the Christchurch suburb of Woolston. 'Smudge woke at 3am feeling very uneasy about something,' Di recounts. 'She tried to tell me that something bad was going to happen by repeatedly jumping on me, but at that stage I was a bit lax in the "cat language" department!' Over the next one and a half hours Smudge continued this behaviour, which perplexed Di:

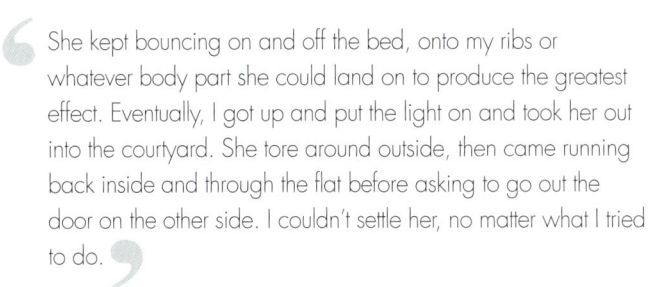

> She kept bouncing on and off the bed, onto my ribs or whatever body part she could land on to produce the greatest effect. Eventually, I got up and put the light on and took her out into the courtyard. She tore around outside, then came running back inside and through the flat before asking to go out the door on the other side. I couldn't settle her, no matter what I tried to do.

Di did notice that in contrast to the stillness of a typical, cold September night, the birds were very active in the trees 'creating a

Smudge.

racket'.[1] She watched them for a while before she made herself a hot drink and an early breakfast. 'Then,' she says, 'at 4.15am, everything went deadly quiet.'

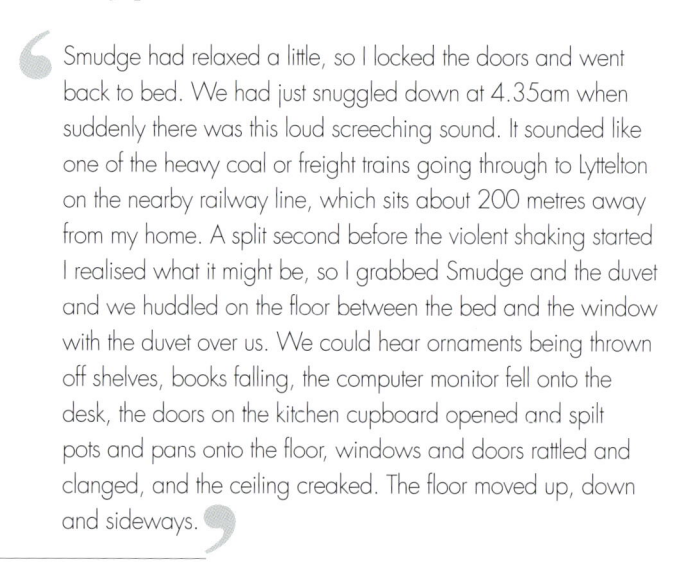

> Smudge had relaxed a little, so I locked the doors and went back to bed. We had just snuggled down at 4.35am when suddenly there was this loud screeching sound. It sounded like one of the heavy coal or freight trains going through to Lyttelton on the nearby railway line, which sits about 200 metres away from my home. A split second before the violent shaking started I realised what it might be, so I grabbed Smudge and the duvet and we huddled on the floor between the bed and the window with the duvet over us. We could hear ornaments being thrown off shelves, books falling, the computer monitor fell onto the desk, the doors on the kitchen cupboard opened and spilt pots and pans onto the floor, windows and doors rattled and clanged, and the ceiling creaked. The floor moved up, down and sideways.

---

1   In Whitehead and Ulsoy's (2013) study on macroscopic anomalies before Christchurch's 4 September 2010 earthquake, they state that unusual heightened activity in birds during the 10 or so minutes preceding an earthquake is a universal observation (p. 170). See also this book pages 111–113.

In the moments after the shaking stopped, Di gathered up Smudge and climbed into the wardrobe with her in case it resumed. When they emerged, Di surveyed the damage and was thankful to find that she still had power and a telephone connection. She was able to contact relatives and inform them that she and Smudge were all right.

Di came to recognise that Smudge's agitation was a precursor to an earthquake and this unusual behaviour became a cue allowing Di to gain valuable seconds before it struck. 'She would sit up and look intently at the ceiling and walls, and then depending on how strong it was going to be, she would either stare at the ceiling and then at me if it was going to be over about 3.5 magnitude, or she would curl back up on the bed if it was going to be any smaller.'

Animals predicting earthquakes

Reports from natural disasters such as the devastating earthquakes that struck Kobe, Japan, in 1995 and Izmit, Turkey, in 1999, indicate there is validity to the claim that observed changes in animal behaviour were precursors to those events. In 2013, N. E. Whitehead and U. Ulusoy conducted research to establish whether the same could be said for the magnitude 7.1 earthquake that struck Christchurch at 4.35am on 4 September 2010.

Research undertaken in 2004 had revealed that many animals (35 species were tested) are highly sensitive to ultra-low frequency electromagnetic radiation, which causes them to display 'unusually itchy and anxious behaviour' (Whitehead & Ulusoy, 2013, p. 167). This type of radiation is thought to be capable of travelling many kilometres from the epicentre of an earthquake through either water or rock.

Whitehead and Ulusoy conducted a survey of people who had precursor stories, including claims of observing unusual behavioural changes in companion animals prior to the earthquake. The researchers also spoke with staff at local veterinary practices and wildlife rescue facilities. While interested in the reactions of animals, Whitehead and Ulusoy also enquired into whether those surveyed had experienced precursors in other forms, such as the phenomena of 'earthquake lights'[1] in the sky or anomalies in the function of electronic equipment (p. 168).

The research produced some significant findings. Whereas 6.4% of those surveyed reported experiencing electronic precursors, and 20% reported that they noticed earth or meteorological signs, 56.5% of the

---

1 'Earthquake lights' is the term given to the mysterious flickers of light sometimes observed prior to the occurrence of major seismic activity. Scientists now speculate this phenomenon may be triggered by shifting soil layers, which create huge electrical charge (Morgan, 2014).

study's informants stated that they had observed what they believed to be an animal's precursor reaction to the imminent earthquake. For example:

> Orana Wildlife Park reported dogs wanting to go outside at 4.00am just before the September earthquake, and subsequently about five minutes before aftershocks. Similarly, their birds tended to go silent for the same time period,[1] and a waterbuck displayed unusual silent defensive behaviour several minutes before aftershocks; this response was so consistent that the waterbuck was termed by one staff member their "earthquake indicator" (p. 169).

Dogs and cats were commonly reported as showing alterations in normal patterns of behaviour prior to tremors occurring:

> There were numerous reports of dogs near observers creating a chorus of barking several minutes to tens of minutes before the quake and aftershocks, but choruses of barking were not always followed by an aftershock, so any reaction was erratic. Amongst the reported animal data ... were 16 stories of owners being pawed awake (mostly by cats) and usually on the face, a few minutes prior to the quake. This was usually said to be unique behaviour for the animal within the ownership period, and is hence rather convincing. Many of a further 40 reports were of owners woken by extreme barking and dogs wanting to be let out of the house (p. 171).

What is particularly interesting is that the authors of this report suggest that being warned of imminent earthquakes by restless dogs and cats has the potential to save human lives:

> In seven cases, the owner let the dog out, but was standing in or very near the door when the earthquake occurred. They were inadvertently led to the (probably) safest part of the house, and thus the dog acted as an accidental safety source. One respondent reported that the incident led to escape from injury when wall ornaments above the bed were dislodged. In Kobe, similarly, dogs particularly tried to make owners go outside with them. One could argue, as one Christchurch respondent did,

---

1   This observation is in contrast to other accounts, where increased bird activity or noise is noted to occur prior to seismic activity (see Di Barritt's story). Both are, however, examples of atypical bird behaviour at different times of the day.

> that being woken could lead to more alertness and a more appropriate reaction when the quake struck (p. 171).

Hence, Whitehead and Ulusoy suggest that 'giving in to insistent pet whims in some cases could also save lives' (p. 175). Whitehead and Ulusoy claim that many Cantabrians placed so much faith in their animals' ability to forecast earthquakes after September 2010 that by February 2011, companion animals were readily being used as an early-warning system.

One further revelation of the study was the finding that twice as many companion animals were reported lost and found in the week *before* the September 2010 quake.

As a result of their findings, Whitehead and Ulusoy uphold the claim that some species may sense seismic activity before it is felt by humans. Theirs is one in a series of on-going research studies into whether earthquake precursors exist and in what form they may prove most useful in saving lives in the future.

Smudge, Di's 'early-warning system', lived through many major earthquakes and countless aftershocks. After that pre-dawn event in September 2010 she endured the 2010 Boxing Day earthquake while home alone. On that day Smudge hid in the wardrobe, which Di had thoughtfully left with its door ajar just in case an earthquake occurred while she was out. 'When I got home there was no power to the house, the water from the toilet had spilled out onto the floor and once again many ornaments and books had fallen or broken. I found Smudge and gave her a huge cuddle and sat down and talked to her for ages to calm her down.' Smudge also experienced the February 2011 earthquake, as well as the two significant aftershocks on 13 June 2011. Sadly, two and a half years following Canterbury's first major quake, Smudge succumbed to renal failure, but Di believes her cat was one of the lucky ones because being locked inside when the significant earthquakes happened meant she was unable to run away. Thousands of cats did flee their homes during these frightening events: some would return home unassisted and others were never seen by their original families again.

Andre

Of the many reactions to earthquakes observed in cats, their most common responses are running away and hiding.

Andre, adopted from the SPCA in 2009 by Rosie and Dave Halligan, is one cat who responded to the 4 September 2010 earthquake by hiding. Rosie says Andre has always been a very timid cat, especially around other people. When the September quake struck, Rosie first feared that

Andre.

Andre might have fled. 'Thank God he was fine,' she says, 'but he did hide under our bed for four days after'. While Andre managed to endure the large quake, Rosie says that he found the relentless aftershocks incredibly daunting, and to this day he is upset if the ground shakes. 'If Andre is on the bed, his reaction to any earthquake is to stare up at the ceiling and then emit a very deep-throated growl,' Rosie explains. This new behaviour is out of character for Andre. Andre's distress following the 22 February earthquake was exacerbated by an eruption of skin sores, subsequently diagnosed as a stress-related condition, and successfully treated by a course of antibiotics.

No place like home

A popular saying suggests that 'dogs bond to people and cats to places'. To imply that such an attachment cannot exist between cats and humans is, however, simplistic. A dog's territory is typically limited to the backyard, whereas cats have much larger areas in which to range and claim as their own. So it is understandable that cats tend to be drawn back to houses or neighbourhoods where they had previously lived; but this does not mean they are less attached to their human companions, as the following story illustrates.

Romeo

Diane Provost describes her female cat Romeo as 'shy', and 'affectionate' towards only a select group of people. When the September 2010 earthquake shook the Provost home in Christchurch's Hillsborough suburb, Romeo took off and did not immediately return. The family had shifted to this property only a year before the 7.1 magnitude tremor. Diane explains:

> We had moved from a house that had many trees, bushes and shrubs – it was in St Martins, two suburbs east from Hillsborough. Romeo had been very happy there and spent her days playing amongst the shrubbery and high up in the trees. Our new house didn't have the same environment and she found that challenging, but she did settle and would spend much of her time outdoors and away from the house in the nearby reserve.

Romeo remained missing for three weeks after the September earthquake and Diane grew increasingly concerned for her well-being. Then a friend suggested she go back to the St Martins house to check whether Romeo had returned to their previous home, as cats often do. Diane drove back to their old house and was surprised to find Romeo straight away. 'As soon as I called her name, she popped out of a bush and into my arms. When we arrived back in Hillsborough she was overly affectionate towards me in a way that she had never been before.'

Romeo.

Romeo was strongly attached to the familiar St Martin's property; it seems that she felt safer there, so returning to this house became her default response to tremors (even though a new cat was now living in this home). Diane continues:

> A pattern had begun. After any significant aftershock, she would immediately vanish and reappear at our old house. This happened 10 times over a period of months. Each time I went to retrieve her became a little more complicated. It took longer to coax her out, to convince her to come close enough so that I could grab her. A tin of fish was always helpful. Whenever we got her home she would act lovingly and would throw herself over me. But then when I went to retrieve her that tenth time, she wasn't having any of it and she ran from me. There was no convincing her.

The new occupier of the St Martins home allowed Diane to leave food out for Romeo while they figured out a way to bring her back for good. The plan involved hiring a cat trap from the SPCA, and following their advice to keep Romeo inside the Hillsborough house for at least one month. Diane also plugged in a pheromone diffuser and always left an inner door open so that Romeo could seek refuge beneath the stairwell in the event of an earthquake. Eventually, Diane let Romeo go back outside and, although she stills runs away when significant aftershocks occur, she now hides in the vicinity of her new home, returning to it in her own good time.

Stormy

Another story of a cat that ran away comes from Jacquie Walters, whose nine-year-old cat, Stormy, vanished after the February 2011 earthquake and returned 12 days later. Stormy had been adopted through the Auckland SPCA in January 2004 when she was one year old. 'She had been maltreated and so was quite skittish at the best of times,' Jacquie says, but after they moved south from the Bay of Islands in December 2010, Stormy had adjusted well to life in the coastal town of Sumner.

Then the February earthquake struck and Jacquie had to vacate her house immediately; she started relocating to a rental house in Mairehau. 'There were no services to our home and it wasn't safe to stay living there,' she recalls. 'I had two children under the age of five to think about.' Unfortunately, when the time came to leave, there was no sign of Stormy.

But like many others whose cats disappeared after earthquakes

Stormy.

and who had to relocate, Jacquie went back 'home' regularly to leave food out for Stormy; the city was still in chaos and the journey from Mairehau to Sumner took about 90 minutes. Stormy did not appear during any of these visits, and Jacquie recalls how her intense fears of having lost her for good, and her hopes that she would find her again, were accompanied by a sense of discomfort and unease:

> There was a feeling that being concerned about a pet at this time was a bit trivial when so much else was going on. I felt guilty that I was worrying about Stormy so much. It distressed me that wherever she was, she was without the comfort of people at night. The aftershocks would have frightened her, of course, and animals have no way of knowing what's going on.

Still hopeful of finding Stormy, Jacquie had posted 'missing' notices on Pets on the Net and Trade Me. On one occasion she thought she had seen her, only to realise that the cat was a stray and probably somebody else's missing companion:

> I saw the cat across the road from our former house in Sumner and called out to it. It was in a very bad way and looked

> malnourished and ill. It wouldn't let me get near it and eventually ran away. It upset me that I didn't know whether or not the cat was Stormy. I realised I had no idea what kind of state she would be in, whether she was injured or hurt, or how badly affected she might be after so long with potentially no food or water.

Jacquie also recalls receiving a phone call from a woman who was working tirelessly to reconnect people with their lost companions and who had seen Stormy's missing cat notice:

> She encouraged me to keep putting food and water out and told me that cats don't generally wander far from home but tend to hide when they're stressed. She told me not to give up hope. It was wonderful that she took the time to call. Her compassion at a time when so many people had suffered bereavement and extraordinary loss was very touching.

With the relocation to the rental property almost complete, future visits to the Sumner house were to become less frequent and the chances of sighting Stormy less likely:

> I'd almost given up, and on the last day of moving belongings I was sitting on the back doorstep. I had decided to wait until it got dark in the hope that Stormy might come home for food. I sat there calling her and feeling increasingly desolate. Suddenly, a little face appeared through the neighbour's fence looking as pleased to see me as I was to see her. She scaled the fence and hopped down into my arms.

Remarkably, after going missing for almost two weeks Stormy returned home fit and uninjured. Jacquie recalls the sense of immense relief: 'I think all the emotions that had been pent up in the days that she had been missing and the pressure I had been under came out as happy tears.'

Elderly cat weathers the quakes

Canterbury's earthquakes had a significant impact on ageing companion animals. Apart from the shock and stress associated with such unexpected and life-changing events, the older cats may be more vulnerable to physical injuries and take longer to recover.

Brett and Heather Douglas' black cat Olive – so named because she resembled a kalamata olive – was 19 years old when the first major earthquake struck Christchurch in 2010. She had grown up in Auckland where she lived as part of the Douglas family until they moved temporarily to Hong Kong, then during the five years her family were overseas, she stayed with feline-friendly relatives in Hamilton. After returning from Hong Kong, the Douglas family relocated to Christchurch and Olive was flown down to be reunited with them. They were incredulous to discover that she now weighed 8.5 kilograms and, Heather says, 'virtually rolled off the plane'. Heather explains:

> Olive was rather a pampered queen, with her own bedroom, a big basket with sheepskin and an electric blanket in the winter months. She happily roamed upstairs and down, but mainly just to find a sunny spot to sleep in or to look for food. One of the highlights of her day was to get in the shower and drink the water. She didn't even mind if people were using the shower at the time – she was happy to join in. She'd also jump up on her special blanket on the couch and watch TV with us. In those days life was safe and wonderful!

However, as the years went by, the ageing Olive found it increasingly difficult to move up and down the stairs and she preferred to remain indoors.

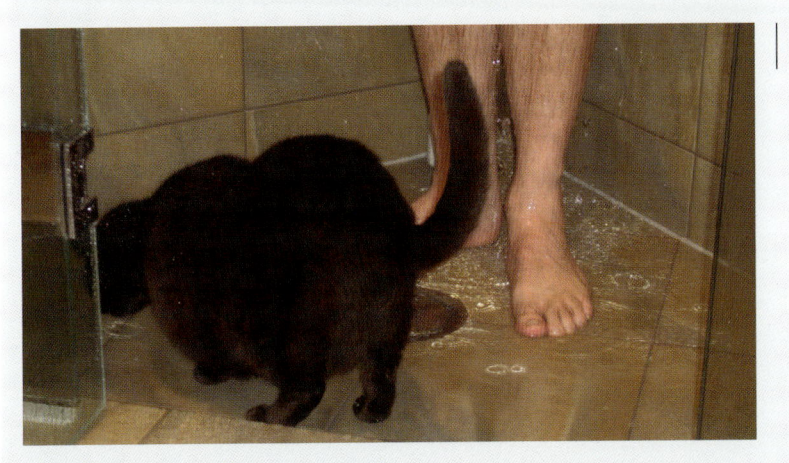

Olive enjoying a drink in the shower.

Olive in a sunny spot.

When the magnitude 7.1 earthquake struck Christchurch on 4 September 2010, Olive suffered a stroke. 'It was terrible. She immediately lost partial vision in one eye – we found her staring into space in a trance.' In a valiant attempt to return Olive to good health and restore her quality of life, Brett and Heather, and their veterinarians, explored every possible option. She underwent many tests, including X-rays and blood tests, and was prescribed medication to assist her recovery. 'Olive really wasn't good with pills,' Heather recalls, 'and she would clamp her mouth firmly shut, refusing to play ball!'

As the months progressed, Olive's health did not improve. The relentless stream of aftershocks compounded her trauma, until finally it became too much for her. 'She lost weight, developed twitches and became depressed and lethargic,' Heather recounts. 'We were extremely worried about her. Her back legs stopped working and we had to encourage her to keep moving and not to give up. Olive tried so hard, but it was exhausting for her. She couldn't even make it to the kitty litter. She just wanted to sleep.'

Just over a year after the September earthquake, on 17 October 2011, the difficult decision was made to have Olive euthanised at the age of 20. 'We were both totally devastated and cried, the vet cried, the receptionist cried, everyone cried, but Olive had decided she'd had enough.'

Twenty is a laudable age for a companion cat, but it is likely that the trauma experienced by Olive in response to the earthquakes not only resulted in the stroke that left her partially blind, but also hastened her decline.

Happy reunions

Some cats who had fled during the earthquakes managed to find their way home after days, weeks or months away. Others were rescued by community members or came to be in the care of one of the many dedicated animal welfare organisations that responded to the Canterbury earthquakes (see chapters 1 and 2). When cats were reunited with human guardians, they sometimes bore physical and psychological scars, signs of the trauma they had endured.

Stella

Stella, Karla Osmer's cat, is one such cat who eventually returned home, injured and traumatised by her ordeal. Her original guardian had developed an allergic reaction to cat fur, so passed Stella on to her parents. However, Stella was bullied by the resident cats there, and came into Karla's home as an adult, aged approximately 18 months.

Karla took Stella to Heathcote to live with her and her son Nathan, then 12 years old. The earthquake of 22 February 2011 prompted Stella, already a timid cat, to shoot out of the cat door and flee the property. The family's other cat, Echo, also disappeared that day.

Karla, who currently works for the Earthquake Commission, was at the time a self-employed web designer. She was in her home on Port Hills Road in Heathcote when the February quake struck:

> I was sitting at the table working on a clothing website. The microwave toppled down, just missing me. I got to the door and hung on, and clung like that all the way through the quake. Because we lived in Heathcote the house got the entire upward lift, but the school where my son was at the time got the highest lift. So when the shaking stopped I picked my way through everything that had fallen and ran down to the school and found Nathan. Thankfully, none of the children were hurt, and I stayed there until all of them had been picked up. When I brought Nathan home there was no sign of the cats, they were well and truly gone.

Karla and Nathan's home was so severely damaged in the earthquake that they had to go and stay with a friend in a less seriously affected suburb of the city. During the week after the February event, Karla went back to Heathcote daily to look for her cats. Echo came back on the third day.

In early March, Karla and Nathan returned to live at their property in the valley, where they had to share a sleep-out and caravan, as the house was uninhabitable. 'The sleep-out was also damaged and leaked, so whenever it rained it was a bit depressing,' Karla recalls. 'The roof of the house had broken tiles – it was munted really. But we got a toilet from the City Council and we went and washed at the shed where the Council set up temporary showers.' Despite these rougher living conditions, Karla wanted to stay in Heathcote in order to be there if Stella returned. 'But she didn't,' Karla says. 'At that time I shut myself in another world. I wouldn't watch the news because I didn't want to see any of the awful things.'

Karla continued to put food out for Stella and checked several lost-and-found pet registries regularly. 'There were *so many* animals in Christchurch who had just fled their homes,' she recalls, and the food she left out for Stella attracted two other feline earthquake refugees who would appear from out of the gully near the stream at the rear of her property. 'I think it must have felt like a safe place for the animals, enclosed like that. They used to come out but they were really scared.' Karla recognised one of these cats from her Trade Me searches, so she called the person who had listed her. A few weeks later, this same woman told Karla that she thought she had seen Stella under the bridge of the motorway that leads to the Lyttelton tunnel three kilometres away.

By this time, Karla and Nathan were house-sitting for three weeks in Linwood but travelling back to the bridge to look for Stella every night.

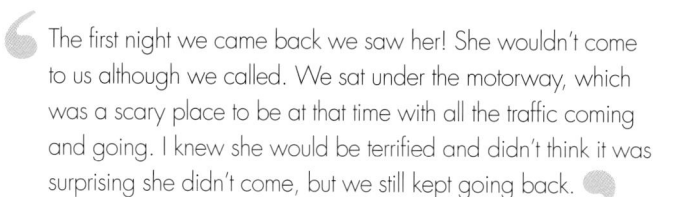

> The first night we came back we saw her! She wouldn't come to us although we called. We sat under the motorway, which was a scary place to be at that time with all the traffic coming and going. I knew she would be terrified and didn't think it was surprising she didn't come, but we still kept going back.

Six weeks on from the February quake and once again living in Heathcote, Stella and Nathan were still trying in vain to entice Stella out from under the bridge. Her reticence was perhaps natural but it was frustrating and sad for them. When, on 1 April 2011, Stella hobbled into their home on three legs, one leg caught in her collar, Karla was stunned. 'She just walked in through the cat door – it was one of those amazing moments. It was the last thing I expected. By this time I thought she would never return – it didn't occur to me that she had died or anything like that, but she was really sick.' Stella was emaciated and her collar had become snagged beneath her armpit causing a deep infected wound. Karla says,

> I don't know how she would have been able to find food with the collar caught around her neck and leg. Maybe she found fish along the stream. There was no way she could have caught a bird. She could hardly walk let along catch her own food. When I saw her I thought she must have come home to die. She was just skin and bones and this awful wound. But she was home, and to us that was a miracle.

Karla immediately took Stella to her veterinarian who operated to repair the wound. Stella stayed at the veterinary clinic for a week before she could come back home. 'I would go to the vet's and just sit there and stay and talk with Stella. It was the loveliest time,' she says. Stella had one further operation on the lesion and was put on an intensive feeding regime. Mother and son had endured enormous personal upheaval – having lost their house and seen their neighbours and community in chaos – but it was the return of their beloved cat that finally enabled some emotional recovery for Karla. She confides:

> I never cried after the earthquake at all. I was quite strong. But I cried and cried and cried when we found Stella. It was my grieving time for all we'd been through. In some ways it was like now, finally, we were all back together as a family and everyone was OK.

Karla recalls how differently the human and feline members of her household responded to the quakes: 'Echo came back after three days and he didn't seem traumatised at all. He was like my son – when the aftershocks came, Nathan would see if he could ride them out, like he was on a skateboard! I wasn't like that at all – every little shake would have me up against the door again. And Stella – well, obviously, she was very upset.'

In fact, Karla has since observed a more permanent change in Stella's character, which she speculates is connected to her feline friend's earthquake ordeal.

> She sticks much closer to home now. She's far more affectionate. She's still timid and doesn't like loud noises, but now she'll come

Stella with Karla and Nathan Osmer in their damaged Heathcote Valley home, March 2013.

Annie Potts

> and jump up beside us and she would never do that before. I used to have to beg her for cuddles!

This new physical affection is very much appreciated; it is comforting and stabilising for the family. 'Even this far down the track we're still a bit on edge, a little bit unsure. Stella really enjoys the quiet time when we can feel safe. I think we've all felt that sense of safety has kind of been taken away from us.'

Pudd

When the February 2011 earthquake struck, Tarn Mullaly had to wait four hours until she could make it home to check on her 'fur-baby' Pudd, an 11-year-old tabby cat. Tarn, who works at Christchurch Airport, was walking up a warehouse stairway to an upstairs office when the tremor occurred. She recalls her predicament at the time:

> It became impossible to go further up, so I retraced my steps. I couldn't move around without letting go of the handrails and I was well aware of the towering stacks of archive boxes swaying precariously above me on the pallet racking. I looked around the warehouse but no one was there. My first thought was that it was a big quake and I wanted to get home.

'Home' at the time meant living out of suitcases and cartons at her sister's house. 'It was a real challenge to find a place to live after the September quake the year before,' Tarn explains.

Tarn left work and endured an excruciatingly slow journey to her sister's house on St Andrews Hill, a suburb in the city's southeast. The traffic was gridlocked, with everyone trying to get home to reunite with their loved ones. Tarn says: 'The cars were bumper to bumper and I could hear the loud Civil Defence alarms. Each time cars paralleled on the jammed-up roads, the same radio station was playing, but there wasn't any shared humour in that. I exchanged blank gazes with the other equally perplexed, shocked drivers. We were all a bit stunned.'

Damage to the roads, which were flooded and filling up with silt and liquefaction, meant some routes were blocked. All the while, cars continued to enter the roadways as many more citizens exited the devastated city centre. 'One-way streets became two-way and traffic lights were ignored,' Tarn recalls. When she finally arrived at her sister's home, she was greeted by grim faces:

> The house looked like a bomb site. Shards of glass were everywhere and no one knew if it was even safe to enter. I remember gingerly stepping over the upturned washing machine and dryer, and I passed the kitchen where the entire contents of the pantry and kitchen cupboards were on the floor. Crockery mixed with glassware, preserves and dried pasta shells were knee deep. There was plum sauce on the walls – it was chaos. The exterior retaining walls were bulging, and almost all the exterior cladding had fallen off. There was no power and no water.

Finding the house in such a terrible state was distressing. It was clear evidence that it had been subject to violent jolting, which meant that Pudd, who had been inside, had also endured this. Tarn looked for her cat and soon found 'his familiar silhouetted hump under the duvet cover'. He was obviously terrified by the events of that day, so Tarn decided that he would feel safe in his favourite position on top of the pantry. 'There was a small space above the pantry under the ceiling, so I put Pudd's furry cat bed, a blanket, fresh food and water from my own water bottle up there for him. But the bad shaking continued through the night and by morning, he had vanished.' Tarn was devastated. 'I cursed myself for putting him on top of the pantry. I noticed in the morning that the entire cupboard was on a lean. He had already been through so much the day of the big quake and now he was somewhere likely feeling scared and alone.' She embarked on an extensive locate-and-recover campaign, calling radio stations, registering Pudd on lost-and-found forums and wandering in the vicinity of her sister's home daily, calling out her cat's name. Tarn spoke with neighbours and the police. 'I went to the SPCA in Hornby, and made posters and flyers, hundreds of them, but out of 44 houses I delivered flyers to on that afternoon following the big quake, only eight people were home.'

Two weeks on and Pudd was still missing, and the weeks of worrying were taking their toll on Tarn. Her spirits lifted slightly when she received a call from a Samaritan in Wellington who was using her spare time to try and match lost and found animals. The selfless efforts of this stranger inspired Tarn to renew her own efforts to find Pudd:

> Deep down, I knew Pudd was still alive. But I also knew he was in trouble. So I amped up my search efforts and broadened the region – I travelled to Shirley, Dallington, Linwood, Sumner, Redcliffs, and even followed one potential sighting in Bishopdale … one door at a time. Whenever one of my posters

> was removed, a new one was put up in its place straight away. So many phone-calls, emails and time spent searching the internet! Five weeks passed, but I wouldn't give up.

Determined to find out what had happened to Pudd, Tarn also reluctantly started examining the 'deceased pet' information lists as well.

Following a number of false sightings, and seven weeks after Pudd had vanished, Tarn received a late-evening phone-call about another potential sighting of Pudd, this time in the vicinity of Bridal Path Road in Heathcote, not far from where she was in St Andrews Hill. She set off immediately and was met there by a man called Russell, the kind person who had phoned her. He had even taken a photograph; however, the picture of this scrawny stray convinced Tarn that the cat he had seen was not her missing Pudd who had weighed an impressive 10 kilograms at the time of his disappearance. Russell and Tarn were both aware that the cat in the photograph could nevertheless be someone else's lost companion, so they decided to try and coax the feline out from beneath the house where he was sheltering. 'As soon as I called the cat it responded with a shrill reply,' Tarn recalls. 'Russell said it must be my cat because it hadn't reacted like that to anyone else's voice.' At this point Tarn crawled into the claustrophobic space:

> And then this strange-looking cat was trotting towards me! I kept calling and it kept coming towards me. It took me five minutes before I realised that this painfully thin cat *was* actually Pudd. He had recognised my voice but it wasn't until we shared a familiar greeting where he rubs the side of his face over my index and middle finger that I recognised him. I was in shock and a little out of breath. He was so skinny, hardly alive.

Tarn's once big and healthy cat was unrecognisable, and his weight had dropped to a meagre 4.3 kilograms during his time as a stray. Pudd was extremely unwell so he was placed under veterinary intensive care for assessment and rehydration. When he was released from the clinic, Tarn took Pudd to her new house:

> I was a little concerned as it was another strange place for Pudd, but he was just so pleased to be with me again. It was obvious that he was still in some pain as well. He stayed with me the entire first night and never moved – he'd never done that before! In the morning he was reaching his paw out to my face and looking at me with his sunken eyes and he had so much

Pudd in June 2011, seven weeks after he was found.

loose skin. It was an extremely sad moment but also one filled with extreme joy.

Pudd had survived as a stray for a total of 49 days and was found approximately four and a half kilometres from his home. Tarn says:

> I'm told I was grinning like the Cheshire Cat when I first arrived back at work after Pudd was found! But as soon as I sat down I think I burst into tears. I can't actually remember doing that but I'm told I did. I'm so lucky that Pudd was found and I'm thankful to all the wonderful people I met along the way who cared about the city's animals. I'm grateful for their encouragement, help and support.

When guardians are reunited with their displaced cats, they can only wonder how far they may have travelled and what they have endured while missing; their scars tell only some of the story. It was clear from the injuries that Stella and Pudd had sustained, and from their poor physical condition, that they had experienced great hardship in the many weeks they lived as strays. Stormy was fortunate to emerge relatively unscathed, having spent close to two weeks homeless.

The late Louie in better times at the James' home in Avoca Valley. The home has now been 'red-zoned'.

Louie

Sandra James' ginger and white cat Louie was at their home in Avoca Valley, Heathcote, when the February quake struck in 2011. Sandra and her partner Dave, who were accompanied by their cocker spaniel, Bebe, had just sat down for lunch with Dave's parents at a cafe in Little River on Banks Peninsula. Sandra recalls:

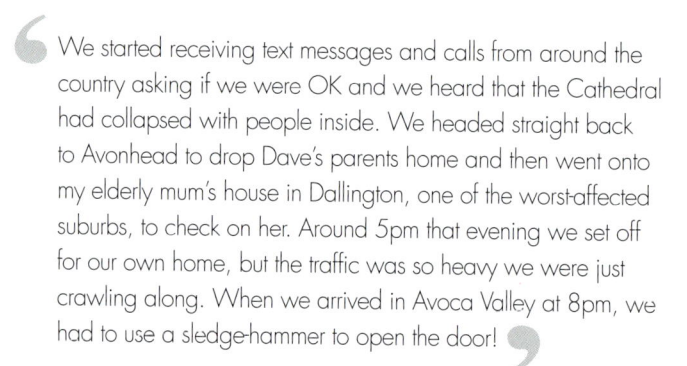

> We started receiving text messages and calls from around the country asking if we were OK and we heard that the Cathedral had collapsed with people inside. We headed straight back to Avonhead to drop Dave's parents home and then went onto my elderly mum's house in Dallington, one of the worst-affected suburbs, to check on her. Around 5pm that evening we set off for our own home, but the traffic was so heavy we were just crawling along. When we arrived in Avoca Valley at 8pm, we had to use a sledge-hammer to open the door!

The family home was devastated, and to make matters worse, Louie was missing. 'It must have been terrifying for him,' Sandra says. 'The epicentre was at the top of Avoca Valley, only 1.4 kilometres from our home. The ground-accelerating forces in Heathcote were far stronger than in the city.'

The James' home was also precariously positioned. 'We were on a slope and so the house was structurally damaged,' Sandra explains. On Thursday 24 February 2011, two days after the quake, the property received a Section 124 notice, known as a red sticker, due to concerns about the risk of future rock falls:

> The police arrived about three that afternoon and told all residents on the hill side of the street to evacuate our homes. We were given two minutes to get out because of the risk of rock collapse. I remember looking up the hill thinking about Louie up there. He loved to roam around the hills and so I thought he would be hiding somewhere up there. It was terrifying when we were evacuated by the police – all I could think was that poor Louie could be in danger of rock falls.

Sandra, Dave and Bebe relocated to a rental property in Avonhead that same day, but they returned to Avoca Valley every morning and night to leave food for Louie. Then six days after the earthquake there was a sign that he had been back to their damaged property. 'I knew Louie was around because he had thrown up on the garden path', Sandra exclaims (a 'sign' that people who live with cats will recognise). At dusk that evening, Sandra and Dave returned to the valley and Louie came down the garden path to meet them when they called his name. Perhaps Sandra's suspicions were correct and the cat had sought refuge somewhere in the Port Hills, but wherever he had been, Dave and Sandra were overjoyed to have him back. Sandra set about ensuring that Louie had a safe temporary place to stay, and booked him into a cattery where he boarded for nearly three weeks while they settled into a rather dilapidated rental property.

Sandra was eager to collect Louie from the boarding facility and did all the right things in order to introduce him to their new lodgings and encourage him to accept this foreign environment. As most cat owners will understand, strategy rather than force was required, and, because cats will be cats, there was still no guarantee of success:

> We kept him inside for two to three weeks and on the third week we slowly introduced him to the backyard of the rental. The rental home itself was not nice and had basically no garden, or rather there were no plants, and it was situated on a busy road. At the end of the third week, Louie ran away when I let him out to go to the toilet.

It was now Sunday 10 April 2011, six weeks after the massive tremor, and it was the second time that Louie had run away. It seemed that the stress of the earthquake and the ensuing upheaval had been too much for him and in his confusion he had again decided to flee. This time, Sandra and Dave immediately launched a locate-and-recover mission:

> We put flyers up at the veterinary centres located between Avonhead and Heathcote, in letterboxes in the local area, at the local supermarkets, and spoke to the neighbours. We walked the streets looking for him. I also advertised in *The Press* a few times and on Trade Me and Pets on the Net. Two to three times each week I would search found cats on those sites.

By late 2012, despite their tireless efforts, they had had no news about Louie's whereabouts. Twenty months from the day that Louie had first vanished after the February 2011 earthquake, Sandra made the difficult decision to gradually reduce the number of 'lost' advertisements she was posting online. 'We were on holiday at Cable Bay near Nelson on Friday 22 February 2013, when we received two text messages from an unknown person,' Sandra recalls. 'We couldn't believe it, but the texts said that it was possible our missing cat was at the SPCA!' Holidays are supposed to be for rest and relaxation, but knowing that Louie might have been found and not being able to confirm this right away was extremely frustrating for them. 'But it was Louie sure enough!' Sandra reports, 'and he'd been found only half a kilometre from the rental property. I really thought he would have headed for the hills he loved, but he hadn't.'

Sandra and Dave had moved from the rental in Avonhead, where they had been living when Louie had vanished, to a new rental home around the corner, one that was much more suitable for their dog Bebe (and, as it turned out, for a cat who liked green spaces and a sunny conservatory to sleep in). Once again, Louie found himself in a new and unfamiliar environment, but this time he stayed. Due to his advancing years, he began to lose mobility as well as the impulse to self-maintain his lovely ginger coat; but Sandra groomed him regularly to keep him feeling good, and he enjoyed passing the time resting in the sun.

Sandra and Dave's land in the Avoca Valley has since been declared unfit for residential dwellings. Sadly, the family has suffered a further loss since they were told of this decision. 'Louie was put to sleep in August 2013, aged 15,' Sandra says. 'It was so nice that he was able to spend his last few months with us in warmth and comfort. He was such a determined cat and a real survivor. Having old animals is tough. I wish they could be with us longer.'

Diamond Harbour friends

Milly came into the Cole family as a stray; 'she' was found hiding beneath the bushes in the garden outside Jan Cole's son's flat in Christchurch city. Jan explains: 'My son Ben was moving out and coming to stay with me for a while. He rang up one day and said he was also bringing a cat in a cardboard box and she was not pleased. In fact, she was very cross.'

Milly, who turned out to be a boy, was thought to be around nine or ten years old when found. While initially disgruntled at being moved, he eventually settled in at Jan's country cottage in Diamond Harbour, across the harbour from Lyttelton, and was content there until 4 September 2010. 'After the earthquake, Milly disappeared,' Jan recounts. 'I called and called but he wouldn't come. Around two weeks later, he appeared at the side of the house wailing and doing this funny creeping walk whilst looking from side to side. We called it "The Earthquake Walk".' Despite returning to the property, Milly was reluctant to cross the threshold into the cottage. 'When he eventually entered, he checked the whole house to see if it was safe. By then we'd cleared up the worst of the mess and picked up everything that had broken, so it looked relatively normal.' But Milly remained highly anxious. 'He'd always been a nervous cat and this trauma made him worse.'

Milly seemed to be one of those cats who sense seismic activity in ways humans do not. 'In the beginning he'd run as soon as the shaking started, but then he got better at sussing out whether an impending tremor would be worth dashing for or not,' Jan says.

Diamond Harbour friends: Milly, Pudding and Molly.

When the 22 February 2011 earthquake struck, its epicentre very close to the Cole home, Jan was delivering census forms in Diamond Harbour. 'I hurried back to my house to find the ranch-sliders smashed to smithereens,' she recalls. 'I was terrified that Milly might have been killed as there were huge shards of glass like daggers littered all over the floor.' Milly was not injured but he had fled, though this time he returned home much sooner than after the September event. Then as the aftershocks continued through February, another character found her way to Jan's home:

> This pretty tabby kitten appeared, who must have been about seven or eight weeks old. To our delight, she stayed, but related better to Milly than to us. When she first came inside, she only had eyes for Milly! We named her Molly, after the little girl who lives next door, who adores cats.

Milly and Molly quickly bonded, and before long the two were inseparable. In March Milly had to be admitted to the veterinary clinic (among other things, he had developed an itchy skin condition post-quakes). 'While he was there, Molly learned to rely on Ben and me for cuddles, as her surrogate "mum" was not around,' Jan says.

Jan suspects 'a rumour must have spread on the feline grapevine' because while Milly was residing at the veterinary clinic, yet another kitten appeared in her garden:

> She was black and white and would sit motionless at the edge of the lawn looking at us. Her big round eyes looked perpetually worried and her white whiskers stuck out horizontally from her face. We'd give her food and after several weeks she plucked up the courage to come inside. She was terrified of us, but played with Molly, who washed her as if she were a sibling. Gradually, after some months, we began to earn her trust, but when I took her to the vet to be sterilised she was terrified. They rang up very diplomatically and said they'd put dissolvable stitches in so they wouldn't have to take them out!

Pudding and Milly.

The Coles named their feisty new feline companion Pudding. 'She is now a real lap-cat, but still insists on lying on the outside edge of the bed at night, ready for a quick getaway,' Jan says. 'During the worst of the shakes, it was interesting to watch the behaviour of my cats. I used to take my cue from them when a quake began to roll. If they ran, so did I. In the end they would not move for less than a 4.2 magnitude, but if it was a more violent one, they were off.'

Second-chance cats

Domestic cats in New Zealand are most often 'free-range' animals, able to come and go at will, and as we have seen they are in a position to run away when scared by an event such as an earthquake; if they do run away they may not always be able to find their way back home and unless they are found by their guardians they face the tough life of a stray. Stray cats are a cause of concern for many people and if they have not been responsibly sterilised, they will breed and add to the feral cat community. Among those cats who find themselves displaced and leading the tough life of a stray, there are a few lucky ones who get a rare second chance as the following stories show.

Barney

One roaming cat, later named Barney, suffered a terrible ordeal as a result of the earthquake on 22 February 2011. His adoptive companion Rachael begins the tale:

> Barney was wandering around behind the PlaceMakers store in Cranford Street, probably looking for mice or lizards, or a warm corner to have a nap that day, most likely unaware of the disaster that was about to happen. When the earthquake struck, somehow the violent shaking and lurching caused him to become trapped, covered by several concrete blocks, one of which pinned his tail to the ground and prevented any chance of escape.

Barney was trapped in a concrete prison without food or water, in discomfort and pain. Yet somehow he endured this ordeal for six days until PlaceMakers' staff heard him meowing. 'The concrete blocks were lifted to reveal him underneath,' Rachael explains. 'He was very frightened, dehydrated, hungry, and in pain from his badly injured tail, but this nameless cat's luck had changed!'

Staff immediately rallied around Barney – who was initially called 'CC' (for Cranford Cat) – and he became something of a feline celebrity at the PlaceMakers store. For the first day or so after his rescue he stayed outside, where he was given food and water. It was quickly deduced that, despite his tribulations, he was a sweet-natured and affectionate cat. 'He had obviously been well-loved,' Rachael says. 'He was smooching around the staff and enjoying all the attention.'

As news of Barney's tale spread, another Christchurch business, Our Vets, donated a bag of food and provided discounted medical treatment for Barney's injured tail. 'It was important that no infection

Barney.

set in, but eventually the damaged portion of his tail went cold and fell off at the injury site,' Rachael explains.

Apart from losing two-thirds of his tail, which was so badly damaged that there was no possibility of saving it, Barney made a full physical recovery. He was listed on 'missing pet' websites in the hope that he might be claimed. However, when his original carers were located, it turned out that, as a result of the quakes, they were no longer in a position to care for him. The next hurdle was therefore to find Barney a new, permanent loving home. 'Finding someone to adopt him became a problem because everyone was affected by the disaster and dealing with damaged homes and lives in turmoil,' Rachael says. A staff member named Aaron took 'CC' to his house, where he was looked after by his son Brocton for a few weeks, but the family cat who already lived in this home was unhappy about the newcomer. 'So our friend Aaron asked if we could adopt him,' Rachael recalls.

> We'd been intending to get a new cat, although we wanted a kitten, but CC's story struck a chord. We went to visit him and immediately he came straight up to us and smooched around our legs. He began purring and we realised *he* had chosen *us*! The first thing we did was rename him Barney, a new name for the beginning of his new life.

Pussdah – the cat who rehomed himself

Sara Wagstaff was living on Scarborough Hill at the time of the February 2011 earthquake (see also Sara's story about the Heathcote Riding School in chapter 6). Not long after it struck, she invited some friends over for a comforting get-together. When these people arrived they were unwittingly accompanied by a friendly Burmese cat. 'It was like he'd just got out of the car with them,' Sara says, 'and, because this breed is known for getting into stranger's cars, I wondered if this was how he came to be here. We certainly hadn't seen him in the neighbourhood before.' Sara gave the cat a treat and he slept beside her on the couch for a while. Later that night she placed him outside, thinking he'd return to his own home, but the next morning he marched straight back into her house. As she recalls,

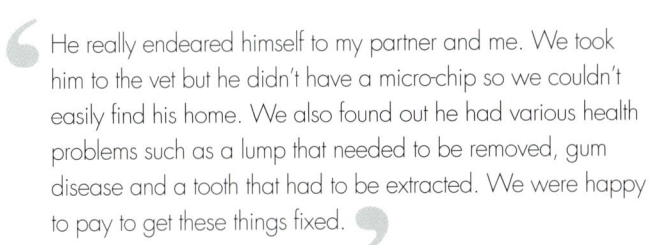

> He really endeared himself to my partner and me. We took him to the vet but he didn't have a micro-chip so we couldn't easily find his home. We also found out he had various health problems such as a lump that needed to be removed, gum disease and a tooth that had to be extracted. We were happy to pay to get these things fixed.

Despite becoming increasingly attached to the cat, Sara investigated online to see whether she could locate his owners. 'There was somebody advertising they'd lost a cat named Frank from near here,' she recounts. 'I called out "Frank!" to see if this cat recognised the name, and he immediately looked up and came running over to me'. Sara admits having mixed feelings about this outcome. 'I spoke to someone who suggested I just pretend I hadn't seen the ad, but I thought if this was me I'd really want to know my cat was all right. So I contacted these people, but they were adamant that their Frank had been in perfect health and wouldn't have required any veterinary attention'. Sara was perplexed by the fact they did not want at least to come and see the cat in case he was their missing companion. As for the cat: 'Our vet explained that cats will stay where the service is good,' she says. 'This cat had rehomed himself.'

Over the next three months Pussdah, the new name given to the Burmese, ensconced himself firmly in Sara and her partner Alan Parker's lives. When the first of two major aftershocks occurred on 13 June 2011, he was inside the house with Sara. Alan arrived home shortly after, and the couple decided to go for a restorative walk along the boardwalk in Sumner. 'We had just stepped onto the boardwalk when the second 6.4 quake happened,' Sara recalls.

> We watched boulders coming down from Scarborough Hill, saw all the dust and rubble – it still gives me goose-bumps – and my first thought was Pussdah! So we shot up the hill, having to stop the car and remove huge rocks from the road in order to get home. The neighbours in our cul de sac were all sitting outside on the curb as we approached our house. We saw that the concertina doors and all the windows of our house had been thrown open. There was disarray everywhere, it was quite unbelievable.

Pussdah's 'selfie' (Sara and Alan in background).

Fearing the worst – that Pussdah had fled in terror – Sara and Alan jumped out of the car and ran inside. 'He was hiding behind a couch, bless his heart, and so we picked him up and put him in the ute with food and water, and he curled up in the foot-well and went to sleep', Sara says. 'He hadn't run away, but for several days afterwards he walked around like a praying mantis – very close to the ground.'

Sara and Alan are now well prepared for the risk that future earthquakes or other emergencies might cause Pussdah to flee. They have micro-chipped and registered him to their address, taken photos of him in case he goes missing, and had a cat-door installed so that he can escape.

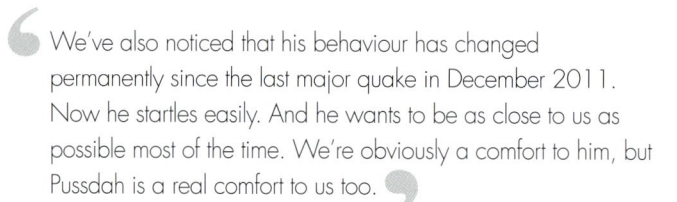

> We've also noticed that his behaviour has changed permanently since the last major quake in December 2011. Now he startles easily. And he wants to be as close to us as possible most of the time. We're obviously a comfort to him, but Pussdah is a real comfort to us too.

Red-zone cats

The effects of the earthquakes on the cat population spread far beyond the immediate area of Christchurch. Over the years following the September 2010 event, Alison, a resident of Kaiapoi, observed how cats left behind in North Canterbury towns such as Kaiapoi and Rangiora responded to the changes brought about by the natural disaster. She says:

> In Kaiapoi the September earthquake did not on the whole terrify cats and leave them homeless in the way that February's quake the next year did. In fact, they found themselves living independent lives in what had become the red zone. When they sought refuge, they sought it in the houses on TC3 land on the edge of the red zone. People moved out, often from rented accommodation, and abandoned their cats along with their unwanted furniture and clothing. The cat saga in Kaiapoi began some months after the September 2010 earthquake and kept on going for close to two years.

Red-zone kitten Little Dark Lord.

Alison was away in Nelson when the quake hit in September 2010, but that did not mean she would escape being at the centre of her own animal earthquake story. Upon her return 10 days after the quake, Alison's husband passed on a message from Cat Care Incorporated, an organisation involved in trap–neuter–return (TNR), fostering and adoption of feral/stray cats in North Canterbury. They were seeking a foster home for a mother cat and her six kittens abandoned by tenants who had deserted a quake-affected rental home.

Alison agreed to take over the care of the nursing mother and her litter, but soon realised that the kittens were being rejected. 'They were inert and unresponsive,' Alison explains. 'The mother cat's milk had dried up and she was emaciated. She wanted nothing to do with the kittens and hid under the bed. I pushed a saucer of meat and a bowl of kitten formula under the bed and left her to it.' Since the mother cat was unable to feed her kittens, Alison took over the responsibility of feeding them every four hours until the mother's milk came back in and she took over again. Alison remembers: 'The kittens flourished, but the mother cat took a while to come right. She remained gaunt in spite of receiving considerable amounts of food. The vet diagnosed scarring on the kidneys – probably as a result of severe dehydration in the days after the earthquake. She thought she would do well, provided she had an easy life and no more kittens.'

Red-zone kitten Barbara.

The mother cat, renamed Milly, was sterilised and vaccinated. Eventually, she found a loving home with a neighbour who had recently lost

Chapter 3 : Feline tales

Red-zone kitten Elvis.

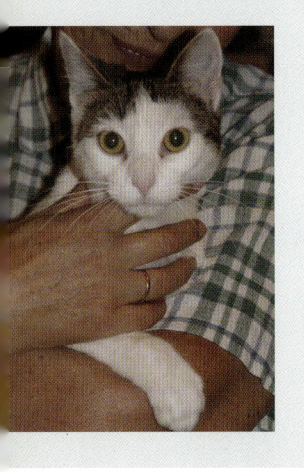

Gracie, the red-zone kitten adopted by Alison.

her own elderly cat. 'She is now round and plump and much given to sleeping on the backs of sofas,' Alison reports. Finding the perfect homes for six rambunctious kittens was to prove more challenging. 'Normally, my personal and professional networks bring plenty of kitten-takers to my door,' Alison says, 'but at this time finding the kittens' homes in Canterbury was something of a nightmare'.

Alison's involvement rescuing cats and kittens affected by the earthquakes did not end after the September 2010 event and the adoptions of these rescued kittens. In late 2012, almost two years after the February 2011 quake, Alison was talking to friend in the red-zoned area of Kaiapoi:

> She told me that she had been feeding an abandoned black and white fluffy cat for some time. I recognised this cat because I had been tracking her for a year after befriending her mother and looking after that litter of kittens. Over the next few days, my friend pointed out three half-grown kittens and said that she had been feeding them. We were concerned that the mother cat appeared to be pregnant again, plus my friend was planning to move out of her red-zoned property after Christmas.

Eager to ensure the cat family's welfare, Alison's friend managed to capture the mother cat who was taken to the SPCA. Alison then set traps for the kittens, which lured in a black and white male immediately, followed by a splotchy coloured female; however, the third kitten was not caught. At first Alison was concerned because the two kittens she had rescued were anti-social, a characteristic which can complicate later adoption. 'I took them with me up to Nelson over the summer and worked with them,' she says, 'first in cages and then in a bedroom, and they soon quietened down.' The male kitten was named Elvis when he was adopted out in Nelson. The female kitten would be called Gracie and would remain with Alison.

> I have had to keep her – but she's a very sweet cat indeed, and perhaps the most affectionate cat I've ever had.

Charlie and Russell

Charlie, the feline companion of Huntsbury Hill resident Robyn Stewart, disappeared when the September 2010 earthquake struck. Robyn posted him as 'missing' on numerous social media sites and lost-animal forums, describing him as a neutered male ginger cat with a distinctive missing tooth. A few days after Charlie had been listed as missing, Robyn's daughter Bella received a call from a lady affiliated with Cat Help (see chapter 2) about a cat who seemed to fit his description. There seemed to be a good chance that the cat this agency had rescued could be their Charlie – he was a neutered ginger who also had a missing tooth! However, the expedition to view the cat took a rather unexpected turn. Robyn explains:

> We went to a house in Phillipstown, close to AMI Stadium, which was largely given over to immaculately clean cages containing heart-breaking numbers of cats and kittens. In one cage was a painfully thin ginger cat with oil in his fur and leaking eyes. The cat had been found in the roof of the building in an engineering yard in Waltham where he had been hiding under trucks, which was why he was covered in oil. He was pitiful, but he wasn't Charlie, so we left him there.

Robyn and Bella were bitterly disappointed by this false lead to their much-loved companion, but although their visit to the residential 'cat shelter' did not reunite them with Charlie, it did have a positive outcome. 'We drove home with Bella sobbing all the way,' Robyn recalls. 'When we got home my husband took one look at the state of us and told us to go back and get the cat who wasn't Charlie.'

So it was that the family adopted this poor, soiled and neglected cat, gave him a name, and helped him to recover:

> Bella called him Russell. His fur gradually lost all traces of oil and his eyes cleared up. He now had enough to eat, although he was never greedy and he remained thin. He proved to be a sad, nervous boy, especially terrified of men. When EQC visited we shut him away, but as one of the assessors was also called Russell, shouts of "Did Russell get out?" proved a little confusing!

Sadly their hopes of finding Charlie alive were dashed when his body was found at the bottom of their neighbour's steep section two months later, and they were unable to ascertain how Charlie had died.

Meanwhile Russell was now in their care. It took some time for Russell to settle into his new home and this often prompted Robyn to speculate about his history: 'We longed to know what had happened to him. Had he run away from home after the earthquake or had he always been a stray? He was neutered when found and he had a gentle nature. We did our best, but he just never seemed very at ease, although he stayed. But he resolutely refused to acknowledge his new name!'

When the 22 February 2011 earthquake struck, Robyn arrived home to discover with dismay that Russell had vanished. Worse still, damage to their Huntsbury home meant the family had to relocate: 'We stayed in the house for five days, constantly calling Russell, but he never came. We then moved to Ilam but returned to Huntsbury every day to retrieve more of our possessions. We still called Russell and had our neighbours looking out for him too. When he didn't reappear we alternated between miserable thoughts of him going back to being a stray and a conviction that he had been near the chimney when it collapsed and was dead under a huge pile of bricks.'

Fortunately, his fate turned out to be the lesser of two evils. Russell had not been injured or killed by falling bricks, but he had fled and returned to the streets and the difficult and wretched life of an urban stray, and with his vagrant background it seemed even less likely that he would return to them. 'After 19 days we were retrieving our final load from the Huntsbury house and I was standing in the kitchen surveying the wreckage of every single piece of china and glass that I had ever owned when I thought I heard a meow from another room,' Robyn recalls.

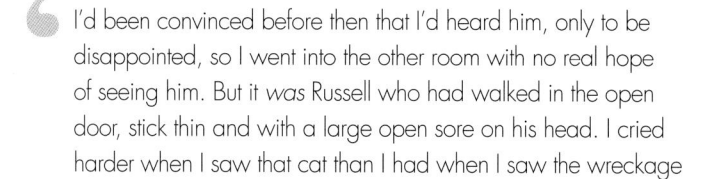

> I'd been convinced before then that I'd heard him, only to be disappointed, so I went into the other room with no real hope of seeing him. But it *was* Russell who had walked in the open door, stick thin and with a large open sore on his head. I cried harder when I saw that cat than I had when I saw the wreckage of my house and all my possessions.

For the second time in just a few months, Robyn set about rehabilitating this troubled cat. Russell's latest adventure added another layer of mystery to his story: 'Who knows what he survived before he came to us or what happened to him in the almost three weeks he was missing,' she wonders. 'I wish he could tell us. Who can explain why he returned on the last day before we were to stop making daily visits?'

Over time, Russell has adapted well to his new life with Robyn and Bella. 'He is slightly more relaxed than he used to be but I don't

Charlie who disappeared (left) and Russell who found a new home (right).

think he will ever be a calm cat,' Robyn concedes. 'We try to give him a nice life and we love him very much.'

Bobby on the beat

One Christchurch cat became the appointed mascot of the New Brighton Police Station during the region's earthquakes. In this intriguing detective story, mystery surrounded the charming black and white cat – presumed to be male – who suddenly appeared at the police station in April 2011. Constable Pamela Cox, who was working at New Brighton at the time of the cat's arrival, began to unravel the mystery. Pamela says the cat was first given the name 'Bobby' by the station's cleaner (after 'Bobby on the beat', a term used to refer to a police officer on foot patrol) but the name was changed to 'Penny the cop cat' (after Lady Penelope from *Thunderbirds*) because all the staff thought the moggie was 'too pretty to be a male!' Penny was featured in a news story, published in the *Star* on 1 January 2012, as it was thought that she – or he – was an earthquake refugee who had been living somewhere in or around Central New Brighton School.

Penny achieved celebrity status at the station, where her presence and company were welcomed. She had a calm and affectionate personality, which led Pamela to deduce that the cat had most likely lived with a human family prior to joining the police. It was at this point that she took Penny to a veterinarian and it was revealed that the cat they had deemed to be male, then a female, was a male after all. Appropriately, they reverted back to calling him the name first bestowed upon him: Bobby. During the veterinary visit, it was also discovered that Bobby had been implanted with a microchip. Pamela's hunch had been correct – Bobby did indeed have a human family and the quest to track them down began. Yet another breakthrough in the case helped Pamela piece together more details of the feline's past. She explains:

Bobby on patrol.

> Some weeks after the story appeared in the paper, one of the detectives at work "announced" that he had brought the cat in from home because it was a stray that had been turning up at his address in Ohoka. He genuinely believed the cat was a displaced earthquake refugee. He hadn't told anyone this when he brought Bobby in, but just decided we needed a station cat and what better way to rehome him.

Subsequently, scanning of Bobby's microchip revealed he was registered to an owner in Ohoka not far from where the detective lived. Pamela contacted Bobby's family to inform them of his welfare and whereabouts; it had been months since his arrival at the station and she was certain that they must be concerned and missing him.

> When I spoke to his owner she told me that Bobby, who she called "Cat", had run away because she'd shifted house and moved in with someone with two dogs. "Cat" didn't like the dogs and so kept running away. The way the cat kept turning up at the detective's house, made him think he was an earthquake refugee.

The news that Bobby had a human family was met with mixed feelings by the staff at New Brighton Police Station; they were relieved for him, but would miss their new-found friend. However, earthquake refugee or not, the course of Bobby's life was about to take another

Bobby and Constable Pamela Cox outside the New Brighton Police Station.

twist! 'Because Bobby had now established himself at the station, his previous owner asked us if we wanted to keep him on as the station cat,' Pamela explains. 'She thought he might just keep running away if he returned to her new home. Of course, we were really happy to do this, as by then everyone had become quite attached to him.'

From the moment Bobby had arrived at the station he had pawed his way into everyone's hearts, and he was never going to be left wanting a loving, safe place to stay. At one point, Pamela felt it might be best for Bobby to be living in a 'proper' house rather than at the station. She considered taking him home herself but already had two cats of her own. Thus, Bobby remained at police headquarters in New Brighton until Pamela learnt she was to be relocated to the new Central Police Station in the city. As his primary caregiver, the one who fed and looked after him, Pamela was reluctant to leave her feline rookie behind; however, in the final twist to this tale, New Brighton's police sergeant, who had also been captivated by the station's endearing feline mascot, stepped up to offer Bobby a permanent home.

Bobby's story shows how well-intentioned people may sometimes make genuine mistakes about the 'refugee status' of animals found after disasters. This is another way in which animals may find themselves inadvertently displaced and even rehomed following quakes, and their original guardians may never find out what has happened to them. Luckily, because Bobby was micro-chipped the mystery of his status was solved and his guardian located, and it was possible to agree on a new home arrangement for him that would be in his best interests.

For the love of Pinky

When Sharon McFarlane was living at Burnham Military Camp in 1994, a stray kitten a few months old bravely ensconced himself in her multi-species family after marching inside to share her other seven cats' food. 'He was very assertive and sweet at the same time,' Sharon recalls, 'and beautiful with his pink nose and grey fur with white markings. He used to sit up proudly, reminding me of an Egyptian cat.' Even though six of her other seven cats were related to each other, Pinky had no trouble joining in with them. 'He liked to sit outside on the kitchen window ledge and look in at me while I was at the sink, and he would meow loudly to let me know if something wasn't OK,' Sharon remembers. 'Each day he would follow the sun around the house with the other cats.'

It was Pinky's love of the sun that eventually claimed his nose. Pink-nosed cats are prone to a form of skin cancer and despite preventative measures taken by Sharon, he developed cancer in his later years (he was a determined cat, unwilling to relinquish the pleasures of life such as warm knees and sun-bathing). The veterinary practice that Sharon attended was able to operate to remove most of his tumour, and with a monstrous-looking nose but unbothered by his appearance, Pinky continued happily about his daily routine; he was the last surviving cat of Sharon's large cat family. Pinky's story does not end there, however; he was to come into the life of Annie Potts and provide the inspiration for this book.

Sharon, who had moved to Beckenham in the late 1990s, was travelling through Vietnam and Cambodia when the 22 February 2010 earthquake struck, destroying her art deco home. At the time, Pinky was being cared for by a house-sitter who had to leave Christchurch immediately post-quake. It was at this point that Annie took Pinky home to Lyttelton with her for the short term. When Sharon returned to Christchurch, the shared housing she moved into temporarily was unsuitable for her elderly cat. But it had taken Annie and her partner Philip less than a day to fall for the confident – at times pushy – and always funny, snuffling character. Pinky seemed content in their home. Annie and Sharon met one day in early March 2011 to discuss the future 'custody arrangements' for Pinky. They agreed it would be in Pinky's best interests to retire to Lyttelton, and Sharon would have 'visitation rights' whenever she liked.

Immediately, this elderly cat took to his port-town duties very seriously, loudly patrolling the hallway and bedrooms of the house, but declining to go outside. The frequent aftershocks that rocked Lyttelton that year did not appear to bother him in the slightest. Pinky, the sun-loving outdoors roamer, simply chose to become an indoor cat, cherishing warm spots on beds, junk food, and offering a very vocal chat before bed. He was a stoic, extroverted character who accepted his new environment and the other cats and dogs who lived there without fuss. In mid-2012, at 18 years of age, when Pinky finally succumbed to the cancer affecting his nose, Sharon, Annie and Philip were by his side. His ashes have been shared between them.

Best friends Annie Potts and Sharon McFarlane shared care of 18-year-old Pinky after Sharon's Beckenham home was destroyed in the February quake.

Annie Potts

In summary

These stories show some of the ways in which cats were affected by the Canterbury earthquakes. Responding in fright to the unexpected shaking, and acting to ensure their own safety and survival, many cats hid or ran away, sometimes getting lost in foreign territories, unable to find their way home again. Some of these displaced felines were eventually reunited with their human guardians or were welcomed into new homes. Others became strays whose existence would be focused on the need to find food, water and shelter, and avoid injury and infection.

The consequences of earthquakes affect human guardians and their cats equally. They place enormous strain on cat rescue organisations, and cause terrible stress for those who lose companion cats and seek desperately to recover them. And when cats suffer displacement – whether long-term or temporary – this drastic change in circumstances inevitably has an adverse impact on their health and well-being. Sometimes, feline personalities and behaviours may be permanently altered as a result of the trauma and distress experienced in disasters.

However, such changes are not always entirely for the worse – as we have seen, human guardians also report that previously distant and nervous cats have become less shy and sometimes even gained confidence in the aftermath of earthquake-related stressors. While stray or abandoned kittens and younger cats are more likely to find homes than older cats (both in 'normal' times and following disasters), stories like those of Louie and Pinky show that in the Christchurch disaster, at least in some cases, the city's displaced or deserted elderly felines also benefited from the compassion and generosity of local people.

In summarising these feline tales, we also want to draw attention to the intense emotions that contributors describe feeling when they found their missing cats: specifically, relief at the return of a loved companion seemed to allow the release of their feelings about their own plight. For example, as Stormy's guardian recalls, when her cat reappeared 'all the emotions that had been pent up … came out as happy tears'; similarly, Stella's human companion says, 'I never cried after the earthquake at all but I cried and cried and cried when we found Stella'. And Pudd's guardian recounts: 'I'm told I was grinning like the Cheshire Cat when Pudd was found! But as soon as I sat down I think I burst into tears.' Their relief and joy in finding their cats seemed to outweigh their response to having suffered huge material loss. Russell's carer reports: 'I cried harder when I saw he was back than I had when I saw the wreckage of my house and all my possessions.' These responses show that for many of us our companion animals are crucial for our personal well-being, our sense of security and contentment. Their reappearance signifies the return of a loved family member, and allows the chance to return to routine and normality (or create a 'new normality') following extreme adversity; most importantly, our joy in their 'homecoming' is a sign of the special 'togetherness' inherent in our companionable relationships with animals.

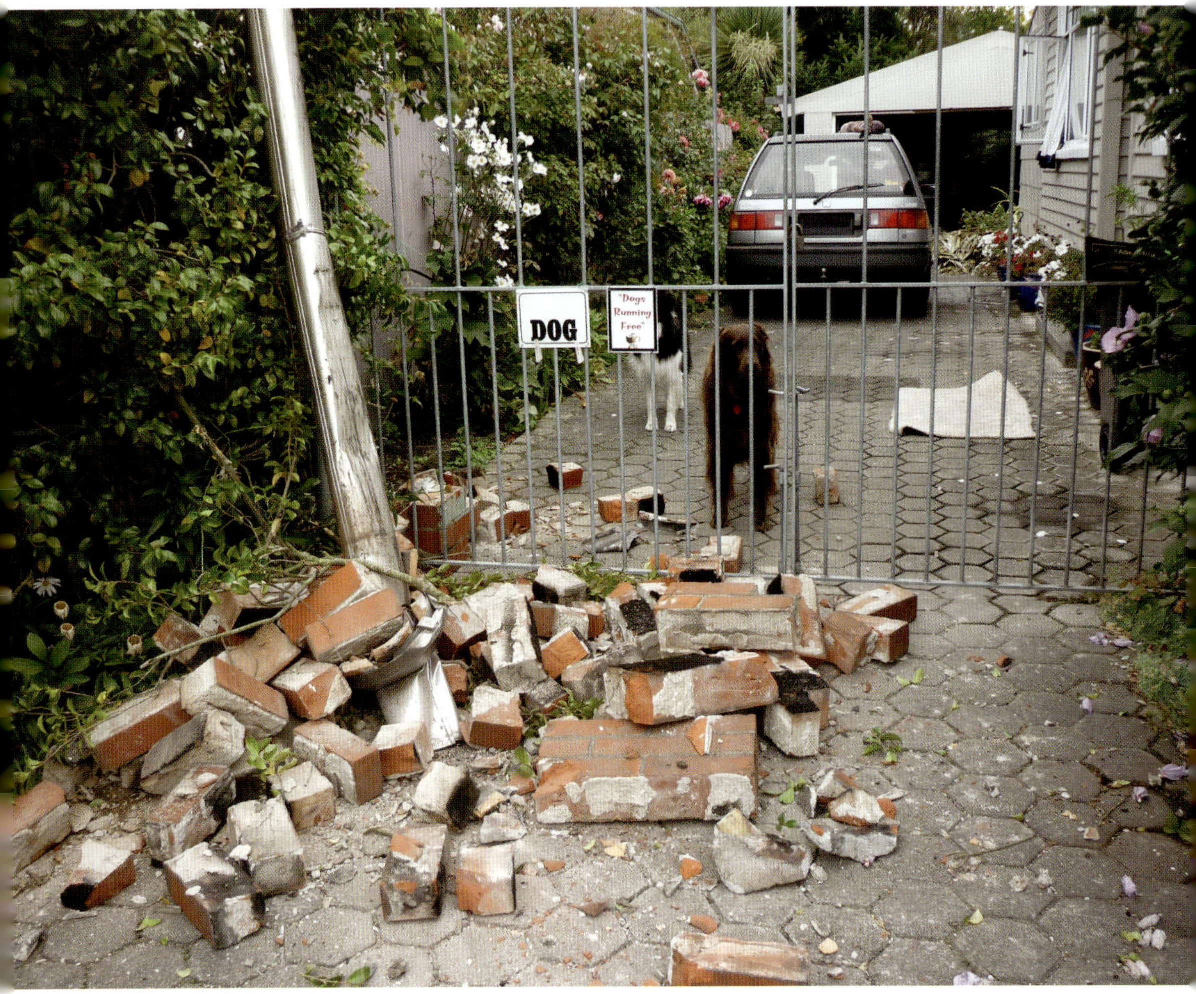
DOG
"Dogs Running Free"

Chapter 4
Canine tales

The domesticated dog has a reputation for being the most loyal species to live alongside humans. Dogs, unlike cats, are necessarily social animals, accustomed to living in groups, or 'packs'. Many experts on canine behaviour will attest to the claim that while dogs can be taken out of packs, their preference for living among others never subsides. It is the natural sociability of these animals that helps them to integrate so well into human families and homes. Moreover, the extraordinary capacity of dogs to bond with humans and enjoy numerous activities with us makes this species particularly able to help humanity in various assistance or 'service' roles in disaster situations.

Although this chapter focuses mostly on the stories of 'everyday' dogs affected by the earthquakes – no doubt considered champions by their own families – we begin with a brief tribute to the canine heroes of Urban Search and Rescue (USAR), a specially trained unit comprising teams of highly skilled dogs and their human handlers (see also chapter 1). Christchurch's own USAR team was first on the scene after the catastrophic February 2011 earthquake and their search for survivors among the city's damaged and collapsed buildings during relentless aftershocks was a dangerous exercise. This local team was later joined by USAR dogs and their handlers from Auckland, Australia, Singapore and Japan.

On 22 February, and in the days and weeks after the earthquake, USAR teams searched more than 80 sites in and around Christchurch's central CBD. Their efforts were largely focused on the Canterbury Television (CTV) premises on Madras Street and the Pyne Gould Corporation (PGC) building on Cambridge Terrace, the two locations where the tremor had claimed the greatest number of human lives

Opposite page: Canine friends Milo (front) and Tybar (back) survey the rubble from a collapsed chimney in Somerfield on 22 February 2011.

Donna Moot

11am on 4 September 2010. Rescue workers and dogs survey the damage in Madras Street.

Alex Hubert

due to collapse of buildings. The coastal hillside suburb of Sumner was another focal location for the search and rescue teams as there had been destructive rock falls there, with one person known to have been killed. In an issue of *Pawprint* (the newsletter of the New Zealand USAR Search Dog Association), dedicated to the Canterbury disaster, dog handler Sara Rad reflects on the experiences and the valiant efforts of her canine colleagues: [1]

> I was impressed by how [my dogs] Sasha and Tommy knew this was no longer a training session. They listened to our directional control commands and took their time searching all nooks and crannies. There were so many distractions and yet nothing stopped them from their task. I quickly realized that all of our training over the years had paid off and the bond and trust that we have with our dogs would make all the searches that we faced slightly easier (Rad, 2011).

The phrase 'rescue and recovery' is most often associated with the

---

1 The dogs trained to work in search and rescue all have unique stories, see Sessions and Bullock (2013) *Quake Dogs*.

work of these courageous USAR dogs, but tales of other heroic canines also emerged from the Canterbury earthquake experience. Guide dog Kiwi may not not be an official rescue dog but Blair McConnell, whose sight is impaired, owes his life to this Labrador retriever. Blair, a sales representative based in the Telecom Exchange Building on Hereford Street, was on the phone to a client when the city began to crumble on 22 February 2011. In an interview with reporter Michael Field, Blair recalls diving under his desk to find that his guide dog Kiwi was already there. 'I grabbed his harness [and] we got out of the building and into the middle of Hereford St with hundreds of others when the second big aftershock hit' (cited in Field, 2011).

Despite the chaos, eight-year-old Kiwi remained completely focused on Blair's safety and well-being, leading him through the rubble and debris along the banks of the Avon River and away from the stricken city. Guide dogs are highly skilled but it is hard to imagine that, even with such training, one would respond so calmly to such a sudden and catastrophic event. Michael Field writes: 'Kiwi went to work and it took nearly three hours for the dog, who is nearing retirement, to get a terrified and disorientated McConnell home.' Eventually, the pair were assisted by a passing motorist who offered to take them home (Field, 2011).[1]

Canine casualties

In Christchurch post-quakes a number of dogs found themselves wandering on foreign streets and in unknown territories, having jumped gates and fences or because secure yards had been compromised by the shaking. Many of these panicking dogs came into the care of organisations and facilities such as the Council's Animal Control shelter and the Dogwatch sanctuary, as discussed in chapters 1 and 2. While it pales in comparison with the number of cats who fled during tremors, the scale of canine displacement was nevertheless substantial.

Thankfully, it was possible for hundreds of disoriented dogs to be returned to guardians promptly because they were micro-chipped. Social media initiatives also assisted to reunite lost canine companions with

---

1   Following the February earthquake, the Royal New Zealand Foundation of the Blind (RNZFB) played a crucial role in helping its blind and partially sighted members and their guide dogs adjust to life in a devastated city. RNZFB says that the earthquakes in Canterbury 'brought home how vulnerable vision-impaired people are when disaster strikes', especially as new obstacles such as lack of public transport, as well as detours and changes to pathways, all have to be re-negotiated on a daily basis. These altered land marks, unusual routes and new obstacles also pose great challenges for guide dogs. To assist the region's 40 or so people living with guide dogs, RNZFB deployed professionals who could assess how the dogs were coping in the aftermath of the quakes, and then retrain them to understand and work with the transformed city, including the pathways and routes they would normally go on (www.fetchmag.co.nz).

their human families. Various online databases were established using existing sites like Trade Me and Facebook, and new databases were set up such as SAFE's Animal Aid and the *Press*'s 'Quake pets: lost and found' registry. New Zealand's foremost nationwide pet database, Pets on the Net, reported that more than 1300 notices about missing or found animals were posted on its web pages after the February earthquake (www.petsonthenet.co.nz). By 30 November 2012, of the 1300 animals that had become earthquake refugees 600 had been successfully reunited with their human companions.

First-hand accounts posted online of those who witnessed terrified dogs running in the streets in the hours after the earthquakes are heart-rending. Malcolm, a sales manager at the CTV building which collapsed killing 115 people in February 2011, recounts his experience on the QuakeStories archive (accessible via the University of Canterbury's CEISMIC Digital Archive).[1] His wife called him that day to ask if he could fetch her some clothes from home and bring them to her at the QEII building where she worked. He delayed a scheduled 1pm meeting by half an hour to tend to her request. 'The rest of the team decided to stay and catch up on some paperwork,' he writes. 'None of them survived.' Sixteen of Malcolm's colleagues lost their lives that day. 'If it was not for my wife … I would have been the 17th victim from Canterbury Television lost in that building that day' (QuakeStories).

At 12.40pm, just 11 minutes before the deadly earthquake struck, Malcolm left the building and was almost home when the shaking started. 'Besides the extreme difficulty maintaining a straight course in my car,' Malcolm recalls in QuakeStories, 'my most vivid memory was the number of dogs running in all directions, across the road, jumping fences, yelping in fear.'

Another eyewitness account of February's event comes in an online post from journalist Kip Brook, who was struck by a 1.8-metre tall bookcase during the tremor and hurried from his office to find his family: 'The roads were leaking sand and liquefaction. Some cars had fallen into holes as the ground had opened up. The power was down, traffic lights were out and there was mayhem at intersections. A big dog, spooked, was hit by two cars but didn't survive the third hit' (http://www.getfrank.co.nz/editorial/features/christchurch-earthquake-scene-setter).

There are many stories of people witnessing their own dogs attempting to flee in response to the earthquakes. In an extreme case, an 11-month-old golden retriever puppy, Charlie, was so terrified by the 4 September 2010 tremor, which caused a bookshelf to fall beside

---

[1] CEISMIC is the Canterbury Earthquake Images, Stories and Media Integrated Collection (see http://www.ceismic.org.nz).

him, that he launched himself through the living room window. Fortunately, he was not home alone at the time and his carer Caroline Fleetwood was able to quickly tend to his injuries. She told the *New Zealand Herald*: '[Charlie] had blood all over his legs and ears. I had to hold the side of his nose on' (Muir, 2010).

When a large aftershock struck on 23 December 2011, Annie Potts was just leaving a veterinary appointment at the Animal and Bird Hospital (AABH) in Woolston. As she was turning into busy Ferry Road, a large, terrified dog scrambled across in front of her car and stopped short in the middle of the asphalt. A veterinary nurse from AABH was able to get the dog on a lead and as the dog was micro-chipped tracked his owner to a residence in the next street. When Annie drove him there she discovered that the dog, who had been inside the house alone during the tremor, had flung himself at a window in panic, and it had burst open allowing him to escape the property. Although not injured, the dog remained very distressed, panting heavily, until his guardians were able to return home from work to comfort him.

Bonnie

In 2010, Alison Chambers was living in the Christchurch suburb of Cashmere, caring for her three-year-old Jack Russell terrier, Bonnie. When the 4 September earthquake struck, Bonnie was sleeping in her basket in the laundry. The dog was so frightened by the event that she urinated in her bed and again in the doorway, where she cowered until Alison was able to let her go outside.

When dawn broke, the new day offered a taste of normality as

Bonnie.

Bonnie enjoyed her daily walk. However, upon returning home, it became evident that Bonnie no longer felt her basket in the laundry was a safe place to rest. Bonnie had not forgotten the fear she had felt being shaken in the dark. She decided to seek out a new safe place to sleep, and after some deliberation, Alison says, she 'took to the settee in the spare room'.

The frequent aftershocks continued to distress Bonnie. To help calm her canine companion, Alison maintained their routine, such as enjoying a Sunday walk together over the Bridle Path to the port town of Lyttelton. These trips were special for Bonnie who was allowed to lick the froth-topping on Alison's takeaway coffees.

When Christchurch's second major earthquake struck on 22 February 2011, Bonnie was at home perched on the window-seat gazing out at the view. 'The lamp on the window-seat fell over and Bonnie jumped off and headed for the stairs to the garage,' Alison explains. The earthquake had shaken open the door leading into the garage and, because the exterior garage door was also open, Bonnie was able to escape. Alison's home was situated opposite Latter Spur Track, which is connected to Victoria Park. The open-spaced grass reserve across the road must have seemed like a sanctuary to Bonnie compared to the chaos of falling books, breaking glass and china occurring in her home. Alison and a band of caring neighbours called Bonnie for two hours and eventually she did return, but was visibly upset and nervous as aftershocks were still rattling the city.

In response to another large aftershock the next day, Bonnie squeezed underneath the fence and fled again. 'Her second escape was more traumatic,' Alison reports. In the process of getting off the property, Bonnie had wounded her head. Neighbours discovered her drenched from the rain and shivering at the end of the street. Alison immediately set about blocking any possible escape routes to prevent further breakouts.

Just as some cats appear to sense impending earthquakes, their behaviour providing an 'early warning system' for their guardians, Bonnie became a reliable indicator of seismic activity when out on daily walks. Her sudden desire to end a walk and return home indicated there had been an aftershock, albeit one that had occurred without Alison's detection. Sure enough, Alison reports, upon checking GeoNet (www.geonet.co.nz) she would find confirmation that an aborted walk had coincided with an aftershock. Bonnie refused to sleep in the laundry again but did return to her basket, which was now in Alison's bedroom. She also gradually grew calmer as the frequency of the aftershocks lessened, which Alison attributes to her being given delicious treats whenever the ground shook and to the maintenance of their routine. 'She still reacts to aftershocks more than three years on from the big quake and she looks for a treat, which she always gets,' she says.

> We recently moved and Bonnie has settled into her new home and is much more relaxed, but I think like us, once you have been through this type of experience you never forget; and Jack Russell terriers have very long memories.

Bonnie was psychologically affected by the earthquake on 4 September 2010 and found it difficult to trust the place where she had previously slept soundly. She injured herself while trying to get away and her repeated escapes could easily have ended in tragedy. Sadly, there are many more dogs who were psychologically and physically harmed as a result of the earthquakes. *Quake Dogs* (Sessions & Bullock, 2013) reports on four British bulldogs, Bentley, Mercedes, Opel and Silvia, who were at home in crates when the 22 February 2011 quake struck. Their human companion returned to the house to find them trapped 'chest deep in liquefaction'; moreover, the dogs were so deeply traumatised they later began to lose their hair (p. 34). The issue of protecting companion animals left at home alone is discussed in detail in the conclusion to our book.

Auckland dogs rally round

Although based in Auckland, Robyn Sabin and Lena de Fonseca devised a way for North Island dog enthusiasts to help dogs in Christchurch who had been adversely affected by the earthquakes. Robyn explains, 'We were really touched by the animals' plights. All around New Zealand people were trying to do their bit. It always seems that animals are last to get help, so we thought we would organise a dog walk to raise money.' The date was set for 31 July 2011, five months after the tragic February quake, and was advertised largely through Robyn's pet store, via posters, Facebook and word of mouth. Approximately 150 people and 80 dogs congregated on Orewa Beach and set off on a collective walk along the seashore and around the estuary. As a result of Robyn and Lena's efforts, and the generosity of the participants who each made a gold coin donation, $450 was raised. 'We knew the animal welfare agencies were struggling with caring for so many surrendered and homeless dogs, so it was great that people wanted to come along and support the cause,' Robyn says. 'Some people took part who didn't even have a dog of their own – they borrowed the neighbour's dog! There was so much community spirit.'

Pickle

One of the many dogs traumatised by the earthquakes was Patricia (Trish) Waters' Jack Russell terrier Pickle, who was aged 11 when the first earthquake struck in September 2010. Trish had acquired Pickle as a six-week-old puppy while living in Diamond Harbour on Banks Peninsula, about half an hour's drive from Christchurch city. She remembers fondly Pickle's unique and spirited personality before the quakes: 'She would run around Diamond Harbour and through Godley House if she escaped from home. I would get phone calls from people along the street saying Pickle is just heading through someone's garden and towards somebody else's garden! Inevitably, someone would bring her back. She never came back on her own!'

Trish and Pickle later moved to live in Heathcote Valley, and when the 4 September 2010 earthquake struck early in the morning, Trish recalls how the house was severely shaken. Once the tremor subsided, she immediately thought of Pickle who slept in the spare room at night. 'My first thought was "She's dead", because I couldn't believe she hadn't barked. She'd slept through the whole incident, which I just found astounding!' Thus, Pickle initially seemed to cope with earthquakes, but before long, her demeanour began to change in a worrying way. 'She started jumping at everything,' Trish recalls, 'every car door slam, and aftershocks, and she just got worse and worse'.

The following February, Trish went on holiday and booked Pickle into a boarding kennel. It was here that Pickle experienced the

Pickle.

22 February earthquake. 'They rang me from the kennels to let me know that Pickle was not injured, but they also said that all the dogs were shaken up.' Trish was told that a veterinarian had checked all the kennel's boarders and prescribed the dogs sedatives. She returned home from holiday to find her house was heavily damaged; the jolts had been so intense that the piano had travelled across the room.

The upheaval in the house was matched by Pickle's inner turmoil, and despite the sedatives, that late summer quake marked the start of a severe downturn in Pickle's psychological health. 'From February on, for 18 months, I agonised,' Trish says. 'Pickle wouldn't sleep, she cried all night, she shivered and shook. I tried a new vet, who did his best to help her. He put her on more sedatives. I had her on various herbal remedies as well.' None of these treatments seemed to help, and by mid-2012 Trish was desperate. 'I couldn't afford to keep spending money when it wasn't doing any good, so I talked to Pickle's previous vet who knew her well and had treated her over many years, and he said the time had come to seriously think about putting her down.'

To hear that Pickle's condition had become so dire that euthanising her was now a valid option was devastating news for Trish. Understandably, she tried to find another solution:

> She's not sick, I said to the vet. She's bright as a button. 'But she is sick,' he told me. 'She's mentally sick.' And she was unhappy all the time. Pickle cried every time a car went by. We had railway lines nearby and she'd be scared of the noise from the trains. She'd be lying in her basket, and next minute she'd be running up and down the house, and you could see where she'd scratched behind the wall.

Pickle continued to deteriorate. 'When the aftershocks came she cried and cried and was paw licking. In the end, I knew it was going to be inevitable. I'd put it off as long as I could and I asked my son-in-law if he could find a vet and take her.'

Trish's son-in-law called numerous clinics but none of them said they would euthanise Pickle under these circumstances. Trish understood their reservations, so she got back in contact with Pickle's previous veterinarian for his advice, and he agreed to do it. 'I was very upset even though all my friends were telling me I'd done all I could, and I had. I asked the vet to do it that day as I didn't want Pickle to suffer any longer.'

Trish decided that rather than traumatise the terrier further with a final car trip to a veterinary clinic, she would instead drive her to the kennels with which she was familiar. Pickle stayed there in the care of staff she knew until the veterinarian could attend. 'I left her somewhere she would feel good, playing with the other dogs,' Trish recalls. 'I just left her happy and having fun.' Trish had her companion buried under the magnolia tree at the kennels because that was where she used to like to play and sit. 'I missed her so much, and I still do,' she says, 'but I know I did the right thing. I don't have any regrets'.

Trish and Pickle's story is one of frustration and heartbreak. Trish believes she was left with no option but to free Pickle from her chronic state of distress and anxiety. The decision to euthanise a companion animal is for many people the most difficult and heart-wrenching one they will ever make – but for most, it is motivated by deep love and affection for a treasured friend whose suffering in life seems unbearable. Committing to care for a companion animal may require us to judge when it is best to end their lives. Humans are not often called to make similar choices regarding the death of a human loved one, and there are no hard and fast rules as to how to do this for animals. Societal and cultural attitudes continue to devalue the grief experienced when a companion animal is lost but it has been recognised that 'playing an active role in the termination of a pet's life may cause distress, guilt, and depression in the pet owner' (Podrazik et al., 2000, pp. 365–366).

Petra

Petra, an 11-year-old whippet, and companion of Sue Barr and her partner Matt, is another dog whose sense of security was profoundly affected by the earthquakes, and she suffered significant weight loss due to chronic anxiety. Sue explains: 'She was on anti-anxiety medication after the September quake but was totally done in by the February and June quakes and she became terrified of being in our house or left alone at all.'

Because Petra was at home alone when the February 2011 event occurred, it cannot be known exactly how she responded to the sudden shaking, but she was certainly further traumatised.

Since Petra's fear and insecurity continued to worsen, the time came to seriously consider other options for her long-term well-being. 'I decided it was in her best interests to find her a new home,' Sue explains, 'especially as she kept losing weight even while on anti-anxiety medication. One afternoon she even tried to eat her way out of the house in panic'. Although it was a difficult decision to make, and Sue continues to miss Petra deeply, finding a new home for this quake-tormented whippet seemed the kindest solution. 'Now Petra lives in Golden Bay on a farm with a fantastic couple and another whippet,' Sue reports.

Petra.

'She has put on weight and is happy again.' Sue believes the significant impact of the earthquakes on Petra's mental health was demonstrated by the ease with which she adapted to a new home. 'She was a loyal, one-person dog, very connected to me before the quakes. However, she had become so fearful of the aftershocks and had attributed them to something about our house that she hardly showed any separation or pining anxiety when she went to Golden Bay.'

Shelter

Fox terrier Shelter was a much-loved companion of Sumner resident Gina Armon and her son, Jamie Armon-Rangi; if not for the earthquakes they feel they might have enjoyed his company for years longer. The story of how Shelter came to be adopted into the Armon family provides an example of the sense of instant connection that can spark between human and animal. Gina says,

> Jamie and I had just moved back to Christchurch from Tauranga, which meant we could finally have a dog. That was pretty exciting! So my dad, Jamie and I went to the dog pound. Jamie saw a puppy in the first kennel closest to the door where I think they put the sad ones. He was a little fox terrier, only nine months old, sitting right at the back of the kennel and shaking because the other dogs were barking. Jamie sat down there beside the cage and wouldn't budge.

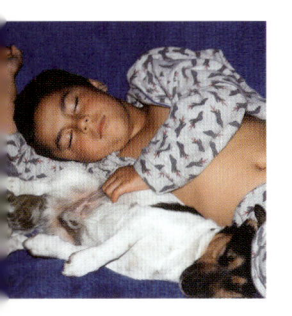

Jamie, six years old at the time, clearly felt an immediate bond with this puppy, and while Gina and her father continued to look at the rows of caged dogs, he stayed with the terrier in the cage by the door. 'I carried on thinking that I was going to see my dream dog,' Gina smiles, 'but when we returned to where Jamie had sat, he had tears streaming down his face, and he announced, "Mum, we have to get this one".'

Gina was open to the idea of adopting the fox terrier because she wanted a small dog who would not jump all over her elderly grandfather. After returning to the pound later that day with her grandfather so he could have the final say, Gina and Jamie were pleased that the terrier met with his approval.

When Gina enquired about the puppy's history, she was told that he had been abused by his his first owner until he was rescued at nine months of age. Gina and Jamie were committed to giving this dog a fresh start and they also gave him a new name:

> The day we took him out to the car to meet Granddad, he had a lead on that said "shelter". So Jamie thought that was the puppy's name. I didn't tell him that the place was called The Dog Shelter, and so that's what we ended up naming him. It got shortened to Shelts.

Despite his troubled past, Shelter settled quickly and happily into life with his new human family. 'Because he'd been abused, he was very timid and he didn't do well in crowds for a while,' Gina recalls.

Jamie and Shelter.

'Luckily, he was still young enough that he outgrew a lot of that, with the help of loads and loads of love. He certainly had his quirks, but he was a brilliant dog.'

Shelter lived with four generations of humans under the one roof. Gina and Jamie, and Gina's father and grandfather shared a large two-storey house. 'Shelter would run up and down the stairs and see who was in which room and then decide who he'd sit with,' she recalls.

Seven years after the adoption, everything changed for Shelter when the magnitude 6.3 earthquake struck Christchurch on that Tuesday afternoon in late February 2011. Gina recounts:

> We were living across the road from where a big boulder came down. I was at work and Jamie was at school, and Shelts was home alone, where he usually was during the day. We left the back door jimmied open so he could go out into the back yard. By the time I got home, my neighbour Tania McClean had run over to get Shelter, because she knew he was alone. She told me that she had found Shelter partially buried by a brick wall that had come down inside. He was in my room where mirrors and everything had come down.

Shelter was not physically injured by the fallen wall and debris, but he was traumatised. When dealing with aftershocks, he took his cues from Gina and Jamie. 'He'd always stand like he was going to move but wait to see what we would do.'

The Armons were forced to vacate their home. Three days on from the earthquake, they were living with friends and temporarily prevented from accessing their previous house, which was now fenced off. Shelter enjoyed the relocation, as Gina and Jamie's friends had a dog of their own with whom the terrier had grown up.

However, the February earthquake was the catalyst for a series of events that were to have a terrible impact on Shelter's health. When the terrier was two years old he had been diagnosed with a heart murmur, although Gina says this condition had not caused him any problems until they moved in with their friends after the quake. 'Then Shelter developed this rash on his paws, which I thought was caused by the long grass around the house we'd moved to. I put it down to that because he'd never had this kind of problem before.'

The veterinarian prescribed antihistamines, which worked while Shelter was taking them but the rash returned with a vengeance whenever the medication was withdrawn. 'I took him back to the vet and they'd give him some more antihistamine and they also put him on steroids. They said because of his heart condition, they didn't want him on steroids for too long.' Sadly, the rash was persistent, returning time and time again. 'It was terrible,' Gina recalls. 'Jamie and I would bandage his legs and he'd pull the bandages off.'

Gina eventually learnt that it was not the grass that was causing Shelter's allergic reaction – it was the red dust coming off the cliffs as a result of the tremors. Bacteria in the dust were causing the skin condition and it seems that Shelter's was not an isolated case, as Gina's veterinarian advised her that this reaction to the dust was a common repercussion of the earthquakes.

As time progressed, the consequences of Shelter's debilitating skin condition and its treatment became more evident:

> One Saturday Shelter started making this funny wheezy noise so we gave him the last of the antihistamines we had. The next day he was looking more distressed and still wheezing and coughing. We were going to take him to the vet on Monday if he was still like that, but when I went to work after the weekend I thought he would be alright. Later that morning Jamie rang me to say that Shelter was really sick.

From work Gina made an urgent appointment with a veterinarian at Animal and Bird Hospital, and arranged for her friend Susie Zumbraegel to take Shelter there. However, the dog's rapid deterioration took them all by surprise. 'Jamie rang me again at work to tell me to go right away. Looking back now, I think to leave Jamie with Shelter in that state was the worst mistake of my life.' Tending to Shelter in such a distressed state and knowing the dog was fighting for his life was deeply upsetting for Jamie, whose special connection to the terrier had grown stronger over the course of their lives together. When Susie arrived to take Shelter to the veterinary clinic, Gina says: 'Jamie took a really long time to say goodbye. He knew Shelter wasn't well, and he was just so attached to him he believed the vet would fix him.' In the car on the way to collect Gina before driving to the veterinary practice, Shelter stared at Susie the entire journey. She patted his head, trying to reassure him.

When Gina saw Shelter, she knew it was serious. After examining Shelter, the veterinarian told Gina her beloved dog would not live out the day. Although she had known Shelter was extremely ill, the words still came as a shock. The long-term use of steroids to treat Shelter's skin condition had exacerbated Shelter's pre-existing heart condition, resulting in congestive heart failure. Gina called home and delivered the distressing news to her son, who immediately set off by bus for the

Shelter in old age.

Animal and Bird Hospital to say a final farewell to his friend.

A few weeks before Shelter's sudden deterioration, Gina had got a tattoo of a flower – an iris in remembrance of her grandparents who had died several years earlier. It was therefore a poignant moment when veterinary clinic staff led Gina and Jamie into a condolences room where there were fresh irises. 'I burst into tears,' she remembers. The irises were symbolic for Gina and Jamie, a sign for them that Shelter would have the company of her grandparents after passing over. 'They're going to be there for Shelter,' Jamie said.

Gina believes that the earthquakes contributed to Shelter's premature death. She says: 'The medication for his rash sped up what would probably have occurred in another five years due to his heart condition.' There was little alternative at the time except to give Shelter the antihistamines to ease his chronic and acute discomfort; however, the Armons cannot help but wonder whether their loved companion might still be here with them if the earthquakes had not occurred.

Accommodation woes

Hundreds of people experienced the loss of companion animals as a result of the Canterbury earthquakes. Sometimes the loss was permanent, when animals were killed (or their lives foreshortened by quake-related illness), or when they fled, never to return. Some people had to give up their companion animals due to changed living situations. Many people who had to abandon quake-ravaged homes at short notice were forced to surrender their companion animals; unless they had the option of living with friends and family (who would also take in their dogs), it was difficult to find pet-friendly emergency accommodation. In many cases, the stress experienced by some people in the aftermath was so overwhelming that they had to permanently relinquish their pets. Post-quake accommodation for people with dogs continues to be an immense problem in Christchurch. Even now, several years on, shelter and advocacy organisations like Dogwatch (see chapter 2) are still reporting higher numbers of surrendered dogs due to lack of dog-friendly rental homes in the city for those whose houses have been 'red-zoned', or are only now being rebuilt or repaired.

In *Quake Dogs*, Laura Sessions and Craig Bullock (2013) highlight the problem of accommodation in the story of dogs Stanley and Jack whose Somerfield home was deemed unsafe after the February 2011 earthquake. The dogs and their human companions were forced to move seven times in the following year. During this time, the dogs spent three months with a family friend without their human companions, a few months at a boarding facility in Nelson, time in Oxford at a donkey farm, a stint at a kennel in Rangiora, a few months with a foster family in Spencerville sourced through a paper advertisement, many months without their family at the Somerville house while repairs were being made, and one month with family friends in Church Bay (Sessions & Bullock, 2013, pp. 188–91). After seven months of relentless disruption, the dogs were eventually reunited with their human family in their repaired home.

Many more dogs were moved in and around Christchurch after the earthquakes, or were temporarily transported outside the broken city. The bureaucratic problems causing delays to building and home repairs, and the vicissitudes associated with dealing with insurance companies and the Earthquake Commission, continue to complicate accommodation issues and negatively impact on human–animal relationships in the city.

Treating canine casualties

The Christchurch disaster, as shown by the stories in this chapter, had terrible consequences for the community's dogs, causing many of these loyal companions to be separated from their loving families, and affecting their psychological and physical well-being. Given the many positive experiences and emotional rewards dogs that bring to their human companions, it seems appropriate to include a story about a person whose work focuses on 'giving back' to dogs, especially to those adversely affected – physically, emotionally and socially – by the major quakes and the thousands of aftershocks occurring in their wake.

Kathleen Crisley's 'lifelong love of all things "dog"' has culminated in her Christchurch-based holistic massage and rehabilitation practice, Canine Catering (the business also produces healthy treats for dogs). With qualifications from the United States in therapeutic and sports massage for dogs, pet nutrition and behavioural assessment, Kathleen combines Western diagnostic and treatment approaches with traditional Chinese medicine in her evaluation and care of dogs, whether they are elderly, recovering from surgery, or affected by other conditions.

Following the Canterbury earthquakes of 2010 and 2011, many concerned guardians of dogs asked Kathleen for advice. 'It's very common for dogs to present with problems that have a physical as well as emotional dimension,' she says. 'This has certainly been my experience with dogs post-quakes as well.' While symptoms varied, the common factor connecting the dogs that Kathleen treated was anxiety. 'In some cases, veterinarians had prescribed anti-anxiety medication for stressed dogs or those exhibiting withdrawn behaviours,' she explains, 'but as the aftershocks continued on and on for weeks, people didn't want to keep medicating their pets without finding alternative ways to help them cope as well'. In other cases, dogs presented to Kathleen's practice in physical discomfort. 'It was very common for them to have incurred soft-tissue injuries from running around earthquake-damaged properties. This happens when physical exertion combines with muscle tension brought on by anxiety.' Dogs were also brought to Kathleen when their latent conditions began to surface in the aftermath of the quakes.

> Dogs who were probably already suffering from arthritis and more chronic conditions prior to the quakes, and were usually very stoic and hiding their discomfort, began presenting with pain symptoms. Christchurch dogs were under great physiological stress at this time, and every dog reacts differently.

With each new canine client, Kathleen completes a thorough initial assessment in their own home environment. She says this provides important information before she even begins to lay hands on a dog for therapeutic massage. Interviews with the guardians of quake-affected dogs revealed several interesting patterns. 'Some people reported that dogs were exhibiting new behaviours, such as excessive licking of the front paws – a condition that, when it becomes chronic, causes a lick granuloma that damages the skin,' Kathleen explains. 'Other symptoms I noted included refusals to eat, social withdrawal, and more aggressive behaviour towards certain members of the family, objects or other dogs.'

One case Kathleen remembers well involved a dog named Bracken who was showing typical symptoms of chronic anxiety. Her family home was a property close to the Greendale fault, the locus of the September quake. She was sensitive to noise and had already been traumatised prior to the earthquakes by a farm accident for which she had been treated with anti-anxiety medication by her veterinarian. When the city was disrupted by seismic activity, Bracken's symptoms became so pronounced that she was happier away from the family home, especially because the house's steel construction resulted in significant noise each time an aftershock occurred. 'At home, Bracken was alert and unable to settle,' Kathleen reports. 'She was also jealous when the other dog in the household was given attention, and at times she seemed suspicious of her owners if they tried to entice her to parts of the property she was most afraid of. When I met Bracken, I could clearly see the distress in her eyes.'

Kathleen devised a treatment plan that would encourage Bracken to relax. This involved massage sessions focused on acupressure points in order to 'soothe the central nervous system', activity toys to direct her attention away from worries, food treats as positive rewards when she engaged with a toy therapeutically, and the use of an anti-anxiety wrap designed for dogs.

Another regular client Kathleen had been treating before the earthquakes was a dog suffering from discospondylosis (a degenerative condition of the spinal column where bone spurs develop on one or more vertebrae); his condition deteriorated significantly when his family had to move to temporary accommodation while their home was being repaired. 'The family's routine had changed dramatically – they were leaving for work at different times and Bertie's daily walk schedule was new,' Kathleen recalls. 'Despite their best efforts to normalise things by bringing his bed and toys to the temporary home, his environment was just too different. He was edgy and anxious, and his muscle tension had resulted in a flare-up of back pain.'

Bracken receiving a therapeutic massage from Kathleen Crisley.

This case shows how the well-being of animals was affected long after the initial impact of the quakes. Now, rather than treating fear of tremors, Kathleen's focus has shifted to dogs whose anxiety and behavioural problems stem from upheaval caused by quake-related events such as moving to temporary accommodation during house repairs or permanent relocation, and disruption to normal routine within the usual home environment while repairs are completed.

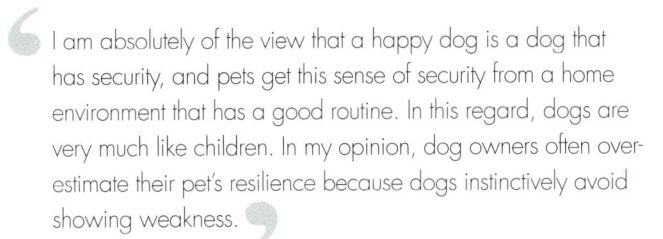

> I am absolutely of the view that a happy dog is a dog that has security, and pets get this sense of security from a home environment that has a good routine. In this regard, dogs are very much like children. In my opinion, dog owners often over-estimate their pet's resilience because dogs instinctively avoid showing weakness.

Kathleen Crisley's own companion, Daisy, who died in 2014.

Kathleen has her own 'canine earthquake story' to tell. She was in Kilmore Street in the central city at lunchtime on 22 February 2011. Managing to get back to her car after the massive tremor, she drove in congested traffic to her home in northwest Christchurch, only to find Daisy, her 10½-year-old dog, very upset; she had been running through the house looking for a way to escape the chaos. 'Luckily, I had "fixed and fastened" all heavy furniture well before the first major earthquake and so whilst a lot of things were displaced from shelves and cabinets, Daisy was never in danger of being hit by falling furniture or paintings.' Based on her professional knowledge of dogs' responses following the September earthquake, Kathleen decided it was important to keep calm and maintain a sense of normality for Daisy. 'Therefore, in the late afternoon I took her for a walk and was stopped by a neighbour who had a mixed breed dog with him. This dog didn't have a collar but was clearly a loved pet as he'd recently been bathed.' Neither the neighbour nor Kathleen recognised the dog and so Kathleen decided to take him home to her fenced property until she could locate his owners. 'With every aftershock, both dogs would come to me for comfort. Our bed was crowded because they'd each come up with me against the pillow.' When Kathleen walked the dogs she noticed the newcomer, who she nicknamed Shake, was limping. She used her therapeutic low-level laser on his paws, assuming they were sore, and also bathed them in salt water.

Shake's identity was revealed when the local veterinary clinic opened several days later and Kathleen had him scanned for a micro-chip. Unfortunately, the dog's chip was not registered with the national New Zealand Companion Animal Registry (NZCAR) but she was eventually able to locate his guardians through the local SPCA and Animal Control office. 'I could then match the dog, named Trick, to his family, who arrived within a couple of hours to collect him,' she recounts. 'Before that though, I had another man, referred to me by the SPCA, come around to check whether Shake was his missing companion. It was hard watching his face go from hopeful and excited to crushed when he realised this dog wasn't the one he'd been hoping to be reunited with.'

Trick's story is one of many that demonstrate how important it is to have companion animals micro-chipped and registered both nationally and locally. His collar with identity tags had been removed the night before the February earthquake when he was being bathed, and were left off so his fur could dry thoroughly. However, the gate on the property where he lived collapsed during the tremor and Trick had fled in fear.

At the end of February 2011, Kathleen's own dog Daisy suddenly became lame, an X-ray revealing she had advanced arthritis. Daisy had always been active and had been receiving joint support supplements, but following the earthquakes she required a much more rigorous programme to keep her mobile and combat the pain. While the exacerbation of Daisy's physical condition is likely to be related to the trauma she endured during the 6.3 seismic event, it is worth noting that she did not display any signs of suffering ongoing anxiety. 'That's because I willed myself to remain calm with her and just comfort her when she wanted it – when she sought me out – rather than making a big deal of every aftershock,' Kathleen explains. 'Routine is very important for dogs and they are also pack animals. We are part of their pack and they watch what's going on for the pack very carefully.'

Trick.

Kathleen has some advice for those living with dogs directly or indirectly affected by the Canterbury quakes:

> In the first instance, try to put yourself in your dog's place. Think of all the things that are going on around him or her in the context of their normal routine or life. Put simply, if you were used to sleeping for eight hours a day when your family is away at work or school, imagine how distressing it would be to have workmen at the property next door, talking loudly, hammering nails and using power tools, plus walking very close to your territory. You'd be on edge and unlikely to rest, and that lack of rest will weaken the immune system.

Kathleen also emphasises that owners play a crucial part in a dog's recovery. 'A professional like me only sees the dog for a short period of time,' she points out. 'It's what the dog does after a treatment and being able to observe even small changes in that dog's behaviour or health that's important. With each subsequent treatment session, and based on an owner's feedback, I build on a picture of what is working for the dog. An engaged and observant owner will help their dog's rehabilitation.'

Tui and Douglas

Douglas Horrell is one Christchurch resident who has sought to help his dog recover from quake-induced anxiety by watching her behaviour and modifying his own; in doing so he has found that his relationship with his nine-year-old greyhound-cross Tui has deepened. Douglas says that greyhounds are deemed the 'couch potatoes of the dog world because they sleep most of the day and store their energy up for short bursts of running'; they are gentle dogs who often find themselves in need of adoption after being retired or rejected from professional racing. Douglas adopted Tui from SPCA Canterbury.

On 4 September 2010 when the first major earthquake struck, Douglas and Tui were together at home. Douglas recalls:

> Tui, like me, went straight from deep sleep to a high level of anxiety. Her natural inclination was to run away but there was nowhere to go as our brick and concrete tile house shook and rumbled like a train. I yelled her name and grabbed her collar. We stood in the doorway together. Her whole body shook and trembled.

Tui's experience of that violent quake affected her profoundly and, as she and Douglas endured the cycle of aftershocks, her symptoms of anxiety escalated. 'She would shake and pant and refuse to eat her food,' Douglas recalls. 'She lost weight, not that she had any spare, and I would give her a bone to distract her, which she would compulsively bury and dig up again. As she dug deeper and deeper under the house she came up against the concrete foundations, which caused scarring on her nose.'

During the quake on 22 February the following year, Tui was at home alone. Douglas rushed back to the house from work as soon as he could and took Tui with him to stay with a friend in Hinds, just outside Ashburton. They had left the shaking city behind but the effects of the previous day soon surfaced.

> The next morning Tui passed urine with blood in it. I took her to the vet who X-rayed her and took a urine sample the colour of beetroot juice for testing. I was worried as I knew this could be a symptom of major organ problems. The results indicated that she was okay. The blood had been the result of some kind of tissue trauma and it was working its way out of her system. The vet said it was likely that when the quake happened she had gone off like a rocket in the confined space, probably charging full speed into furniture or a wall.

Tui.

Douglas learned from greyhound rescue groups that dogs of this breed have a heightened natural tendency to flee when they are afraid, and that this can lead to extreme anxiety when they experience a threatening situation and cannot escape.

Working out how to help Tui with her anxiety has been a long journey. 'I trained myself to never outwardly display fear and anxiety at the aftershocks,' he says, 'as I realised that Tui was picking up my fear and turning it into her own. However, my protective instinct for Tui heightens even just imagining being back in that quake period again. I'm still concerned that the stress of the earthquakes has taken years off both our lives.'

However, Douglas recognises that his companionship with Tui has been instrumental to their recovery:

> Life has improved vastly for Tui and me. She was my companion through some of the strangest times I've had. Long walks after the February quake kept both of us sane. Together we watched army tanks roll through the city, and listened to wind rustling through trees in Hagley Park – the only sound to issue from the evacuated heart of Christchurch after it was red-zoned.

The calming coat

Many people found that their dogs, as loved and loyal companions, helped them to cope better with earthquake stress. In turn, Becky Hadfield and her friend Jo Harris came up with a way to ease the anxiety of dogs traumatised by the tremors, beginning with Becky's Dalmatian, Poppy.

Poppy, who was handpicked in 1999 from a litter of Dalmatian puppies in Kaiapoi, was a fun-loving character while growing up. However, Becky says that her positive disposition was transformed by the Canterbury earthquakes:

> Poppy was typically an extremely friendly and outgoing dog, always interested in being amongst the family activities as "one of the gang". But sadly she changed dramatically when the earthquake happened in September 2010. We lived on Rocking Horse Road on the estuary waterfront in Southshore, and felt a very violent rolling motion with every quake and aftershock.

The area where Poppy was living was so badly damaged that the family home was condemned to be demolished. As a result of the magnitude 7.1 pre-dawn quake and subsequent months of aftershocks Poppy had not fared so well either:

> During earthquakes she became a trembling jelly of a dog. She refused to go upstairs into our lounge and kitchen area. She preferred to be outside the house, and had to be coaxed into the home. Poppy became my shadow, on edge all the time. The only way I could calm her and stop the trembling was to literally sit with my arms wrapped around her, holding her tightly in a hug. We tried to keep her routine the same, and she was fine on a walk. It was just in the house that she experienced anxiety. You could literally see her slow down and stiffen up as we approached the house. Any loud bangs set her off. We were together in the house for both the September and the February quakes, so it became a real place of fear for her.

After numerous episodes of coaxing a terrified Poppy inside the house, and many hours spent holding her tightly between her legs in a comforting bear hug, Becky had the idea of creating a device to mimic this 'safety hug'. Enlisting Jo's help, Becky developed a dog coat to help soothe earthquake-affected dogs. Becky explains:

Poppy wearing her calming coat.

> ❝ The Canine Calm Coat was really born of necessity. I couldn't see how I was going to offer Poppy the reassurance of my "bear hug" all the time. I also had two children to reassure. So, after researching the benefits of compression for soothing anxiety, and talking to Jo, who is a medic with a wealth of experience in techniques to deal with anxiety in autistic children, we experimented on Poppy with a number of compression coat designs. ❞

Becky and Jo's creation was trialed on dogs at the SPCA, Dogwatch and veterinary clinics, and was also used by some animal behaviour specialists and dog trainers. They were keen to find out whether the coat, which brought so much comfort to Poppy, would work on a broader scale. Convinced of its effectiveness, Jo and Becky decided to patent the design and now manufacture the coats in Christchurch.

The coat that Becky devised to help her dog deal with the trauma brought about by earthquakes now has the potential to help other dogs cope with disastrous events. 'It is a really satisfying project,' Becky says, 'and of course my dear friend Poppy is a very happy and willing pin-up girl for the product.'

Canine therapy

There is no doubt that animals helped the Christchurch community to recover after the earthquakes. Dogs such as those working with teams like Urban Search and Rescue saved people's lives in the immediate emergency, and in the aftermath of the quakes they also provided solace and a sense of normality in people's everyday lives – or what was left of the 'everyday'. Animals are effective therapists just by being themselves; in times of crisis we feel better just spending time with them in a relationship that does not depend on speaking or human language. This is not to say that animals cannot communicate with us (those of us with pets know they can and do) but they communicate in non-verbal ways, which we find just as significant and comforting as speech. Those who were lucky enough to remain with their companion animals post-quakes have conveyed how precious these relationships were to them throughout this time, providing affection, stability, security, acceptance, distraction and reassurance.

Aja

One Christchurch dog who exemplifies the therapeutic capabilities of companion animals is Aja, a brindle bull terrier–Staffordshire terrier cross, who was rescued by Animal Control in Nelson after being abused as a pup. She was adopted by Alan McGregor and Linda Zampese and their twins Lara and Luca (who were seven at the time of the quakes). Being close to the Port Hills, the family was badly affected by the February earthquake in particular. Their house was a chaotic mess and they had

Aja, with Lara and Luca Zampese.

to live without water and power supplies for two weeks. According to Linda, Aja loathed the tremors: 'She turned into an agitated and quivering mess each time an aftershock occurred.' Linda also wonders if Aja is able to sense seismic activity before it happens because the dog becomes visibly agitated prior to any shaking the humans can feel.

Whenever the ground shudders or quivers, Aja runs to the children for cuddles and reassurance and they are able to comfort her quickly. Likewise, when Lara and Luca have been upset by the major quakes – one twin's ability to sleep was very disturbed for a period – Linda says that their close relationship with Aja provided tremendous stability and comfort. The mutual friendship and support Lara, Luca and Aja give each other has assisted both the children and their dog to cope with the aftermath of the quakes. Helping companion animals through anxious times also has the important benefit of teaching children about empathy and the value of caring for others.

Guinness

We close this chapter with a story about Guinness the Irish wolfhound and his human companion Sean Scully. The duo is well-known at home – and now nationally – for helping victims of the February 2011 earthquakes. Named after the famous Irish stout (full-bodied with a creamy topping), Guinness's 80-kilogram mass was matched only by his charm as he accompanied Sean on a mission to assist Christchurch residents in the aftermath of the quakes.

In 2011 Sean was living at a property just outside the suburb of Prebbleton, approximately 15 kilometres southwest of the city centre. Sean's home escaped the devastation of the February earthquake and, aware of his good fortune, he offered to help a friend; realising the scale of the disaster, and moved by the plight of the elderly in particular, he then joined the wider efforts to help those struggling with the clean-up and worked to clear liquefaction from private properties and public streets. Sean contacted radio personality Pam Corkery for assistance, and her broadcast appeal resulted in more than 200 wheelbarrows being donated; Sean also sourced donations of other supplies such as shovels and tools from hardware companies. As he explains:

> A lot of people seemed more comfortable with donating items rather than money. They knew that things like wheelbarrows and shovels would be immediately useful and felt happy that their donations would go directly to people who desperately needed them.

Christchurch's 'Earthquake Dog' (Guinness).

Sean Scully

An important, if less tangible, aspect of Sean's campaign to help Cantabrians recover from the shock of the earthquake involved walking through the streets with Guinness by his side. The gentle canine giant's captivating appearance and affable personality brought welcome respite for many who were feeling overwhelmed by the disaster. 'Guinness is a friendly and calm-tempered dog who attracts attention wherever he goes,' Sean says. 'He has this ability to allow people to open up, and he acts a bit like an ice-breaker. People are just really drawn to him.' He believes the impressive canine's presence allowed people to take their mind off their terrible situations, even if it was only for a short time. Guinness was particularly popular with children.

These days, aged eight, he accompanies Sean to work on a daily basis:

> I have started my own company in Christchurch doing mostly commercial earthquake repairs. Guinness holds a variety of titles in the company, such as "Health and Safety Manager" and "Contract Manager", and in much the same way as he did after the earthquake, when people come into the office and see him there he defuses their frustration over having to deal with earthquake repairs nearly four years on.

Because of their heroic and generous efforts in the weeks after the February earthquake, Sean and Guinness each received Local Hero medals at the New Zealander of the Year awards in 2011. The time they spent working alongside the Student Volunteer Army resulted in Guinness being named the Army's unofficial mascot. To Cantabrians, he is simply known as 'The Earthquake Dog'.

In summary

The stories recounted in this chapter demonstrate how those dogs who remained with guardians and families in the city post-quakes provided crucial comfort and security at a time of upheaval and trauma. (Conversely, the loss or enforced separation from a loved dog could exacerbate personal and familial distress.) Such support was usually reciprocal, with people focused on protecting their dogs and ensuring their well-being in the aftermath of tremors.

In situations where guardians were unable to console their dogs' debilitating anxiety during the ongoing aftershocks, they had to decide how to act in the best interest of their pets – in some cases this resulted in reluctantly relinquishing loved companions to new homes outside the city, away from the shaking; in other more tragic cases, dogs were euthanised because people in desperate circumstances felt they had no alternative option.

When quakes and aftershocks occurred, many dogs obeyed the instinctive urge to flee from a terrifying event, running away from houses and properties, only to find themselves in foreign locations without knowing how to return home. These dogs who escaped in panic were at risk of being hit and killed by cars. This raises the issue of how best to protect dogs in such circumstances and whether they should be confined indoors, a subject we will return to in the conclusion to this book.

Finally, it is important to note that, several years on, companion animal guardians in Christchurch are still facing many of the same kinds of stressful issues and concerns that confronted them immediately after the major earthquakes, such as having to find affordable rental accommodation where pets are also permitted, and working out how best to deal with the consequences of the quakes on their pets' health and psychological well-being. Fortunately there is an abundance of highly qualified and experienced animal behaviourists, canine therapists, veterinarians and veterinary nurses in the city who can help dogs and their people recover and 'recharge' post-quakes. These experts stress the importance of micro-chipping, maintaining routine, and finding ways to reduce our own anxiety so that we can comfort our companion dogs and give them a sense of security.

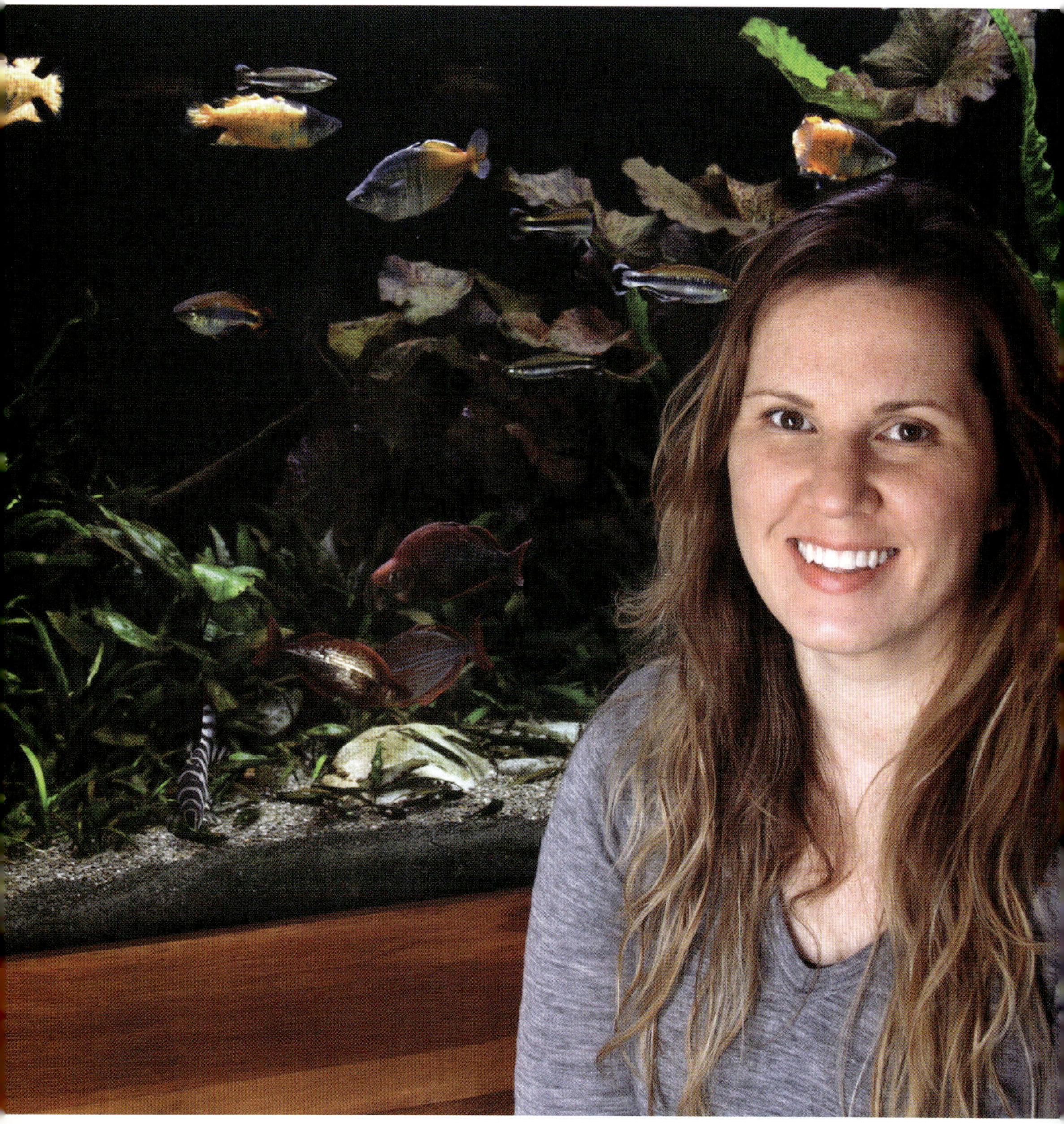

Chapter 5

From turtles to hedgehogs: other species affected by the quakes

In New Zealand when we talk of 'pets' we tend to think of cats and dogs, but our most numerous (or popular) companion animals are, in fact, fish, with an estimated 1,678,000 fish kept in the nation's homes (NZCAC, 2011). We share our lives with multiple companion species, including birds, turtles, horses and rodents. Sometimes animals farmed for food (sheep, cattle, chickens, turkeys, ducks and goats) escape their typical fate and become lifelong companions instead. In addition to domesticated animals, cities are inhabited by wildlife – native and introduced birds, fish, reptiles, insects and mammals – and may also contain within them, or on their outskirts, zoos or wildlife parks featuring exotic species. This chapter explores what became of some of these other animals when the Canterbury earthquakes struck.

Turtle Rescue

Turtles are one of the most ancient reptile species and are impressively long-lived. The lifespan of a captive turtle is generally shorter than that of his or her counterpart in the wild, but they can survive for up to 40 years. Turtles kept as companion animals (typically red-eared sliders, eastern long necks and Reeve's) require ample room in their home environments; they also need conscientious care from someone with specialist knowledge.

The necessity for such expertise means those who choose turtles as companions tend to be dedicated to meeting the unique requirements of these animals. Cantabrian turtle enthusiast Donna Moot belongs to the Federation of New Zealand Aquatic Societies whose members worked to assist quake-affected fish and reptiles; she ascribes her own fondness for these reptiles to their unique personalities and ways of

Opposite page: Jennifer Hamlin, president of the Federation of New Zealand Aquatic societies, rescued more than 300 displaced fish following the earthquake on 22 February 2011.

interacting with humans, as well as to the therapeutic restful benefits of turtle-watching. Some of Donna's turtles live inside her house and others reside in ponds in her backyard.

Donna has extensive knowledge of these reptiles and is dedicated to their care, and she is considered one of New Zealand's 'turtle experts'. This is a title she seems reluctant to embrace, but she does concede that she has gained a vast understanding of turtles and turtle husbandry over the 28 years she has been keeping them. Donna's involvement with rescuing these animals started nine years ago when a routine visit to a veterinary clinic with her own companion turtles resulted in a request for her to foster turtles surrendered to SPCA Canterbury. She soon realised there was a need to establish an official organisation in Christchurch specialising in the protection of these creatures, and so Turtle Rescue was founded.[1] 'In the first year, only two [turtles] came to me, but after that the numbers grew. I never say no because then a turtle might be sold on Trade Me and end up being passed from person to person. Or it might become unwell. It could end up being dumped in the Avon River – this has happened before. The Department of Conservation staff have fished them out and brought them to me. Abandoned turtles have also been found in Governors Bay wandering in the bush.'

Dumping pet turtles in the wild is inhumane as these creatures have been captive-bred and are not used to fending for themselves. This careless practice may also harm the ecosystem of wilderness areas as turtles are not endemic to New Zealand. Donna cautions that while turtles make great companion animals, they are a big commitment and people should ensure they are accurately informed about their needs before acquiring them as pets. It frustrates her when people think turtles can be fed once a week, live happily in dirty water, or in tanks containing stones that might be ingested. In addition to caring for abandoned and rescued turtles, a large part of Donna's voluntary work includes educating people about their proper care. 'When teaching, I personalise the turtles, as this helps people to realise that these unconventional pets are living, feeling beings.'

With her extensive expertise and experience, it is no surprise that Donna was the person to whom turtle-loving Cantabrians turned for help post-quakes. This was a chaotic and stressful time for Donna, who describes the effects of the quakes on her life as 'phenomenal':

> Early on the morning of the September earthquake, I had someone walk up to the gate at my house with a box while I

---

1 See https://www.facebook.com/Turtlerescueandrehoming

> was still in my nightie! This woman knew of me because she had previously visited here with a school group. She had with her a couple of turtles who had been rescued from a collapsed building in the suburb of Sydenham.

These two turtles were to be the first of hundreds sheltered, rehabilitated and rehomed by Donna following the upheaval created by Canterbury's seismic activity. 'I estimate I dealt with between 200 and 250 turtles,' she reports. Fortunately, Turtle Rescue, which relies on public donations, has enthusiastic volunteers who were able to help out during this hectic period. Donna explains:

> I have students assist here at different times. I'm a member of a fish aquatic society and we had a couple of working bees here after the earthquakes to get the ponds up and running. I do the day-to-day stuff, which has meant running up to 14 tanks in the house. I come home from work – I'm a registered nurse working in community mental health – and can still be up at 2am cleaning tanks.

When the February 2011 earthquake struck, Donna was at home in her garage where she keeps a few of the turtles as well as spare tanks and equipment. She was thrown onto the ground with everything tumbling around her:

> Tanks exploded and a lot of the lights on tanks fell inside them. The glass of one tank that I kept in a bedroom had shattered and water from this tank went through the wall into the next room and soaked the carpets. Liquefaction was rising in the backyard and the water damage to everything was immense. Ironically, my water supply had been cut off, and so had the phone connection. It was fortunate that I didn't lose power though because it meant I could immediately have heaters on drying the carpets.

The damaged tank in the bedroom contained turtles who had just arrived from Dunedin. On closer inspection Donna noticed that one of these turtles was in trouble:

> The basking area of the tank had slid down and her leg was jammed between two pieces of glass. It was really hard trying to move the glass – and frightening – because I kept thinking

it was going to break or shatter some more, and cut her leg off. I was also pretty sure the leg was already broken anyway because it was on an awful angle. But this particular turtle had arrived with severe calcium deficiency, and in fact this probably saved her. Because her bones were so soft, they didn't break. Any other turtle would have suffered a broken leg in these circumstances.

Turtle refugees at Donna Moot's home in February 2011.

Such an injury would have likely resulted in euthanasia, Donna explains. 'Broken legs are difficult to treat here. Overseas they could help her, but in New Zealand we are really limited in our ability to treat reptiles.'

Donna recalls that almost immediately after the February quake people began phoning her and turning up on her doorstep. 'Many of the city's residents were suddenly homeless and didn't know what to do about their turtle companions. They brought me turtles in shoeboxes in the car.' Donna's own house was water-logged, and soon it was also inundated with reptile refugees. 'I had turtles in plastic containers all over the lounge. It was hard remembering which turtles were which. In tanks you can tell them apart, but put them in boxes and they all start to look alike. But of course, I couldn't turn people away.'

The chaos caused by the earthquake was compounded as more and more people arrived with turtles. Relief appeared later in the afternoon in the form of local friends. Donna recalls:

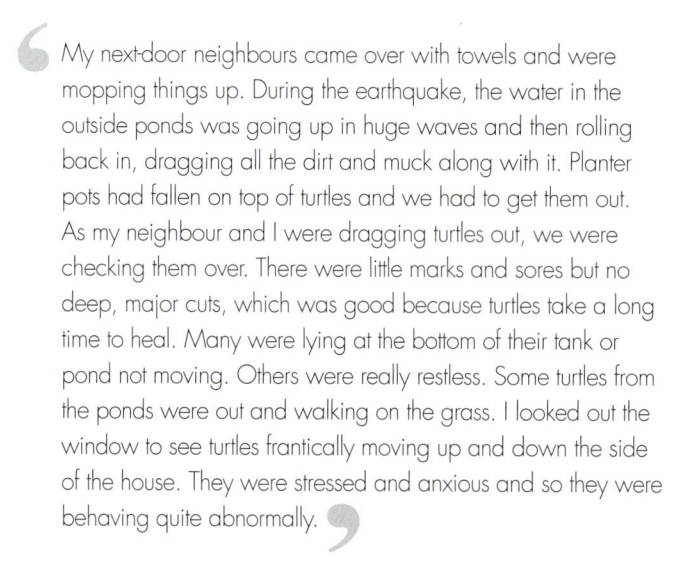

> My next-door neighbours came over with towels and were mopping things up. During the earthquake, the water in the outside ponds was going up in huge waves and then rolling back in, dragging all the dirt and muck along with it. Planter pots had fallen on top of turtles and we had to get them out. As my neighbour and I were dragging turtles out, we were checking them over. There were little marks and sores but no deep, major cuts, which was good because turtles take a long time to heal. Many were lying at the bottom of their tank or pond not moving. Others were really restless. Some turtles from the ponds were out and walking on the grass. I looked out the window to see turtles frantically moving up and down the side of the house. They were stressed and anxious and so they were behaving quite abnormally.

On the third day following the February quake, Donna found herself with approximately 45 turtles in her care. It soon became clear that this

Donna Moot with one of the turtles who lives in the ponds outside her home.

Annie Potts

was beyond her capacity, especially as she was still without a water supply to her home and only had one tank that was not broken (the turtles were taking turns in the water). She decided to contact Chris Burne who owns Hothouse Turtles in Hawkes Bay, intending to seek assistance with housing for at least 3 of the 45 turtles. To her delight, Chris managed to arrange for all of them to be relocated to the National Aquarium in Napier. The next hurdle was arranging air transit for the reptiles. Freight costs were considerable and the airline's priority was the evacuation of people. With nothing confirmed, but with plans for transporting the turtles prepared, it was not until Donna received a phone call from Chris Burne at around 12.15pm on Friday 25 February that the massive exercise to shift the turtles north began.

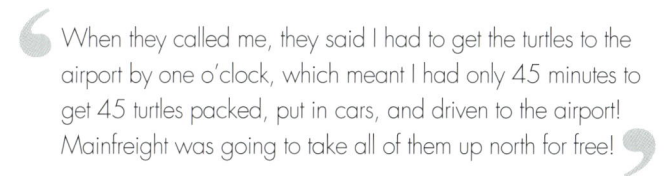

> When they called me, they said I had to get the turtles to the airport by one o'clock, which meant I had only 45 minutes to get 45 turtles packed, put in cars, and driven to the airport! Mainfreight was going to take all of them up north for free!

During this time, Donna was also liaising with Dave Bradshaw who was tending to the remaining animals at the severely damaged Southern Encounter Aquarium and Kiwi House in Christchurch city. Donna explains:

> Dave had four big female turtles he was keeping alive by going in to the aquarium every eight hours to ensure the generators were running. On the morning of the possible evacuation, volunteers went online and asked if anyone knew how to contact Dave urgently. I said please tell him that I need the turtles here immediately if they are going to be evacuated. Thankfully, he arrived on my doorstep just in time to make the flight to Napier!

News of the turtle evacuation captured the interest of a television crew filming animal rescues by the SPCA. They contacted Donna to see if they could document the evacuation event. 'After I said they could come, zoom, they were here and there was a camera-man following me everywhere', she recalls.

Once all the turtles destined for Napier were hurriedly packed and labelled, and with little time to spare, the turtle convoy set off for the airport:

> It happened very quickly. Two cars packed with turtles behind me were struggling to keep up. There was additional stress with a camera-crew member in the car filming and knowing that they were going to put the events in a television programme. It actually was just like it's portrayed in the documentary they produced: *Am I going to make it in time or not?* When we arrived at the airport it was also stressful as I was working out which turtles were aggressive, which ones were sick, and transferring them from our containers into polystyrene boxes. I had a marker and was frantically trying to label them. Just trying to keep track of all the turtles was difficult and, of course, it was hard having to let some of my own turtles go as well.

After the evacuation and during the drive back home, Donna immediately noticed the strangeness of not having turtles around. She was looking forward to having the opportunity to take stock of her own situation and beginning the massive task of returning some degree of order to her life and home. However, her solitude was short-lived. As she pulled up the drive to her house following the stressful dash to the airport, there was already somebody waiting to surrender another turtle. 'But it was only one,' Donna laughs, 'it wasn't 45!'

Half the turtles that left Christchurch after the quake in February 2011 were Donna's personal companions, including her special shelled-friend, Minnie. Also among the evacuees were Spencer, and earthquake refugees, Jessica, Bruce and Hope. Spencer is a red-eared slider (an American species) who acquired his name because he was found after the quakes wandering around in Spencer Park, a coastal reserve northeast of the city. Donna describes Spencer as 'quite unique' because he is placid and relaxed with other turtles. 'Typically, turtles are territorial and they don't actually need friends. They are perfectly fine on their own. In the wild, turtles live in ponds and if they get a bit stroppy they can just move away from each other,' she explains. 'We put them in tanks and force them to live together, which means they often clash and they can fight to the death.'

Spencer has a deformed shell, some muscle wasting and an overbite affecting his mouth. He is missing some claws as well. 'I can tell by looking at him that he must have been living in really shallow water because of the muscle wasting and the fact that he couldn't swim', Donna says. 'The overbite deformity is caused by a vitamin deficiency. He must have been sharing with another turtle, which is probably why he is missing a lot of his front claws.'

Piecing together Spencer's history is a bit like forensic profiling; Donna has been able to establish many theories about Spencer's history based on his behaviour and appearance. 'He is dark coloured and their shell darkens as they age,' she explains. 'They are green, yellow and

Donna Moot in the tank room, which was badly damaged in the February quake (photo taken in March 2013).

Annie Potts

red when they are young, but as they get older, by about 10 years of age, the males start to get quite black. So Spencer must be over 10 years old.' It is impossible to know how Spencer came to be wandering in the public park. He may have been dumped there, but Donna says that many people underestimate how skilled turtles are at climbing, so he may also have simply escaped.

Jessica is an eastern long neck turtle who came to Donna after the 22 February 2011 earthquake. 'Her family bought her as a baby from a pet shop. They were living in Heathcote and building a big five-foot tank for Jessica when the earthquake struck. Immediately after the shaking stopped, they searched for Jessica, found her under piles of glass and rubble, and brought her to me thinking it would be for just a few days. She's still here.' Due to the extensive damage caused to their house by the earthquake, the family was forced to shift into a bus parked in the driveway of their wrecked home. A year or so on from February's quake they were still living in the bus, although Donna reports that currently (2014) they are in rental accommodation while continuing to wait for their own home to be rebuilt. 'The family has been through a lot and I'm happy for Jessica to stay as long as she needs to,' Donna says. 'They come and visit her and one day she will be able to return to them.'

Named after the insurance assessor who found him, Bruce is also an earthquake refugee. He was left behind in an abandoned house in one of Christchurch's red-zoned suburbs, along with a female turtle whom Donna called Hope. 'These two had such lovely personalities,' Donna recalls. 'They didn't come to me until Easter of 2012. It was so sad that the water they'd been living in was just grey slime, but someone – possibly squatters – must have been going in to feed them because they had obviously been eating crayfish – this was causing the stinking water and fish smell. It was just revolting.' Consequently when Bruce and Hope were rescued they had severe diarrhoea and required veterinary care. Donna explains that the local SPCA paid for veterinary treatment for the first eight days for any rescued turtle she looked after, while further expenses were her responsibility to meet. 'I had to treat these two as if they were infectious and isolate them in a room and tank of their own. Everything was kept separate. Although they didn't end up having *salmonella* or *campylobacter*, I just couldn't risk anything spreading through a population of 40 plus turtles. That would have been awful.' Unfortunately, Bruce and Hope had to be separated because it was not possible to re-home them together, but they are each now adopted into new families.

Donna stresses that for her, rescuing turtles is also about supporting people:

> Every turtle that comes to me comes with a person. Turtles don't walk up my driveway on their own. Those people all have their own stories. After the earthquakes, I was dealing with traumatised people who couldn't process things so well. I was seeing the destruction that people were living with and I was supporting them and interacting with them, offering them a little bit of help.

The fact that most 'exotic' species kept as companion animals are confined for the greater part of their lives means that they are particularly vulnerable to the dangers of earthquakes. Donna stresses the importance of minimising damage to turtles and their tanks in the event of tremors. 'I'm using really sturdy frames for the tanks to sit on – they're no longer on frames with flimsy little legs,' she points out. 'It's important that the tank is not going to slide.'

Turtles and fish were two species of companion animals requiring special care in desperate circumstances after the earthquakes in Christchurch: birds and rats, similarly kept in confinement as companion animals, were in need of emergency assistance too (see also chapter 6).

Woolston's avian advocates

Between them Lyane and Paul Scarlett have accumulated 35 years of experience caring for birds. Lyane is a an avian veterinary nurse at the Animal and Bird Hospital in Ferry Road, and Paul is owner and operator of Canterbury Bird Supplies, in the eastern suburb of Woolston. Their shared passion for, and expertise in all things avian has led to their home functioning as a kind of suburban rescue facility and advice centre for pet birds. Although the number of birds under their guardianship changes frequently (but usually hovers around 50), at the time when Paul and Lyane related their earthquake experiences there were up to 70 birds being cared for on their property.

Most of these birds, which include 50 budgies, eight cockatiels, some quails, finches and chickens, live in outside aviaries; a few are Paul and Lyane's own companion birds and live inside their home. 'A lot of the birds here have been given to us,' Lyane explains, 'and we have also taken on birds that have been found and advertised through the vet clinic I work at, but have remained unclaimed. The chicken we've got now was an earthquake refugee who was brought to the vet clinic. She was found wandering around the streets after the February earthquake, and I also care for a budgie who was rescued at the same time. He was a baby and wasn't eating on his own, so we had to syringe-feed him. I think he must have escaped when the quake struck.'

Lyane and Paul Scarlett with their companion parrots, Cappy the Indian ring-necked parakeet (left) and Barry the Barraband's parakeet (right).

Annie Potts

Numerous avian earthquake casualties have been nurtured by Lyane and Paul over the past few years. Some of those given refuge had homes, but for various reasons their owners decided or needed to surrender them. 'People turned up here after the earthquakes asking to leave birds with us – they'd say "We're off", or "We can't take them with us",' Lyane recalls. 'Some of them told us we were welcome to find their bird a new home, but 9 times out of 10 we ended up keeping them ourselves. I think people felt comfortable leaving their birds with us because they knew that we were bird lovers and that we were happy to take as many as we could comfortably house.'

While relinquishing responsibility of companion birds was a common occurrence after the earthquakes, Paul asserts that people surrendering birds, because they no longer want them or are unable to care for them, is an ongoing issue in 'normal' times too. 'Cockatiels are commonly rehomed because they tend to suffer from anxiety. People know we have lots of birds and so they come around and ask if we can put their cockatiel in our aviary too because he's lonely and they work all day. So we get a lot of birds that way.'

Also known as Weiros, cockatiels are members of the cockatoo family and native to Australia. They are popular as a companion species because of their engaging personalities and relatively small stature, being larger than a budgerigar yet smaller than a galah. For the most part, cockatiels are intelligent and affectionate birds when kept in captivity; however, as Lyane and Paul point out, they are prone to anxiety. This predisposition makes these birds particularly vulnerable to trauma during and after tremors. Lyane identifies cockatiels as typical victims of an avian phenomenon called 'night frights':

> Because caged birds can't see in the dark, when they are startled by sudden loud noises during the night, they get frightened and start flying around the cage in panic. It's really difficult to calm them down, and because cockatiels are more prone to night frights for some reason, any unexpected noise or movement means that they're more likely to freak out. They bounce around the cage and can damage their wings.

At the veterinary clinic, Lyane saw at least seven cockatiels who had endured severe scares resulting in wing damage after Canterbury's earthquakes. Fortunately, Lyane says there are practical measures people can take to reduce the likelihood of injury to cockatiels (and other parrots) as a result of aftershocks. 'It's recommended that to prevent "cockatiel earthquake syndrome" you give your bird a light, like a child's night-light,' she says.

Paul witnessed at first hand how caged birds reacted to the magnitude 7.1 earthquake in the early hours of 4 September 2010:

> After the shaking stopped, I went straight outside and saw that all our cockatiels were splattered up against the front of the aviary with their wings spread out. Just a few of the budgies had done this, and the rest of them were still on their perches looking stunned.

Lyane recalls their birds' reactions after the daytime earthquake on 22 February 2011: 'I was outside watching them during the aftershocks. They would go quiet, jump a little bit, but after about 30 seconds they went back to tweeting again as if nothing had happened.' She believes the birds felt safer in the daytime because they knew that they had the ability to take flight. 'It's that fight or flight response – so if a quake happens at night they spin out, but if it happens during the day, it's not that bad for them as they can see what's going on and where they can fly.'

Cockatiels are particularly prone to 'night frights' when aftershocks strike in the dark.

Lyane Scarlett

While none of the Scarlett's birds received serious injuries as a result of the February earthquake, there were casualties associated with the previous year's September event. 'We lost many baby budgies then,' Lyane says. She explains:

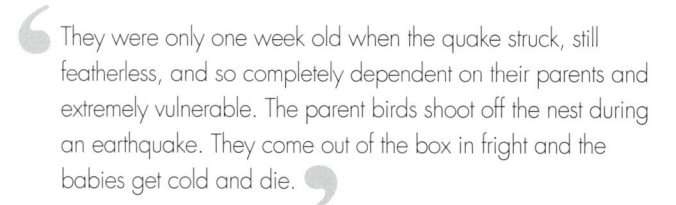

> They were only one week old when the quake struck, still featherless, and so completely dependent on their parents and extremely vulnerable. The parent birds shoot off the nest during an earthquake. They come out of the box in fright and the babies get cold and die.

While cockatiels and budgies were frightened by the quakes and aftershocks, particularly when they occurred after dark, chickens were very stoic – in contrast to their proverbial cowardliness, chickens are in fact staunch birds by nature. Lyane reports that her free-ranging chickens were not particularly bothered by the earthquakes, which reflects the accounts of others who observed chickens' reactions (see also Debbie Yate's story in chapter 1). Annie Potts' hens in Lyttelton stayed on their perch during the September quake, and in February 2011 continued to roam around the grass as if nothing untoward had happened. Nor have there been any reports about chickens uttering alarm calls during or after tremors.

In some of the worst-affected eastern suburbs, where many families were forced to evacuate their houses, Paul says that local communities really stepped up to help, particularly where chickens were concerned:

> People took over the care of chickens because their neighbours had to leave their homes after being red-stickered or during repairs. When they came to see me here for supplies, I'd ask them how long they'd had chooks for, and many replied they'd just inherited a flock because their neighbours had had to leave.

Lyane agrees that caring for the city's animals after the earthquakes required a community effort. 'The vet clinic where I work became a depot for animal food. We were giving out food to people in need. I remember some kind residents in Redcliffs were feeding a streetful of abandoned cats.' Lyane and Paul also contributed to ensuring companion birds were sustained in the immediate aftermath of February's event. 'I gave people sacks of bird food,' Paul recalls. 'One person couldn't get to the money machine because of the chaos around here, but he came back to pay when things settled, which was really nice. It actually took a while for business to return to normal. Sales totally dropped because people were just too scared to go anywhere. We were open but it was a waste of time for a couple of weeks.'

In addition to supplying food on credit, Lyane and Paul provided advice and guidance to bird enthusiasts and concerned members of the public, drawing on their expert knowledge of particular species. They responded to numerous calls for help with birds caught up in a variety of situations. 'One time a man came around with a cage of budgies for surrender,' Lyane recounts. 'Another time people arrived here after finding caged birds in an abandoned house. We also had to help with an aviary full of birds someone had simply abandoned.' Soon after the February quake, the Scarlett's aviaries were full to capacity. They then found alternative homes for birds through the Christchurch Bird Club and other bird enthusiasts.

The gravity of the abandoned-bird problem was very distressing at times. 'There was one house where birds had been left and were dying on the ground – they had no food or water,' Paul remembers, 'the people had obviously just deserted them'. Lyane adds: 'I've heard many stories about people taking off without a thought for the welfare of the animals they leave behind. I guess for some, the earthquake was so traumatic that they put themselves ahead of everything else, which is tough to understand when you're an animal lover.'

While far too many birds were irresponsibly abandoned, others were victims of circumstance, such as those housed at Christchurch Polytechnic Institute of Technology in the city centre (see page 49). 'There was also a budgie left in a business building on Manchester Street for four days,' Lyane says. 'No one could go and retrieve him, for safety reasons. Thankfully, he didn't die. Budgies have the ability to go without water for quite some time because they are desert birds, so when he was finally rescued, he was fine.'

Paul recalls the distress of one Dallington resident whose companion birds were not so lucky and were beyond rescue when he found them:

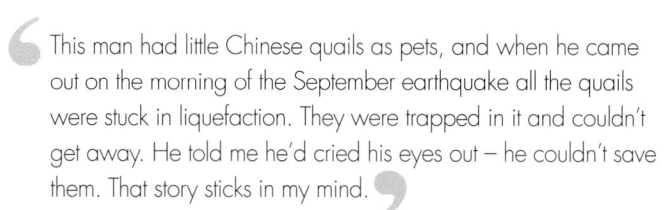

> This man had little Chinese quails as pets, and when he came out on the morning of the September earthquake all the quails were stuck in liquefaction. They were trapped in it and couldn't get away. He told me he'd cried his eyes out – he couldn't save them. That story sticks in my mind.

The Christchurch experience has shown that preparation is a key aspect of mitigiating the risk of animal injury and distress in the event of a natural disaster. Planning for earthquakes, especially in seismically active regions such as Canterbury, Marlborough and Wellington, can mean the difference between health and harm, or even life and death, for companion animals. Lyane and Paul stress the need to be prepared in order to prevent injuries to birds living in captivity. 'I know of cages that were thrown over during the quakes and the birds caught inside them were killed,' Paul cautions. 'We anchored our cages. We've wired both cages in our hallway to the wall. We've also bought cups to go under the feet of cages with wheels, to stop them rolling in a quake.'

New Zealand Rat Rescue

A disaster on the scale of the Canterbury earthquakes exposes and exacerbates the negative preconceptions that many people have about certain types of animals; such prejudices may have a direct impact on how these animals are treated during and after these events. Perhaps the best example of this correlation is provided by pet rats. After the earthquakes, because many people consider rats to be a 'throw-away' species, some pet rats were in dire need of special help and advocacy.

New Zealand Rat Rescue is a registered charitable trust dedicated to improving the lives of pet rats all over the country. In September 2011 when two Auckland-based members of Rat Rescue, Stephanie Manley and Lily Song, were interviewed on Television New Zealand's *Close Up* programme, they exposed many of the common misconceptions and prejudices that people hold about rats. Species of the *Rattus* genus are creatures of paradox in human culture – despised as pests, they are at the same time the sacrificial 'heroes' of science and medicine, and the companion species of choice for many people. Even tame pet rats are easy targets for abuse, as Stephanie pointed out in the interview on *Close Up*: 'Rats are classically $10 pets. We know of cases where someone has bought a rat from a pet shop just in order to play a prank on a colleague on April Fool's day.' In the same interview, fellow rat-rescuer Lily elaborated on these rodents' presumed dispensability, stating that many tamed rats are simply released into the wild when they are no longer wanted, despite the fact that domesticated rats have not learnt how to forage or care for themselves outside captivity. Lily also commented that rats are stereotyped as dirty and disease-mongering. 'In fact,' she explained, 'they clean themselves often, more than most people wash their hands in a day'. Lily also described how people react to her rescue work on behalf of rats: 'If I said I was a volunteer at the SPCA, people would say "That's lovely", but if I mention I offer a foster home for Rat Rescue, they say "I can help you take care of that – with my cat".'

In fact, rats are intelligent, playful and sociable rodents. It is no surprise then that all over the country enthusiasts are caring for discarded and mistreated rats. Lisette Zwarts is one such devoted member of New Zealand Rat Rescue and she helped companion rats who had been abandoned or neglected following the Canterbury earthquakes. She lives in the port city of Timaru, four hours' drive south of Christchurch, with a timid Italian greyhound, one staunch cat, and 12 rats. Lisette admits that her affection for these rodents stems in part from her empathy for them:

> Like fish, rats are often considered "throw-away pets". People get them easily and then don't realise the level of care they require. Rats actually have really sensitive respiratory systems and they do need a lot of medical care. Plus, caring for rats involves a lot of patience and perseverance, but they are great

fun. They are sensitive too – when I'm upset, a ginger rat I live with comes and licks me. Not many people know that rats also wag their tails, especially when they're excited!'

'And,' she adds with a smile, 'they clean your nails!'

Together, Lisette, Mallori Kaminski, Kelly Donaldson and a fourth rescuer in Nelson, Trudi Hazlitt-Black, make up New Zealand Rat Rescue's team in the South Island. 'Since there are only a few of us in the South Island, we usually talk every day,' Lisette says. 'We rally around all the time to find solutions for rats in need.'

One female rat who came under the care of this group following the February 2011 earthquake is Maggie, short for Magnitude. 'She was in a pet shop when the quake struck,' Lisette explains:

> She was only four months old but she already had a litter of babies. The shop was breeding from her too early and, after the quake, it was clear she was being neglected. She wasn't receiving the same level of care as some of the other larger animals in this store, which was in a badly affected part of the city. I noticed this and was concerned for her. It was a very stressful situation, but fortunately we rescued her after a couple of weeks. Her babies all found homes, but she was traumatised.'

Mallori Kaminski and Lisette Zwarts from New Zealand Rat Rescue's South Island branch, with companion rats Keiko and Maggie.

Annie Potts

Maggie was fostered for almost a year by a member of Rat Club (the New Zealand rat enthusiasts' group), but she failed to develop any connection with other rats or humans during this time. When she started biting people, the fosterer decided she could not continue to care for her. 'I have a lot of experience with rats who are aggressive towards people so I said I would take her,' Lisette recounts. 'At first she was a little scatty and would run away if I put my hand next to her. She was anxious and would bite.' If rats nip, Lisette explains, the important thing is not to pull away, but to press back on them. 'Their teeth are designed to cut deeply, but if you push back at them, they stop.' She attributes some of Maggie's recovery to her relocation to Timaru, where she seemed more settled away from the aftershocks. 'I am also careful not to be domineering or scary, but just to be a presence that is comforting for her. Maggie's a very busy rat, but she knows where to come if she gets scared. She'll race back and sit on my lap! Rats are social creatures and they do need reassurance. She is really lovely and a much happier rat now.'

When the earthquakes struck Christchurch, Rat Rescue members predicted an increase in demand for their services, especially following the magnitude 6.3 event in February 2011. This was not the case, however. One possible reason why fewer than expected rescues took place is particularly concerning. 'I thought we'd have a huge influx and so I had prepared for it,' Lisette remembers. 'I had three cages

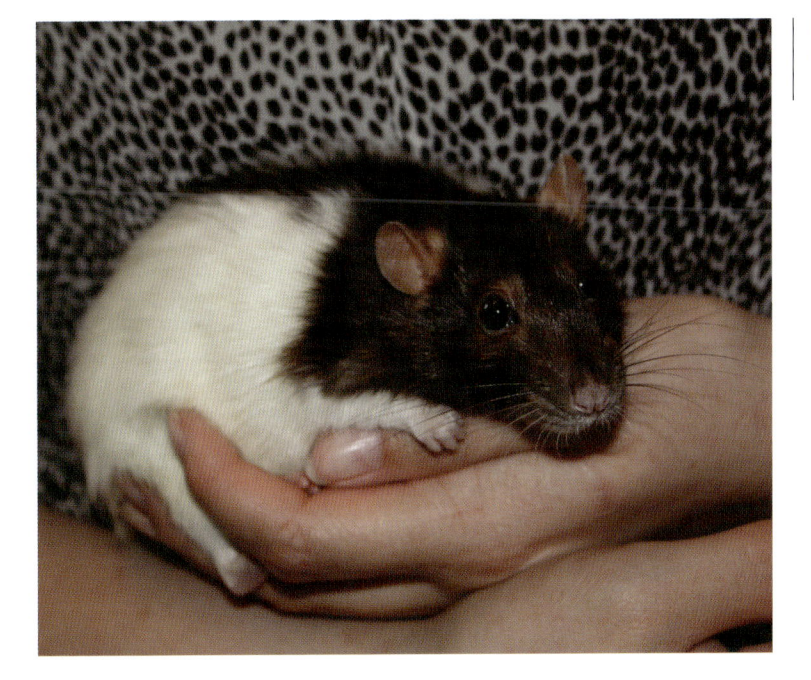

Maggie (short for Magnitude).

Annie Potts

empty and ready, and a couple of other cages that I could use in case of emergency, but I think a lot of people just let their pet rats outside to fend for themselves.' Kelly agrees:

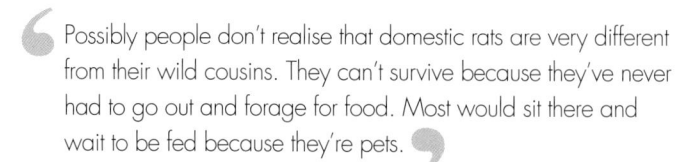

> Possibly people don't realise that domestic rats are very different from their wild cousins. They can't survive because they've never had to go out and forage for food. Most would sit there and wait to be fed because they're pets.

Rat Rescue stresses that releasing pet rats is irresponsible and inhumane. 'They'll probably get eaten very quickly,' Lisette says, 'because that's what will happen if you stick a large white rat in the wild. They are easy targets for predators.'

Sadly, through her practice as a veterinarian, Mallori witnessed specific instances of rat negligence post-quakes. 'I know of rats people dumped on the side of the road,' she says, and there are many more cases of neglect and abuse:

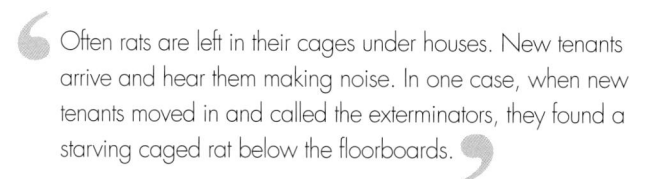

> Often rats are left in their cages under houses. New tenants arrive and hear them making noise. In one case, when new tenants moved in and called the exterminators, they found a starving caged rat below the floorboards.

Again, these instances reflect the widely held perception of rats as 'expendable' creatures.

At the time they were interviewed for this book in 2013, Rat Rescue's South Island branch had saved eight earthquake refugees. While this may not seem like many, to each and every one of those rats it meant a second chance at life. As part of their advocacy for these charming rodents, Lisette, Kelly, Mallori and Trudi also educate people about rats' needs for stimulating home environments and frequent interactions. They urge people adopting these rodents to commit to their welfare for life (the life span of a rat is short – around two to three years) and, post-quakes, they also stress the importance of securing cages so they do not collapse or tip over in the event of aftershocks.

Rabbit expert Bethan FitzGerald

As part of her Honours degree in Arts at the University of Canterbury, Bethan FitzGerald completed a research project on how popular cultural representations of *Oryctolagus cuniculus* – the common rabbit – impact on our understanding and treatment of these animals in real life. Bethan had good reason for choosing this project: she lives with several rabbits, as well as guinea pigs, and is an expert on their natural behaviour in the wild and their appropriate care when kept as companions. It is her aim one day to write a book dispelling many of the unhelpful myths circulating in society about rabbits (see also Bethan's website about raising guinea pigs: www.pigsqueaks.com).

Bethan recalls how the rabbits she lives with responded to both of the major earthquakes affecting Christchurch. After the September 2010 event, her biggest rabbit, Solomon, then three years old, began frequently thumping his feet. 'They thump to warn of danger,' Bethan explains. 'He was very upset by the aftershocks.' She suggests that Solomon may have experienced the tremors as being similar to the jolting that occurs when she moves his hutch around, with him inside it, to different places in the backyard.

Bethan FitzGerald with companion rabbit Icarus.

> The first time he experienced an aftershock *outside* his hutch, when he was roaming around the garden independently, and realised it was actually the ground beneath him moving – that absolutely freaked him out! He was terrified, running everywhere. I had to help him back into his hutch because I thought he was going to hurt himself in his panic.

A sadder outcome was in store for one of her companions on 22 February 2011. Bethan's guinea pig Luna died that day, not long after the lunchtime quake struck.

'I've talked to my vet about what happened and she doesn't think that guinea pigs have heart attacks from frights,' Bethan says, 'but it was pretty horrible and I had to hold her for four and a half hours until she actually stopped breathing. I couldn't leave her alone because she kept flipping herself onto her back, and her jaw had locked, though she was unconscious for most of it.'

In the immediate aftermath of the February event – and at the same time Luna was dying – Bethan also had to contend with water flooding uncontrollably into her family's backyard from a neighbour's damaged swimming pool, nearly submerging all the hutches and threatening to drown the guinea pigs and rabbits.

Bethan noticed that while her rabbits hid during the first major earthquake in September 2010, they preferred after that to 'shelter and watch' during subsequent aftershocks. She attributes this to the rabbits becoming accustomed to the ground shaking beneath them. The guinea pigs have always hidden during aftershocks, but they tend to re-emerge soon after. 'Guinea pigs love to console themselves with food,' Bethan says with a smile.

On the subject of animals predicting seismic activity, Bethan also has an interesting tale to tell about her cats. 'Marmite and Storm used to get up off the chairs they were asleep on and quietly sneak out the cat door – then right away an aftershock would happen! Marmite even tried to wake my mother up before the September earthquake. She was crying and pawing at Mum's face for about 10 minutes before it struck, and she never does this kind of thing.' The cats' pre-quake behaviours were so noticeable to Bethan and her mother that they began having fun trying to guess when aftershocks were going to happen based on the feline activity in the house.

Heathcote Riding School

From humble beginnings 33 years ago, when its owner first offered children rides on her two horses, the Heathcote Riding School has become an institution in the valley after which it is named. Managed by Mandy Harrington and Emma Anderson, it now spreads over 45 acres and is home to 31 horses. Weekends and school holidays are busy, with many children spending all day at the riding school helping out with their favourite ponies. The horses have come to them via word of mouth or through the newspaper; some spend their twilight years on the property while others move on to new homes. 'Sometimes it's nice for them to retire to a quieter place and with only one person,' Mandy says. 'They can get tired of all the riding and the contact with so many different people.'

When the 4 September 2010 quake struck at 4.35 in the morning, nobody was around to witness the horses' reactions. However, staff and helpers were present on 22 February 2011 when the land shook violently almost directly beneath them (the quake's epicentre was 2 kilometres west of Lyttelton). Mandy was pulling a tarpaulin over a stack of hay 10 bales high that day. She had climbed halfway back down the hay stack and was balancing between the hay and a tin wall, in order to tie the cover down, when the rumble started. 'I hugged a tree to stay upright, and the man who was with me yelled at me to get down. I was yelling back at him, "I'm not moving!" I remember the noise was *massive*! And the really scary part was noticing once I was back on the ground that the earth had opened up all around me and that kids were screaming.'

Mandy recalls there were five adults present at the riding school that day. Emma had taken a nervous beginner rider to the exercise arena, where the ground had cracked open in front of them during the mighty tremor.

> The horse bolted and the beginner rider flew off his back, but luckily she wasn't hurt. I'm sure it was the noise. It was so loud being in the valley. The hills were actually shaking and boulders were tumbling down, but it was the *sound* of the earthquake that was most terrifying.

She describes how for a brief while the entire herd galloped as one towards fenced corners, stopped short before colliding with posts, then turned as one, and took off again until constrained by another corner. Despite this noticeable 'flight' response to the extreme seismic activity of that February afternoon, Mandy points out how remarkably quickly the riding school's horses settled down and returned to their usual activities. 'Our ponies didn't get anxious afterwards, although I know of one woman whose horse has been traumatised badly. He lost a lot of weight and still suffers from anxiety,' she explains. 'But the horses here have coped well, probably because they are in a herd and feel safer together.' In support of this theory, Sara Wagstaff, a volunteer helper at the centre, mentions how the horses responded differently to a sizeable aftershock at a much later date: 'They were untethered in a holding area and they did what horses do when it rains but much faster. Like a school of fish they all turned their backs as one!'

After February's quake the riding school was without water and power; the lack of water constituted an emergency due to the need to keep scores of horses hydrated in the late-summer heat. A man whose children regularly rode at the school arrived with a truck containing a large water container, and he returned to replenish water supplies each week while the shortage lasted. 'We left the gates open for the horses to be able to go anywhere on the property,' Mandy recalls. 'That way, when one trough was empty they could wander to the next.' Water was an on-going issue, however, and the riding school's minders also put up notices around the valley asking the public to drop water off to them. 'A local horsewoman, Kathy Byfield, phoned the newspaper and eventually we received a massive water container and some troughs delivered by RD1, a rural supplier. The Woolston fire brigade which services Ferrymead came and helped fill up the troughs. Everyone pitched in to help these horses.'

Heathcote Riding School has its own emergency process should another earthquake occur while children are out riding the horses. Following 22 February 2011, lessons included a drill where riders learned to dismount from their ponies the instant they heard the word 'earthquake' being called out. 'When you're on a horse you can't always tell if there's been a quake,' Sara explains. 'So someone on the ground yells "earthquake" and the children know to get off straight away. We also instruct them to look after themselves first because the horses will take care of themselves.' The riding school had a chance to trial its emergency procedure when another significant aftershock occurred on 23 December 2011. Mandy recounts:

> Some children and one of our helpers were down at the lake with horses. The kids love taking the horses swimming. Someone called out "earthquake" and all the children jumped off their ponies because they'd been practising this drill. And the ponies didn't care – they were perfectly happy in the water!'

The riding school also has its own equine earthquake refugee. Two years ago Mandy rehomed Rocky, a small brown pony found trapped after the February quake in a West Melton glasshouse along with two other horses. Rocky's owners at the time were leasing the land and had simply left; no one knows how the ponies got into the glasshouse, but they were traumatised by the time they were rescued. Mandy recounts the story:

> They were petrified, the other two so much they were initially going to be put down. Rocky went to a couple of other homes before coming to me, but he was too difficult to catch because he was very frightened. He lived for a while in a backyard

that was next to a kindergarten. Sometimes he was taken to the kindergarten for the young children to ride, but ponies are unpredictable and after a while his owners decided the safest way for the children to continue having contact with Rocky was for them to cut a hole in the fence between the crèche and his yard. They then ran a funnel through the hole and the kids fed him carrots and apples this way!'

A relationship break-up resulted in Rocky needing another place to live, and this was when Mandy adopted him. 'He's still scared of people. None of the children here can catch him. He runs around snorting with fear if they try. I love him though, he's my rescue pony, and he will be my grandson's special horse too.' The other two terrified ponies rescued from that glasshouse following the February quake have also found caring homes.

Rocky the earthquake refugee with Sara Wagstaff, Mandy Harrington and her dog Tyson (who is also an earthquake survivor).

Annie Potts

There is no doubt the horses at Heathcote Riding School have provided therapeutic interactions for Christchurch's children in the wake of the devastating earthquakes. They have also dramatically transformed volunteer helper Sara Wagstaff's life. Having relocated to Sumner from Auckland with her partner Alan in the winter of 2010, Sara suddenly found herself unemployed as the agency she had moved south to work for was forced to close after September's earthquake. 'This prompted me to think about what I really wanted to be doing,' Sara says, 'and one thing I'd wanted to do for a very long time was get to know horses. This was a major challenge as I'd always been terrified of them.' One day, taking a relative to see February's earthquake damage to Castle Rock in the Heathcote Valley, Sara chanced upon the riding school and later contacted them. 'It's taken me ages to learn how to ride as an adult, but now I am here most days and I love being with the horses.' With an academic background in both psychology and anthropology, Sara believes that it has been the contact with horses that has helped her through difficult life events in the past three years.

> For a while things felt very uncertain and out of place. Being with animals provides security and helps me put things in perspective. There's a routine here at the riding school and it doesn't matter whether there are earthquakes or not, this routine has to continue for the horses. That always stays the same.

The suburb of Heathcote has been repeatedly ravaged by quakes, and more recently by flooding (which has been complicated by earthquake damage). As Sara points out, maintaining a routine has helped her and the horses adjust to post-quake life; similarly, the daily constitutional taken by Sara and the two horses she cares for provides a sense of stability and comfort for the residents of the valley. Locals will be familiar with the conspicuous trio that departs the riding school each day around mid-morning – a big chestnut horse (Lilly) and a tiny black and white pony (Sydney), with Sara walking in between them. Before coming to the riding school, Sara's horse Lilly had lived for seven years in a paddock far from traffic. As it is no longer peaceful in Heathcote, Sara's mission is to help Lilly adjust to her new noisy home. 'There are now very loud sounds in the valley,' she explains. 'There is the noise from demolition happening all around us. I've been trying to help Lilly get used to the roads and all this noise by leading her down them while I walk beside her.' Lilly and Sydney are paddock-mates and very attached to each other. 'Lilly is more relaxed with Sydney close by on our walks, and I can't leave one of them behind in the paddock because they get stressed,' Sara explains. 'If Sydney is ever left behind he always finds a way to escape and join up with us.' This regular exercise is essential for the miniature pony too, who struggles to maintain a healthy weight, and often finds himself placed in what Sara refers to as 'the Jenny Craig paddock' (an area where he has access to less grass). Sydney has a mind of his own though: 'I have tried riding Lilly while leading Sydney,' Sara admits, 'but he won't have that! He just roots himself to the spot and refuses to move. So, for now, we all have to go on foot together.'

    There is a bizarre twist to the riding school's earthquake story. While the residents of this valley have staunchly weathered the major quakes and thousands of subsequent aftershocks (in large part because of the strong community spirit in this suburb), they remain highly alert to the risks of living in this area. Late one night in December 2011, Heathcote

Heathcote Riding School's paddock-mates and best friends, Sydney and Lilly (with Sara Wagstaff, their 'walker').

Annie Potts

homes were disturbed by a familiar thundering sound approaching the valley – it grew louder and louder, no doubt matched by increasing adrenaline levels in those who heard it as they prepared for another 'big one'. But this was not a seismic event. It was the riding school herd of more than 30 horses, led by a cunning one who had perhaps noticed a gate had been left open, running down the road, kicking up dust in their wake – and keeping the neighbourhood on its toes. Where were they heading? Around the corner and back to the riding school!

Melissa's menagerie – Angel Horse Sanctuary finds a safe haven

Long-term Christchurch resident Melissa Miles was delivering three rescued kittens to a veterinary clinic when the 22 February 2011 earthquake hit. Arriving at the clinic, Melissa saw that the staff were in crisis, dealing with a patient who had been undergoing surgery during the quake. So, with the kittens still in her custody, she drove to her parents' house in the middle of the city to check on them. Her shaken huntaway, Millie, who was staying with Melissa's parents and was on medication for a cardiac condition, met her at the door. Once assured of her family's well-being, Melissa put Millie in her jeep with the kittens and set out for her own home in Lyttelton. All the while, she was repeatedly trying to reach her partner Mark by cellphone – he was 'somewhere downtown'. She decided to stop on the way to check that her nine horses and pony were safe in their paddock in nearby Ferrymead.

The horses and pony had come under the care of 'Angel Horse Sanctuary', Melissa's private endeavour, after being deemed too old, unwell, unwanted or 'mad'. Melissa has provided refuge for horses in need for a decade, although her first horse rescue dates back 16 years. Since the horses and pony had coped well with the September 2010 quake, which had occurred in the pre-dawn hours, Melissa was unsure what to expect. However, the effects of this earthquake were revealed to be worse. Melissa recalls:

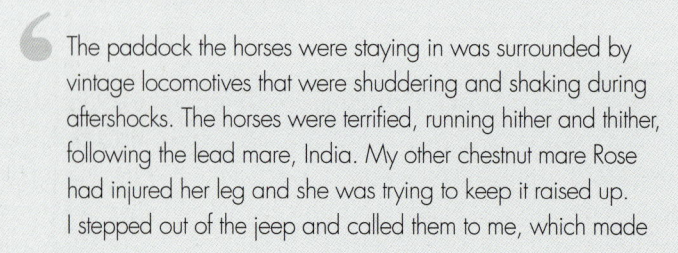

> The paddock the horses were staying in was surrounded by vintage locomotives that were shuddering and shaking during aftershocks. The horses were terrified, running hither and thither, following the lead mare, India. My other chestnut mare Rose had injured her leg and she was trying to keep it raised up. I stepped out of the jeep and called them to me, which made

Chocolade and Rose.

> them settle somewhat, but then they would set off again with each successive aftershock. They couldn't figure out where the danger was coming from.

Melissa assessed Rose's injury but was unable to rinse the wound because there was no water supply. Realising the injury was serious, and with limited resources after the quake, she contacted her veterinarian who arranged to leave some medication for her to collect from the clinic in Belfast.

> As I drove across town to get it, I was too deeply disturbed to fully take in the city, which was in disarray. The roads were filled with holes and there were great slabs of lifted tarmac. Water was everywhere but none of it was safe to drink. I made it through liquefaction and over twisted bridges to pick up the vital medicine for Rose. I figured the faster I went the more likely I'd be able to beat the authorities who were closing off roads. I realised they'd be considered too dangerous for safe passage but I was quick and very lucky to make it to the vet and back!

Melissa was relieved to be reunited with Mark four hours after the quake. She expresses her gratitude for the assistance she received from others during this chaotic and stressful time:

> Help came from many sources. I shifted the horses into a safer paddock, and water and containers [in which] to transport the water to the horses came via Mark's friends. I also had help from two volunteers Zsombor and Zsofi – a brother and sister who had moved to New Zealand from Hungary – who have assisted me with caring for the horses for three years. Along with Mark and myself they bucketed water from a heritage well into 20-litre containers and moved wheelbarrows over rough, shifting ground and across a meagrely framed, fractured bridge barely a hand-span wide!

Earthquake damage to Melissa's home in Lyttelton meant that it could not be occupied for six months. As well as the horses she was caring for four rescue cats at the time, plus several chickens; she decided to leave them at the Lyttelton house as that was their territory and returned regularly to feed and reassure them. During this time, Melissa and Mark took up an offer of sanctuary with friends Barry and Heather in West Melton:

> We arrived with nine horses, the pony, the dog, two guinea pigs and the kittens! Our friends' kind neighbours provided hay and took in the kittens. Other West Meltonites provided grazing when my herd had eaten my friends' paddocks down. I will be eternally grateful for all the kindness my animals and I received. Now the animals are all home again, and the kittens have been rehomed.

Fortunately, after a long and difficult period of medical attention, Rose made a full recovery. Since the February quake, Melissa has welcomed a further three feline earthquake refugees to her home.

Janetta Stead – urban wildlife heroine

> Just imagine being sound asleep in a warm bed, when suddenly it's filled with sandy cold water. This water is so thick you cannot move or get out of your home. You are stuck up to your neck in wet sand. It is pitch black and the ground is shaking. You cannot reach solid ground or keep warm. Most of the animals I took care of and rehabilitated after the earthquakes in Christchurch went through this very experience.

So begins Janetta Stead's poignant story of rescuing hedgehogs and birds in the aftermath of the city's quakes.

Living in New Brighton (one of the suburbs that was worst affected following the February 2011 event), Janetta witnessed the horrific impact of liquefaction on urban wildlife and set about rescuing hedgehogs, ducks and other birds from this disaster. 'Hedgehogs seemed to be the most affected,' she recalls. 'As people dug out the liquefaction from around their homes, they were found in flooded hedges, holes, around gardens, and driveways.'

Janetta points out that these spiny mammals usually have several homes around an area of about three kilometres: 'This is their "patch".' Eager to rectify disparaging attitudes towards hedgehogs, she explains: 'Some people don't like these animals because they think they are dirty, flea-ridden, introduced creatures from Britain, but in fact the hedgehogs in New Zealand don't carry fleas, and the skin disease they are sometimes afflicted with is mange, which is very treatable.' On the question of hygiene, she wryly points out that 'unlike dogs and cats, hedgehogs don't lick their bums!'

Janetta says that while most adults will remember feeding these creatures on the back lawn at night as children in pyjamas, times have changed for the urban hedgehog, who now finds it harder to survive in the suburbs due to landscaped easy-care gardens. For Christchurch's hedgehogs life became even harsher in the aftermath of the city's earthquakes and Janetta was on hand to give members of the public advice and practical assistance. 'Most of the casualties were brought to me starving, covered in mud and sewerage, their prickles damaged or even ripped out. They were very sick,' she recalls. The food stocks that hedgehogs depend on in the wild had been decimated due to liquefaction, or because buildings had collapsed or been demolished in their usual territories. As Janetta points out: 'Winter typically brings tough conditions and weakened chances of survival for hedgehogs unless they can make a warm nest and reach a weight of at least one kilogram before hibernating.'

A hedgehog recovering from disease caused by liquefaction is cared for at Janetta Stead's home.

The same hedgehog, fully recovered.

Prior to the winter of 2011 there were scores of hedgehogs preparing nests around gardens and hedges close to buildings due for demolition, especially in the eastern residential red zone. Janetta and her friends attempted to retrieve as many hedgehogs as possible and move them to more secure ground before they started to hibernate. At one stage, Janetta had eight hedgehog refugees living in her laundry at home (usually they would have been kept in her garage but that had been damaged in the quakes). Another rescuer, Irene Chapman, collected 26 hedgehogs who were sent to the home of a supporter in Balclutha, seven hours' drive south of Christchurch. Today, Janetta is still involved in urban hedgehog rescue and hands out her phone number to demolition workers in case they find any wild animals while knocking down houses and other quake-damaged buildings. 'Hopefully, this will save many more hedgehogs,' she comments.

Avian wildlife in the city was also the focus of Janetta's rescue and rehabilitation work. With advice from New Brighton's well-known bird carer 'Nana Pam', Janetta helped rehabilitate many ducks and seabirds. She recalls that numerous young birds, including starlings, wax eyes, pukekos and blackbirds, were in desperate straits after the tremors. Most of these fragile youngsters were handed on to Nana Pam who, Janetta says, 'has a special gift for looking after birds, young, old or injured'.

Ducks were also displaced following the earthquakes because their feeding grounds and nests had been destroyed, and the urban duck population faced other hardships indirectly caused by quakes. Janetta points out:

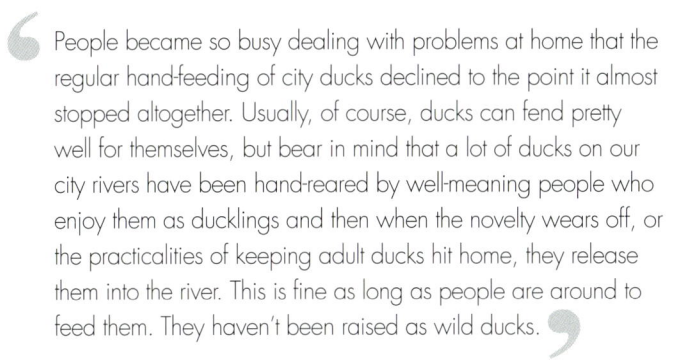

Urban waterfowl were also affected by the quakes. These paradise ducklings were recuperating at the Stead's home in New Brighton.

> People became so busy dealing with problems at home that the regular hand-feeding of city ducks declined to the point it almost stopped altogether. Usually, of course, ducks can fend pretty well for themselves, but bear in mind that a lot of ducks on our city rivers have been hand-reared by well-meaning people who enjoy them as ducklings and then when the novelty wears off, or the practicalities of keeping adult ducks hit home, they release them into the river. This is fine as long as people are around to feed them. They haven't been raised as wild ducks.

Another issue affecting food supplies for urban ducks was pollution of waterways after the quakes. 'Sewerage pipes were destroyed and the Council had no choice but to pump raw sewerage into the rivers,' Janetta explains. 'People also dumped thawed food from their freezers into rivers because the power was off and rubbish collection was on hold.' These factors compounded the ducks' plight, and pollution grew to a point where the human population was also told to avoid all river contact. 'So I had ducks everywhere! I was going through many bags of pellets and bread to feed them, and carting fresh water not only for my family but for the ducks and other wildlife.' The ducks Janetta looked after at home following the earthquakes gradually left of their own accord, but she is still visited morning and night by a handful of clever opportunists returning for treats.

Whenever animals arrived in her care, Janetta recorded their weight, general condition and whether or not they suffered from any

Janetta Stead about to release the shag back to the Scarborough cliffs' nesting ground.

evident injuries, and devised an individualised rehabilitation plan. She remembers finding a spotted shag one day while walking at South Brighton beach. 'He had been washed up on the shore and kids were playing with him. He was so exhausted and starving that he couldn't get away from them.' Janetta believes he may have been a casualty of the February earthquake because the Scarborough cliffs, in the nearby seaside suburb of Sumner, are breeding grounds for the spotted shag. 'His nest may have been damaged or lost when the cliffs collapsed up there,' she surmises, 'or he could have been starving because food was low due to the city's sewerage being pumped into the sea'. The shag was nursed back to health by Janetta and her family:

> When he was ready to be released back to the wild, my daughter and I took to him Sumner beach and walked for half an hour around the foot of the cliffs. As soon as Kelsi lifted him from the box he knew where he was! I held him for a few minutes, and then when I let him go he scrambled straight to the water's edge, swam, then preened himself and dived under. When he resurfaced he was heading straight around the cliff back to the Scarborough breeding site. He was going home! And that was a really good feeling.

Janetta has some advice regarding emergency care of wildlife:

> Remember most vet clinics can assist you. But first be sure to put the patient in a quiet and warm safe place, like a large cardboard box or a cat cage. Use animal heat pads or hot-water bottles to warm the animal. If you haven't got those then an empty plastic milk container filled with warm water will help. Don't try to feed birds – get help from someone who knows the different species and what they require as food. Hedgehogs can be offered wet or dry cat food or even dog roll and water (no milk).

The earthquakes' effects on wildlife habitats

The earthquakes had a terrible impact on wildlife habitats in the city and surrounding regions, affecting wetland species in particular. Even coastal wildlife were not spared – an article in the *Press* claimed that fur seals had been killed by coastal rock falls following the September 2010 event (Carville, 2014). New Zealand fur seals frequent the rocky shores surrounding the mainland and normally encounter few threats to their survival (Department of Conservation, 2014).

One of the earthquakes' more devastating outcomes for local wildlife has been linked to contamination of Christchurch city's lakes, rivers and streams. Earthquake-related pollution caused signficant problems for the Avon River in particular, and unfortunately these issues are ongoing. The Avon is a prime waterway coursing through central Christchurch that provides a habitat for species including ducks, fish (such as brown trout), invertebrates and New Zealand's endemic longfin eel. An Environment Canterbury Regional Council report outlines that the primary damage to the river was caused by a combination of factors: raw sewerage entering the river, the influx of liquefaction and silt, and changes to the river bed and river bank topography (Environment Canterbury, 2011). While each of these impacts has affected wildlife living in and around the river to varying degrees, it is the discharge of sewerage into the river that seems to have had the worst effects for local bird wildlife.

Department of Conservation ranger Craig Alexander catches a royal spoonbill in the Avon-Heathcote estuary, in order to check for signs of botulism after the bird was observed in a state of distress.

Fairfax New Zealand/*The Press*.

Chapter 5 : From turtles to hedgehogs

A royal spoonbill suspected of being infected with avian botulism featured in a *Press* article a year after the February 2011 quakes; the report linked an outbreak of the disease to 'increased sewage levels in the Bromley oxidation ponds, the Avon-Heathcote estuary and the eastern wetlands caused by the earthquakes' (*Press*, 2012). As the *Press* reported, the outbreak of avian botulism had killed approximately 4300 birds in the Christchurch region. (This surpassed the estimated death toll of birds killed directly as a result of the *Rena* oil spill off the coast of Tauranga in October 2011.) In another related article published by the *Press*, it was reported that paradise shelduck, mallard duck and grey teal duck were the species worst affected by the spate of avian botulism – the populations of paradise shelduck and mallard duck dropped by 85% and 49% respectively (Sachdeva, 2012).

The disruption to the environment also created opportunities for one species: the Australian brushtail possum. This marsupial was introduced to New Zealand in 1858 for the purpose of obtaining fur for trade and, having no natural predators here, has flourished and become a regular feature of the New Zealand landscape. Present estimations place the national population of possums in New Zealand at around 30 million (Potts et al., 2013). Whereas environmental transformation after the quakes has had a negative impact on the habitats of many animal species, it has provided possums with more options. In an August 2012 article in the *Press* entitled 'Wildlife returns to abandoned suburbs' reporter Charlie Gates speaks with Landcare Research pest-control scientist, Janine Duckworth. Duckworth suggests that Christchurch city's red zones have become appealing places for possums to settle because there are fewer humans now living there, if any at all. She says: 'It doesn't surprise me that we are seeing more of them as they do try and avoid people. With fewer dogs in the areas that will allow them to move into places they may not have been able to take advantage of in the past' (Gates, 2012). It would seem that in this case, one species' danger-zone is another species' safe-haven.

The royal spoonbill was cared for by Jackie Stevenson from Bird Rescue Christchurch, and was released on the Ashley River approximately two to three weeks after being rescued by Craig Alexander.

Jackie Stevenson

Orana Wildlife Park

On 25 September 1976 Orana Wildlife Park opened its gates to the public for the first time, and since then it has remained New Zealand's only open-range wildlife domain. When it was launched, the park housed 12 adult lions, six lion cubs, two tiger cubs, two donkeys, two camels, two water buffalo and two Shetland ponies. So successful was its opening on that spring Saturday that by two o'clock the following afternoon there was a queue of cars 7 kilometres long waiting to be admitted to the country's first drive-through lion reserve.

Nearly 40 years later, Orana Wildlife Park's 80 hectares is now home to more than 400 animals, representing 70 different species from New Zealand, Australia, Africa, Asia and the Americas (www.oranawildlifepark.co.nz). These include big cats (such as lions, Sumatran tigers and cheetah), non-human primates (including siamang gibbon, lemurs and spider monkeys), exotic herbivores (zebra, scimitar-horned oryx, Rothschild's giraffes, rhinoceroses and sable antelopes), Asian small-clawed otters and water buffalo. The open-range sanctuary aims to provide animals with enclosures that are as close to their natural habitats as possible. Streams, moats and banks are used as barriers so that visitors are able to safely view the animals behaving within more natural environments.

'Orana' is a Māori word that translates as 'place of refuge'. The park, a registered charitable trust and not-for-profit organisation, is dedicated to environmental preservation through conservation advocacy and formal education programmes, has a focus on sustainable use of resources,[1] and is also involved in the conservation of endangered species through its zoo-based breeding programmes.

Orana Wildlife Park is not exclusively focused on exotic species, also containing a walk-through lowland aviary that provides a natural environment for New Zealand's endangered native birds, as well as an alpine-themed kea habitat and a nocturnal house for kiwi and morepork. Brown teal, blue ducks and kiwi are part of the park's captive recovery programme involving endangered New Zealand waterfowl and flightless birds bred at the park for later release to the wild.

When the earthquake struck Christchurch on 4 September 2010, Orana Wildlife Park managed two facilities – the wildlife park on McLean's Island, a few minutes north of the city, and Southern Encounter Aquarium and Kiwi House in Cathedral Square, in the centre of the city. Alyssa Salton, head keeper of native fauna and domestic animals, recalls:

> Because it was so early and pitch-black at the time of that quake, we needed to find the best way to check what the situation at the park was. We started going around the dangerous animals first (in vehicles) and then more and more people arrived to help. The manager of the aquarium also came to Orana Wildlife Park to see if he could get some petrol from us to run generators because they had lost all power. It was a pretty full-on day. At the zoo, power was lost for eight hours.

---

1   This includes a recycling programme and providing herbivorous animals' faeces to the local ZooDoo company for conversion to compost.

Gidro, the black-and-white ruffled lemur killed as a result of the September 2010 quake.

Andrew Walmsley

Tragically, one of Orana Wildlife Park's primates died as a result of the September 2010 event. In panic, a 10-year-old black-and-white ruffed lemur named Gidro attempted to jump from the lemurs' island but ended up drowning in the moat. Another lemur successfully jumped across the water but was later caught and returned to the island enclosure. Aaron Gilmore, former head keeper of exotic animals, explains:

> They were really scared and wanted out of their night-time building. It would have been shaking and the lemurs would have wondered what was happening. There was a lot of alarm calling when we arrived in the morning, so we immediately knew something wasn't right. The spider monkeys and lemurs react very much like humans and so they experienced that whole fear of going back into buildings. You can't force them to return to the buildings, it's something they have to do in their own time. Usually they sleep inside, but for several nights after the September quake the lemurs preferred to sleep outside. The black-and-white lemurs started making nests outside because they associated the house with the noise of the quakes.

In contrast, Aaron noticed hardly any change in the behaviour of the big cats living at the zoo: 'Even after the February quake, the lions just sat there and as long as they were fed, they were fine. They didn't seem concerned about the ground shaking.'

When the 22 February 2011 earthquake struck, Alyssa Salton was down the road from the zoo helping to catch brown teal for the park's endangered species breeding programme. 'When it happened I knew it was a bad one. It felt different,' she recalls. 'We returned to Orana quickly – some staff had to leave immediately because their homes had been damaged.' Alyssa was relieved to find the animals under her care faring well:

> We had kiwi eggs in incubators, so we were rushing to keep the incubators running. We lost power so we had to get generators set up. We were very lucky though – in the September earthquake objects went flying across the incubator room, but our incubator and kiwi eggs were OK. After the February quake we walked in with our fingers crossed – we had one egg in an incubator and another under a male kiwi outside so we were concerned that he might have got frightened and squashed his egg on the way out of the burrow. But when we checked he was still sitting on the egg as if

nothing had happened. Our nocturnal birds tend to go to their burrows when upset, that's their way of keeping safe. I was in the kiwi house during a couple of big aftershocks and it is a very noisy building, so it makes sense they move into burrows to keep safe. But those kiwi sitting on eggs, they are always tucked up in the exact position after shakes as before. They are very dedicated, that is their sole focus, nothing else.'

The brown kiwi chick hatched from the egg that was rocked in the incubator during February's major earthquake was later called Ōtautahi (the local iwi's name for Christchurch). One year later this juvenile bird, whose species is classified as Nationally Vulnerable by the Department of Conservation, was released to live in the wild at Rimutaka Forest Park near Wellington.

Importantly, adverse reactions to aftershocks have lessened over time. Alyssa thinks the animals 'take it more in their stride now. After each aftershock we'd hurry around to check and they would just be looking at us as if to say "What's the fuss?"' The animals like routine and it is important that feeding occurs on time each day.

It is the dangerous big cats that concern park staff the most when any untoward event occurs. Orana Wildlife Park's Manager of Marketing, Public Relations and Visitor Services, Nathan Hawke, explains: 'Our emergency plans focus on getting people into safe houses. The protocol for dealing with escaped animals, for instance, is to ensure everyone gets indoors fast.' Obviously, this strategy conflicts somewhat with the natural instinct to evacuate buildings following earthquakes. 'Getting people *into* a building when there's been an earthquake is somewhat counterintuitive, but it's a priority here to ensure people are kept safe and we must check the integrity of all exhibits whilst ensuring our animals (particularly dangerous ones) are safe and secure,' Nathan says. 'First we always check the enclosures – particularly those of the lions, tigers and wild dogs – and make sure these animals are contained. Then we can start addressing other ways the park and its inhabitants may have been affected.'

Nathan points out that all the buildings at the park – including the exhibits themselves – have been constructed according to New Zealand building codes, so 'if the house next door's still up, then there's a good chance our exhibits are too. We are able to check enclosures and people at the same time because our visitors will be viewing the animals in these exhibits. Staff carry radios and we have vehicles to get around the zoo quickly.'

While Orana Wildlife Park's staff prioritise containment of the

Male kiwi at Orana Wildlife Park determinedly stayed on top of the eggs they were incubating when the earthquakes rocked the kiwi house.

Orana Wildlife Park

When earthquakes strike, Orana Wildlife Park's first priority is to ensure animals' enclosures are secure, in order to keep both the reserve's inhabitants and its visitors safe.

Orana Wildlife Park

more dangerous animals at the park, they also have specific disaster-management plans and practices to support the well-being of anxious or stressed individuals of all species. Aaron has observed that in response to aftershocks, the cheetahs and rhinoceroses routinely run around their enclosures, while the giraffes 'lock their legs and just go with it'. He also wonders whether the waterbuck, like some other 'flighty' species, might sense impending aftershocks: 'They sometimes want to stay in their night-houses instead of moving to the display enclosures in the morning, and then a few hours later we'll get an aftershock. I think they sense something's going to happen.'

Since the September 2010 event, staff and animals at Orana Wildlife Park have had time to adjust to a new Christchurch frequently shaken by underground activity. However, the zoo's sister facility, the Southern Encounter Aquarium and Kiwi House in the CBD, suffered irreparable damage as a result of the 22 February 2011 earthquake. In an online post announcing its indefinite closure, Chief Executive Lynn Anderson praised the staff who had 'poured their heart and soul into Southern Encounter', and in the week after the quake 'worked incredibly hard, going beyond the call of duty and risking personal safety, to rescue and release many of the animals' (Orana Wildlife Park, 2011). (The building has since been demolished.)

Nathan recalls:

> Initially, we were granted access after the February quake – even though the aquarium building had been red-stickered – so the staff were able to progressively remove wildlife located there. A staff member rescued about 70% of the wildlife. The kiwi and native reptiles came to Orana Wildlife Park or were rehomed elsewhere, and the aquatic species were released on a conservation policy basis to various locations.

In her valedictory post Lynn Anderson wrote that many of the fish, including the eels and over 100 Nationally Endangered Canterbury mudfish, were released to the wild (Orana Wildlife Park, 2011). However, difficult decisions had to be made about the remaining fish. Nathans explains:

> Unfortunately, the water quality was deteriorating, the generators were no longer working, and Southern Encounter's building was inaccessible, therefore those species unable to be released or rehomed had to be humanely euthanised.

While most of the animals at Orana Wildlife Park fared well post-quakes, and the reserve's buildings and land have remained remarkably undamaged, the earthquakes have had a marked impact on visitor numbers. Nathan Hawke reports that October 2010 was a record month for Orana Wildlife Park and speculates that the surging visitor numbers that month were partly because the zoo was viewed as a safe place where families could go for the distraction offered by interacting with other species. However, after October 2010 the park encountered reductions in visitation rates. Usually, around 45% of visitors come from outside Christchurch (typically, 30% are domestic travellers and 15% international visitors). Visitor numbers from outside Christchurch fell because the city itself was becoming increasingly viewed as a risky place to travel to; in addition, accommodation options were severly limited as more and more buildings in the city were assessed as dangerous and uninhabitable. The exodus of Christchurch residents from their city also affected the park's income in 2010 and 2011. 'The reduction in visitors has had an impact on our operation, even though at Orana we were fortunate to be able to re-open with only very minor physical damage. We are on good solid land, you can feel the aftershocks, but it's quite different being outside in a park.'

In addition, Orana Wildlife Park has had more than earthquakes to contend with. As Nathan explains, winter snowfalls have caused more physical damage to the zoo than the quakes or their aftershocks:

> We were closed for 10 days in 2012 because of snow. The inriggers on the lions' and tigers' fences got bent right around their enclosures; aviaries were significantly compromised. We had a team of arborists here for a week clearing all the damage from the trees. Animal welfare is our priority, and as long as our animals are fed, have warm houses, are sheltered from southerlies, then they are well, but the snow storms create much more havoc, in terms of damage and clean-up, than the earthquakes did.

Despite the challenges that have faced Orana Wildlife Park over the past couple of years, Nathan is philosophical: 'We've been lucky. We've remained open and exhibits have been fine after the earthquakes. All our staff members have remained safe.' He is also pleased to report that in 2014 visitor numbers are once again trending in a better direction.

In summary

The stories recounted in this chapter demonstrate the extraordinary efforts invested by dedicated animal rescuers, carers and enthusiasts into helping a diverse range of Christchurch's non-human residents after the quakes. It was fortunate that experts on urban wildlife were on hand and willing to protect and nurture the free-roaming creatures of the city.

Unlike cats and dogs, many of the animals discussed in this chapter live in confined spaces such as tanks, aviaries, cages, paddocks and other enclosures. Those who care for these captive animals stress the need to ensure that their homes are carefully secured, before earthquakes or other emergencies occur (see also the conclusion to this book).

It is of great concern that some people simply abandon or dump animals when they are no longer able to care for them (or no longer wish to) rather than trying to rehome them. The experiences of those who looked after birds, rats, turtles, and even larger mammals such as ponies, demonstrate how vulnerable these species are to neglect and mistreatment. It is perhaps in part because they are considered 'border species' (animals existing both in the wild and as domesticated pets) that irresponsible owners assume they will be able to survive on their own if released or abandoned. Such mistaken assumptions are particularly problematic for domesticated rats, turtles and birds, as we have made them dependent on us for their survival.

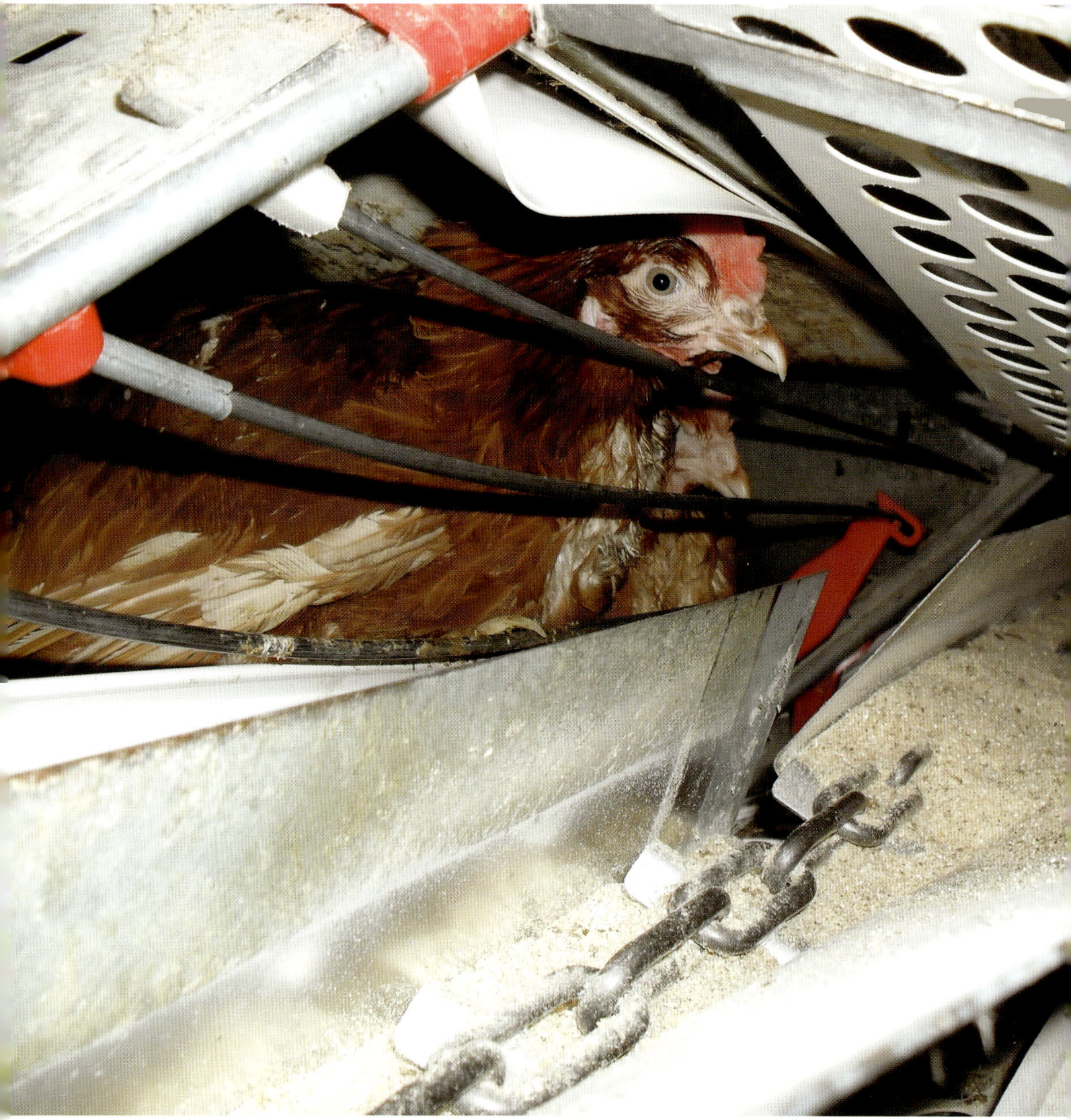

Chapter 6
Those most vulnerable

While this book has so far focused predominantly on the stories of those assisting with the rescue, shelter and everyday comfort and support of companion animals in the aftermath of Christchurch's major earthquakes, it is vital not to overlook the fate of thousands of the region's non-companion animals who were also affected. Although increasingly urbanised, our national identity remains strongly associated with agriculture, not just for economic reasons but also because rural New Zealand and animal farming have featured prominently in our cultural imagery since European colonisation (Potts et al., 2013). The country's 'utility' animals, especially those subject to intensive farming systems, are in fact often those at the greatest risk of injury, suffering and death when human-induced or natural disasters strike – precisely because they are also the most vulnerable. Similarly, thousands of animals are kept in New Zealand's scientific and medical laboratories, university zoology, biochemistry, physiology and psychology departments, and other research institutes, for the purposes of experimentation and teaching. Contact with these creatures is in normal times restricted, and their everyday lives, as well as the experiments conducted on them, are usually obscured from the public and underplayed in the media. It is therefore no surprise that their fate during disasters is also routinely unpublicised.

In *Filling the Ark: Animal Welfare in Disasters*, author Leslie Irvine (2009) begins by asking: 'When a disaster strikes, who should enter the ark?' Presuming *Homo sapiens* is permitted entry first, Irvine challenges us to examine which other species we would generally grant admission and thereby save. She questions how we make such decisions about which animals are deemed worthy of rescuing or

Opposite page:
A casualty of the
4 September 2010
earthquake.

Sacha Dowell

helping and which are not, suggesting that such choices tell us much about how our culture values or favours certain kinds of animals, or particular species, over others. For some people, Irvine argues, it will be as natural to believe dogs and cats should be welcome on the ark as it is to think that humans will automatically be on board. But, she points out, 'while we applaud ourselves for considering this minority of animals who share our households, the majority of animals who play other roles remain invisible to us' (p. 2).

In our introduction we discussed the 'vulnerability paradigm'. To recap, this is the theory that 'disasters' are not merely extreme events caused by external forces beyond our control; rather, they are 'disasters' precisely because they tend to impact differentially on those who are most at risk, those most vulnerable. When we extend this paradigm to include other species, it is easy to see how particular animals are already placed in more susceptible positions pre-disasters (such as hens on battery farms and chicks on broiler farms, mice in laboratory cages, pet rabbits in hutches, or turtles and fish in aquariums). As Irvine (2009) points out, these creatures have little or no choice in determining their living conditions or everyday movements; being confined, they are at greater risk due to the relationships we have with (or, in some cases, impose upon) them. Leslie Irvine's work demonstrates how 'different categories of animals are differentially exposed to hazards and are differentially provided opportunities for rescue or escape' (p. 6). She shows how, although companion animals may be abandoned, displaced and even prematurely or, 'for convenience', euthanised in the aftermath of disasters, they are in general much less vulnerable than animals raised in industrialised farms or used in medical and other forms of research and teaching. To Irvine, because of the different vulnerabilities of various species – a factor that is related to the value and use of animals to us – it is unhelpful to talk about animals in disasters as if all animals face the same risks.

This chapter is dedicated to those less visible, marginalised animals – the creatures we 'grow' for food and those we use in research. The safety and well-being of these 'other' animals – our sacrificial species – should, we argue, receive every bit as much consideration as companion animals when disasters occur.

Animals farmed for food

As mentioned above, one of the reasons why the impact of disasters on the individual lives of thousands of 'utility' animals can more readily be disregarded is that such large-scale suffering and death is often simply not reported or easily visible. Leslie Irvine (2007) has demonstrated how much media coverage and public outcry post-Hurricane Katrina focused on the abandonment, anguish and demise of companion species such as cats and dogs, while there was scant attention or public empathy given to those animals used in the service of humans. When reports did occur of the vast numbers of cattle and chickens drowned or left to starve to death in the wake of the hurricane, such losses tended to be discussed in terms of reduced revenue for farmers or producers. This is not unusual, given that farmed animals are primarily viewed in business or economic terms; nor is it idiosyncratic to North America – the framing and measuring of animal lives and deaths in terms of dollars per carcass/body is evident when disasters hit rural New Zealand as well (Wilson et al., 2009).

Following Hurricane Katrina, while 5000 volunteers converged in Louisiana and Mississippi to help rescue the region's affected companion animals, millions of farm animals perished; the majority of these were factory-farmed chickens. The scenario was beyond bleak: 'those who did not starve or die of thirst and exposure were bulldozed alive into dumpsters. Over 8,000,000 birds died in just *one* producer's intensive farm' (Irvine, 2007, p. 2, emphasis added). While dogs and cats are valued for their unique personalities and companionship (and, as we have seen are in many homes considered to be part of the family), animals farmed for food in Western societies are valued primarily in financial terms. As Irvine (2007) notes, media reports following Hurricane Katrina's impact on Louisiana lamented the deaths of farmed animals as losses in revenue for producers: 'The animals' lives were not noted' (p. 2). Rhetoric in such reports posits that the farmers are hurt (monetarily), while the animals are merely gone.

As in all heavily industrialised countries, New Zealand farms have become more mechanised and technologised. The idyllic farming scenes of earlier landscape art and photography are no longer the norm, especially for egg or chicken-meat farms – having now been replaced by rows of massive sheds containing thousands of birds at one time – some caged in tiers (such as battery hens in the egg industry) and others cramped in windowless sheds (such as chicks raised for meat) (Potts, 2012). The farming of these birds is hidden from public view and the chickens themselves are so divorced from the natural world that they may never see the light of day. It is perhaps not surprising that those creatures most likely to be killed or hurt in natural or human-induced disasters are also those most heavily confined or contained. They are also those least likely to actually be seen by consumers – such as the chickens and other birds kept in intensive-farming operations. Unable to move or seek safety when earthquakes, flooding, fire or tornadoes occur they may panic and suffocate and risk suffering crush and other injuries from collapsed cages.

Most media reports initially claimed that no lives were lost as a consequence of the Canterbury earthquake on 4 September 2010 (it is now thought that the death of one person due to heart attack may have been caused by quake-related shock, see http://christchurchcitylibraries.com/Kids/NZDisasters/Canterbury-Earthquakes/4-September-2010/). However, these reports disregarded the thousands of animals who died as a direct result of this event; thousands more were severely injured and traumatised. In fact, it is known that more than 3000 chickens, eight cows, one dog, a lemur at Orana Wildlife Park, and 150 tanked fish perished because of the September earthquake (Glassey & Wilson, 2011). Importantly, 99% of these fatalities were preventable: for example, 3000 hens killed at Weedons Poultry Farm, a well-known 26,000-bird commercial operation west of Christchurch, were victims of inhumane structural design – as well as safety and welfare failures – inherent in factory farming. Specifically, two out of three stands of cages collapsed on top of each other during the tremor (Glassey & Wilson, 2011).

During the earthquake on 4 September 2010, tiers of cages containing laying hens collapsed on top of each other at Weedons Poultry Farm.

Sacha Dowell

Intensively farmed hens trapped following the 4 September 2010 quake. This image demonstrates how vulnerable caged animals are when disasters strike as they are unable to escape.

Sacha Dowell

Animals confined in cages or sheds are particularly vulnerable to trauma, injury and death during any kind of natural or human-induced disaster. In January 2013, for example, 18,000 laying hens on another intensive egg farm, in Rolleston, west of Christchurch, perished due to smoke inhalation when a wild fire engulfed sheds. In covering this story, the *Press* reported not on the suffering of these birds but on the fact that the couple whose property had been affected returned home 'to find their livelihood in ruins' (*Press* Reporters, 2013). The chickens killed in the September 2010 earthquake and summer fire of 2013 were casualties not so much of those disasters, but of large-scale intensive farming, which involves keeping birds in unnatural and inescapable conditions. In comparison, free-ranging hens, when checked post-quake, were still safely perched in the branches of trees or, if they had retreated to henhouses overnight, had been able to come and go as they needed (see veterinarian and free-range egg farmer Debbie Yates' story in chapter 1). It is a chicken's natural inclination to perch in bushes or trees and these provide a safer environment for them, not just from night-time predators like stoats or cats, but also from mechanical and architectural failures of caged systems.

Of course, unexpected and adverse events can also harm farmed animals not confined in sheds or cages. In addition to the factory-farmed hens who died following the September 2010 quake, eight cows had to be destroyed after they fell while waiting to be milked on a concrete pad in Hororata, less than 1 kilometre from the fault-line (they had

Debbie Yates' free-ranging hens were untroubled by Canterbury's seismic activity (see chapter 1).

Debbie Yates

suffered broken legs and pelvises). Numerous farmers also reported that their livestock were 'spooked' by the earthquake and aftershocks. Cows usually milked twice a day were particularly susceptible to higher milk somatic cell counts, indicative of the presence of white blood cells (leukocytes) in milk due to pathogenic bacteria such as *Staphylococcus aureus*, which causes mastitis (infection of udders). Cracks and fissures appearing in the ground following seismic activity also presented hazards for cows to negotiate (Glassey & Wilson, 2010).

It is important to note that there are other kinds of natural disasters, particularly those due to adverse weather events (for example, floods, droughts and snow storms) that affect New Zealand farms more frequently than do earthquakes. A report by the World Society for the Protection of Animals (WSPA, 2012), quantifying 'production losses due to livestock deaths from disasters in New Zealand', points out that most inland farms in this country can expect to be affected by snow each year. Despite this probability, farmers continue to breed sheep so that lambs are born before spring has properly arrived, making these infants particularly vulnerable to early snow falls. Recently, a late-winter snowstorm in Southland resulted in half a million lambs perishing. While these weather events are often represented as disastrous for farmers, they are not 'natural disasters' in the sense that they are unexpected or particularly extreme for the times of year in which they occur. Since snow storms in August and early September are not atypical, the deaths of so many infant animals is predominantly a consequence of breeding and lambing practices determined by farm business decisions rather than by animal welfare concerns.

Animals used in experiments

In emergencies the impact on animals kept in laboratories receives even less media attention than the fate of farmed animals (Irvine, 2009). The differential value and reporting of animal deaths following disasters was clearly demonstrated after Hurricane Katrina. While it was well-known that thousands of companion dogs and cats had died during or after the hurricane, few people were aware that around 8000 animals held in Louisiana State University's Health Sciences Center School of Medicine had also perished: those animals who did not drown from the flooding, starved to death or were later euthanised. Technological failures – due to natural disasters, system faults or for other reasons – also kill experimental animals held in environments dependent on electricity to provide their air supply and to power the automated machines dispensing their food and water. Unlike our companion animals, the vast majority of laboratory animals who die as a result of natural or human-induced disasters have not been 'known' personally (i.e. as individual mice or rats), so their loss is not felt deeply by those who worked on them. Biologist Lynda Birke (2003) argues that depersonalising or de-individualising animals used in research is an effective cognitive strategy enacted by scientists in order to detach from the realities of manipulating living creatures on a daily basis.

As with farmed animals, whose deaths due to adverse events are recorded primarily as lost revenue hurting producers' pockets or a nation's economy, the deaths of laboratory animals tend to be framed in terms of missing or lost 'data'. The disparity in value of animal lives does not depend entirely on how we categorise different species, because, as we have seen in chapters 1 to 5, the animals people cherish as companion animals are also often the same species used in research and testing (rabbits, rodents, dogs, cats, birds, fish and horses) (National Animal Ethics Advisory Committee, 2013). Determining which animals 'enter the ark', as Irvine (2009) puts it, relies more upon compartmentalising individual animals, or groups of animals, within the same species. Rats, cats and birds to whom we are emotionally or socially connected may enter the ark, while those whom we use instrumentally may not.

Animals used in research and teaching were affected by the September earthquake in 2010. At the University of Canterbury, laboratory fish in some non-secured tanks were killed when these tanks crashed to the floor; freshwater fish also died when the strong shaking created waves that washed them over the side of a tank (this same wave motion caused snapper in another tank to vomit) (Glassey & Wilson, 2011). Electricity supply was disrupted for 12 hours, compromising the heating of tropical fish tanks, although no fish were reported to have died. Immediate welfare concerns related to ensuring that laboratory animals were fed and had water available (food and water dishes were scattered in the tremor, but order was restored within 12 hours). Rat breeding in laboratories decreased by 10% in the weeks following the quakes (possibly due to the continuation of strong aftershocks) and snapper stopped eating for a week (Glassey & Wilson, 2011).

In a somewhat unusual move, given the history of shallow and non-specific reporting of the conditions and treatment of laboratory animals in medical and other research domains (as well as in the news media and public discourse), Aaron Dyer, an animal technician at the Christchurch Animal Research Area (CARA), produced a retrospective report on animal fatalities, injuries and behavioural changes following the September and February earthquakes (Dyer, 2013). (CARA is a facility that houses animals used in medical research within the University of Otago's Christchurch campus, and Christchurch Hospital.) The report, whose purpose is to improve animal welfare outcomes in future emergencies, describes how during the major February quake, rats and mice kept in 'rodent racks' (stacked cages on castors) were violently shaken as racks moved across rooms, though no cages were displaced from shelves to the floor. Food was scattered across the room and many animals were wetted by contents of water containers. Numerous rats and mice escaped their cages when lids were dislodged (these tagged animals were, Dyer states, easily recaptured and returned to their cages).

Several sheep, 19 white rabbits, approximately 600 mice and 185 rats were housed in the CARA facility at the time of the February event. While Dyer reports no animals suffered physical injuries as a direct result of the earthquakes, three sheep were subsequently destroyed – one was undergoing an operation at the time of the tremor, and the other two were deemed to be of no further use because the experiment they had been part of was interrupted by the earthquake. Behavioural changes were noted in the mice following all major quakes and aftershocks (including the 13 June 2011 aftershock, which was equivalent to February's magnitude 6.3 quake). Specifically, mice began showing aggressive behaviour, including 'tail twitching, rearing onto their hind legs, biting and increased cage fighting'. In addition, it is reported that:

> Prior to the September earthquake, our strain of Baib/Cs [mice] were easy to handle and showed little, to no, cage fighting or aggressive tendencies towards each other or their handlers. Experimental male Baib/Cs on a high fat diet exhibited the highest increase in aggression, especially towards cage mates, and as a result had to be housed separately. In addition, self-mutilation occasionally occurred, leading to these animals having to be removed from experiments and euthanized (Dyer, 2013).

Behavioural issues such as these are, as Irvine (2009) argues, less likely to occur in uncaged animals. It is the coincidence of confinement and external forces (the shaking from quakes and aftershocks) that creates a sense of fear and anxiety in rodents, who want to be able to escape (as would be appropriate behaviour under natural conditions).

In summary

The issues and concerns introduced in this chapter highlight the fact that those animals who are exploited and consumed by humans require as much consideration with respect to their safety and welfare during emergencies as do our companion animals, if not more so. While few people have emotional connections to intensively farmed or experimental animals, these are the creatures we have made most vulnerable in the event of natural or human-induced disasters. It is precisely because we have decided to use and consume these animals for the benefit of our own species that we are obliged to protect, rescue and care for them too.

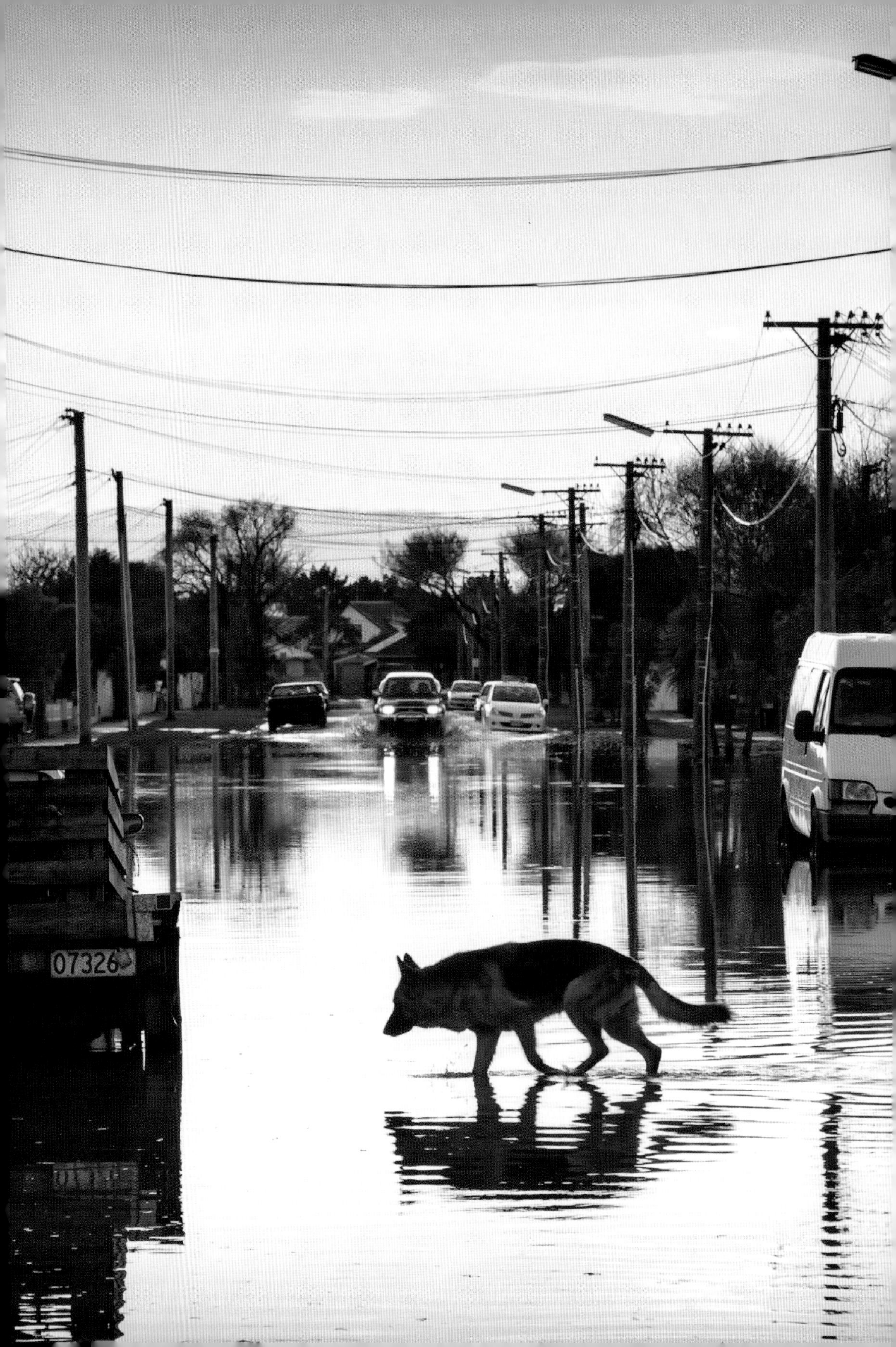
07326

Conclusion
Learning from the Christchurch experience

Christchurch's animal earthquake stories demonstrate how intimately traumatic experiences connect humans and other animals. These accounts also show the strong inter-agency and cross-community cooperation entailed in organising a city's effective rescue response for non-human species. There are numerous instances of welfare organisations, shelter and advocacy volunteers, and caring individuals stepping up to care for affected animals, sometimes even when faced with enormous disruption and challenges in their own personal lives. Help for the city's animals came from many directions: kind neighbours looked after the companion animals of families who had evacuated damaged homes; people rescued abandoned kittens from dangerous buildings or fed homeless strays in red-zoned areas; others offered their time to walk and play with displaced dogs at Dogwatch and the Council's Animal Control shelter. Many local, national and even some international helpers searched online to match missing pets with found animals. Those waiting for news on missing companion animals were moved by the kindness of volunteers who called to support them. Companies and individuals donated money and services to transport, feed and house quake-affected animals. People who were already caring for their own traumatised companion animals also rescued and rehabilitated urban wildlife. And of course hundreds of people in Christchurch and around New Zealand came forward to foster or permanently adopt animal earthquake refugees into their homes.

It is also vital to acknowledge the enormous support that these other species provided to humans after the earthquakes. Interactions with animals, even brief encounters, were reassuring: they offered a sense of security and purpose, continuity and routine, affection, and

Opposite page: 7am on 4 September 2010, just after the first big earthquake. Birch Street, Bexley, Christchurch.

Alex Hubert

distraction from troubles. Those people fortunate to remain in close proximity with their companion animals often benefitted from the strength of these unique relationships in the face of the upheaval.

While the experiences reported here of agencies and individuals who cared for animals during this unprecedented national emergency are necessarily highly localised, the fundamental lessons we can learn from them are not. In closing, we bring together some of the key issues and concerns identified via scholarship in the field of animal welfare in disasters and also by the rescuers, shelter workers, and companion animal guardians whose stories inform this book.

'What about the animals?' Anthropocentrism in emergencies (and everyday life)

The first issue we draw attention to relates to the belief system known as anthropocentrism that pervades everyday understandings and treatment of non-human species, and which has also influenced emergency management to date. Anthropocentrism refers to the premise that human beings are the central or most significant species on the planet (Armstrong, 2008). It has persisted more or less for centuries and can be evidenced in the trivialising of animals' lives and deaths, and the disparagement of meaningful interspecies relationships.

Companion animals

Anthropocentrism exists in legal discourse too, specifically in the fact that animals are still regarded as human 'possessions'.[1] This is despite studies affirming that people experience the loss of a companion animal as similar to the death of a close family member or human friend rather than the loss of a house or other property (Davis, 2011, p. 225). Animal law expert Marsha Baum (2011) points out that 'since property has less value than humans and has no rights, protection of humans will take priority in rescue efforts, evacuations, shelter and relief funds' (p. 108). And in fact, up until now, animals have not been recognised as worthy of rescue and shelter in their own right or even *alongside* humans; rather, they have been relegated to receive help after humans have been 'saved'. The value disparity between humans (as agents or subjects) and animals (as property or objects) was demonstrated by the tremendous loss of animal lives in the aftermath of Hurricane Katrina. It is also revealed in the way the deaths of farmed animals count not in

---

1   This is not the same as saying such legal redress should not exist, however. As long as we continue to view and treat animals like objects, the law is a double-edged sword – both reinforcing this idea of animals as property and also offering a means to prosecute those who disrespect 'property'. Without alternative legislation in place, animals could suffer even more.

terms of the loss of living beings, but insofar as they impact on human livelihoods, as well as on regional and national economies.

Veterinary Emergency Response Team (VERT) leader Hayley Squance mentions in chapter 1 how difficult it has been to ensure that animals' safety and well-being is considered in Civil Defence policy and emergency planning. It has been controversial even to talk about animal suffering when humans are suffering at the same time. As Hayley point outs:

> It's difficult to say "What about the animals"? It's a sensitive issue.

We also heard in chapter 1 how animal welfare agencies such as the Society for the Prevention of Cruelty to Animals (SPCA) experienced the pressure of this social conditioning when they felt they needed to wait and judge the best time to introduce the issue of animals suffering after the quakes.

To date, animals have tended to figure in emergency management frameworks only insofar as their safety and well-being may influence people to make risky decisions and behave dangerously. This is because there is clear evidence from global investigations of evacuation responses during natural or human-induced catastrophes that people are more likely to disregard official directions to evacuate dwellings if companion animals are unable to be removed to safety at the same time. Animal guardians are also more likely at a later time to break through established cordons and enter precarious 'red zones' in order to uplift or feed companion animals who have been left behind. Re-entry to such areas risks the lives not only of those returning to search for animals but also of any rescuers required subsequently to escort cordon-breakers from the region. It is crucial therefore to ensure wherever possible that humans and animals move out of perilous zones at the same time. Despite this knowledge, companion animals, who are considered valued, integral members of most families in developed countries, have nevertheless been caught in the fraught in-between space of object and subject – thing and person; they are at the mercy of our constructed hierarchical animal categories which dictate whether they may move more in one direction (thing/farmed animal/laboratory animal/able to be replaced) or the other (person/companion animal/ irreplaceable and saved).

Importantly, however, assumptions related to the devaluation of animals are increasingly being challenged, helped by significant changes in human–animal relationships that have occurred in the past 40 or so years in Western societies. As it is now more the norm to consider companion animals as integral members of families (and urban households as comprising multiple species), attitudes towards this category of human–animal relationships are shifting accordingly. Dogs and cats, as well as other companion species, are less likely to be viewed merely as children's playthings, accessories, frivolous hobbies, status symbols, or useful watchdogs – prejudices of pre-1970s New Zealand (Potts et al., 2013).[1] Steve Glassey's (2010) survey of companion animal guardians in New Zealand has shown that 99% of respondents counted 'pets' as important family members, with 63% stating that their companion animals were vital supports in times of crisis. It therefore makes sense to ensure animals are protected and factored into emergency planning in a similar way to other 'vulnerable dependants' such as children.

Anthropocentric attitudes towards animals and human–animal relationships are also effectively challenged by many of the perspectives and experiences of those whose stories appear in this book. The overwhelming majority of 'animal earthquake stories' narrated by rescue workers, animal-shelter staff and the city's companion animal guardians, demonstrate the remarkably close bonds between humans and our companion species. The tributes to animal companions demonstrate how our lives are intricately enmeshed with and strengthened by the unique interactions and fondness across species.

Nevertheless, as some stories from this book show, individual 'owners' of animals are also influenced by the culture's anthropocentric ideology, and may fail to take animal interests to heart when disasters strike. In discussing this issue, we draw upon the work of animal welfare emergency expert Sebastian Heath, who has exposed numerous myths associated with discourse on animals in disasters in the United States. Two of these are especially relevant to Canterbury's experience post-quakes. The first myth posits that disasters inevitably result in the tragic separation of animals and their guardians, requiring enormous efforts to reunite them (Heath, 1999). While it is certainly the case that humans and animals become separated in emergencies, and we have seen how intensive the rescue operations and shelter efforts were in Christchurch, the majority of problematic cases reported demonstrate *existing* appalling aspects of 'pet ownership' [sic] (p. 13). That is, many of the animals found after large-scale disasters have been deliberately abandoned or were already strays at the time of the disaster. This point

---

1   However, co-author Donelle Gadenne stresses that throughout her career working as a veterinary nurse, up until 2012, a significant number of companion animals were still being viewed by many clients as utilities for the purposes of hunting or as guard dogs. Moreover, the practice of acquiring a particular breed of dog (or even cat) as a status symbol persists.

was made by professionals at SPCA Canterbury and Dogwatch: disasters highlight the problems already there. On an everyday basis, not only in emergency situations, people abandon animals without any provision for continuity of care. Likewise, irresponsible 'owners' of animals fail to desex cats and dogs, resulting in scores of homeless kittens and unwanted puppies whether or not there is a concurrent disaster.

The second myth Heath reveals is related to the first, and posits 'disasters create new conditions that have never been experienced before' (p. 19). He argues that, in reality, it is more likely that disasters merely exacerbate existing conditions. They appear to produce new difficulties because problems that occur sporadically in everyday life occur in much larger and more noticeable numbers in a disaster; sometimes their existence has been cushioned pre-disaster so that when they emerge so significantly in an emergency situation even front-line responders are surprised (Heath, 1999, p. 10). Again, we can turn to the issue of unwanted breeding, the proliferation of strays and existence of feral cat colonies, all situations that cause the cats involved to lead miserable lives. Many of the cats found in emergencies are strays at the time of disaster, indicating that desexing should be a priority in normal times too. However, the vast problem of stray cats is likely to go unnoticed by the public until an emergency occurs.

Under the Animal Welfare Act (2002) guardians or 'owners' are responsible in the first instance for ensuring the safety and welfare of their animals. However, as we have seen in this book, it is not always possible to remain personally responsible for a 'dependent other' when faced with extreme changes to home, finances and health. Not every responsible guardian of an animal will have access to the necessary resources, including financial support, in order to adequately ensure the welfare and protection of their animals during crises. It is much easier for those with close family support and access to regular sufficient income to take shelter at pet-friendly hotels, temporarily board their companions at kennels or catteries, and pay for any veterinary bills, than it is for those on limited incomes or with restricted social supports.

Regrettably, the notion of personal responsibility is problematic for those animals who are not considered valued family members. There are degrees of closeness between humans and animals in their care. Accordingly, it is not surprising to learn that, in their survey of 'pet evacuation' post-disasters, Heath et al. (2001) found those who showed lower attachment and commitment scores towards their companion animals also scored lower on stated levels of preparedness and motivation levels related to rescuing their animals. Poor levels of attachment and commitment to companion animals also resulted in higher risk of 'pet evacuation failure'. Chance's tragic story in chapter 2 clearly demonstrates how dogs may lead long lives of neglect in homes where they are treated merely as objects or things, and that when emergencies occur, they can, like objects, be merely left behind or discarded.

Thus, delegating the removal and care of animals solely to 'owners' is risky for animals; it leaves welfare at the whim of the owner and depends on how valued an individual animal is to that person. While it is certainly important that responsible guardians retain and manage their own animals' welfare in disasters, it is also likely that some animals will be left behind by less dedicated 'owners'. Such animals require alternative means of evacuation or care, and may rely on compassionate neighbours willing to feed or house them, and on animal welfare agencies able to advocate for and rescue abandoned animals and those left home alone, for whatever reason. Emergency management services need to account for these less fortunate cases who, through no fault of their own, have found themselves in uncaring homes.

Importantly, however, it is also crucial not to jump to the erroneous conclusion that it is mostly those with limited financial, social or other resources who will abandon or dump 'inconvenient' or 'unwanted' animals post-disasters. In fact, guardians who are not monetarily privileged, or who are otherwise socially marginalised, may be those *most* at risk of prolonged and intense grief following companion animal loss. In their 2009 follow-up study of human–animal relationships following Hurricane Katrina, Sarah Lowe and colleagues (2009) focused on the psychological repercussion of companion animal loss for some of New Orleans' most vulnerable people – 365 African-American women from working-class environments. Their research showed that the loss of a beloved animal friend under such circumstances was associated for these women with much more intense psychological disturbances, above and beyond demographic variables. Moreover, losing a companion animal in the 2005 disaster had continued profoundly to impact on these women's lives four years later.

Anthropocentrism influenced the frustrating and sad issue that appeared to surface immediately post-quakes (and that in 2014 continues to create enormous pressure for families with pets), involving the lack of affordable pet-friendly temporary or permanent accommodation in Christchurch. Compassionate landlords willing to rent properties to responsible multispecies families are always in short supply, but the severity of this lack was pronounced following the earthquakes. Due to a scarcity of options for *all* displaced evacuees, landlords were seen to take advantage of the high and urgent demand for homes by raising rental prices and favouring those without companion animals (Carville, 2012; O'Connor, 2013).

Another way in which anthropocentrism has disadvantaged animals caught in disasters relates to the lack of systematic record-keeping and research on how non-human species are affected physically, behaviourally and psychologically by such adverse events. It is mandatory, for example, to record human deaths following a catastrophe; however no such requirement exists with respect to other animals. This lack of data results in turn in deficient understandings of how best to mitigate hazards and risks that could reduce morbidity and mortality of non-human species. In order to begin to redress this knowledge gap, particularly post-quakes and in the New Zealand context, Hayley Squance and her colleagues at Massey University undertook a retrospective survey of dogs' and cats' visits to two veterinary clinics in Christchurch. The researchers found the most evident changes in the health of animals post-earthquakes pertained to increased incidence of bladder and urinary tract infections (especially in cats) and gastrointestinal conditions (particularly in areas prone to liquefaction). Most disturbingly, animal deaths due to natural causes or euthanasia spiked in relation to earthquake occurrences and to relocations required by the Earthquake Commission, indicating that some companion animals were destroyed due to lack of resources or alternatives for their shelter and care. Squance et al. (2013) assert that knowing the medical conditions that disasters exacerbate can lead to plans being put in place to reduce the effects on animals. This information can be used to educate guardians, veterinary professionals, emergency managers and other animal health carers. Measures can be taken as soon as an adverse event occurs, in order to reduce the likelihood of, for example, renal problems developing or worsening in cats, and also to ensure that positive options such as shelter and foster care are readily accessible for those without adequate resources to continue guardianship of animals in the immediate aftermath of disaster (Squance et al., 2013).

Farm animals

So far we have been mainly discussing companion animals. However, anthropocentrism is most evident in practices that exploit animals for human purposes. Undoubtedly, animals who are not classified as members of our families, those we objectify and exploit the most, are less likely to count as the victims of a disaster. For example, it is unusual for media to report on the individual suffering of many farmed animals, yet it is common to read or hear about the financial impacts to farmers or the economy of 'stock losses' following extreme climatic events or disasters. Farmed animals represent income, so their loss is primarily understood in monetary terms. This is not to say that the welfare of these animals is never considered, but farms now operate according to modern business models and, like other businesses, are driven by profit.

During emergencies in New Zealand, Federated Farmers has been in charge of responding in affected rural areas. When the earthquakes occurred in Canterbury, this organisation was leading animal welfare responses in the countryside (and dealing with larger animals), while Christchurch City Council's Animal Control unit and SPCA Canterbury were handling birds (such as backyard flocks of chickens) and companion animals in urban areas. In emergencies affecting both rural and urban communities, effective communication across agencies is essential. For example, Wellington SPCA's Chief Inspector Ritchie Dawson points out that semi-urban 'life-stylers', whose properties fall between a definite urban/rural distinction should plan carefully in case of emergencies, particularly factoring in concerns such as on-going water provision to animals. 'The logistics of water supply for life-style blocks is complex,' he says, 'because if you have a tanker turn up with water during an emergency, then where will the tanker sit for three weeks?'

In addition, vulnerabilities of farmed animals change as farming operations change: they may spike at particular times of year (such as when lambs are being born) and preparations should therefore be made accordingly (Whitman et al., 2013). The health of farmed animals relies on the availability of food and water; adverse events affecting the environment impact directly on animal welfare – if the grass cannot grow due to drought or snow, or if the soil has been affected by liquefaction, volcanic ash, flood silt etc., then cows and sheep need alternative feed (Whitman et al., 2013).

A common concern has been identified across all chapters in this book: animals at greatest risk in disasters are those confined or incarcerated. Pigs, rabbits, chickens, turkeys, ducks and other game birds are among New Zealand's intensively farmed species. Other animals whose movements are restricted on an everyday basis include horses kept in stables, rodents in laboratories, fish and turtles in aquariums, birds and dogs in cages (or 'crates'), and cows being milked by machines, as well as animals kept in boarding kennels, catteries and pet shops. Animals who are unable to escape independently when faced with potential harm from natural events such as wild fires, flooding, snow storms, drought, earthquakes, tornadoes – or anthropogenic emergencies caused by humans (including mass chemical spills, structural collapses, power outages) – are at the mercy of those who own or care for them.[1] The deaths, horrendous injuries and suffering of the hens on the battery farms in Canterbury affected by the earthquake of 4 September 2010 and by the wild fire of 2013 could have been spared if these birds had not been incarcerated. However, given our world is not ideal and intensive farming still exists, those who manage large animal production factories need to ensure confined animals are protected as much as possible from injury and suffering should disasters strike.

The National Animal Welfare Emergency Management (NAWEM) advisory group's submission in response to the Draft Code of Welfare for Layer Hens in 2011 emphasised the need to 'reduce the zoological vulnerability of layer hens', using the high number of fatalities at Weedons Poultry Farm during the September 2010 earthquake as an example, and outlined key ways in which the emergency preparation and management for caged hens could be enhanced in New Zealand. Recommendations included: the need for staff training on emergency management; automated feed, water and light systems that could continue operating for 72 hours if the main power supply is affected; putting specific fire-fighting systems in place; installation of seismic cage restraints for sites within earthquake prone areas; housing sites outside flood- or fire-prone areas; effective litter management on intensive farms; and quick and humane mass destruction (via carbon dioxide poisoning) in the event of extensive injuries and suffering.[2]

Some of NAWEM's recommendations were incorporated into the new Code of Welfare for Layer Hens 2012, but the group's advice that a new Minimum Standard pertaining specifically to the emergency management of layer hens was not taken up by the government's National Animal Welfare Advisory Committee responsible for drafting the code. Moreover, it is important to note that the key reason layer hens are so vulnerable – that is, the fact they are trapped inside cages – was also not addressed in NAWAC's new Code of Welfare for chickens in New Zealand's poultry industry. Instead of abolishing cages altogether,

---

[1] Diseases can also cause problems post-disasters (Dickison, 2010). In commercial poultry farming, the damp and cramped conditions can trigger a series of mutations that result in highly pathogenic forms of some diseases. With the 'avian flu virus', for example, a mild form of the pathogen can rapidly move towards a dangerous and highly transmissible form when it occurs in crowded chicken factory farms (see Lucas, 2009).

[2] In their analysis of the impacts on rural organisations of the 4 September 2010 Darfield earthquake, geologists also highlight the need for New Zealand farmers to have back-up systems in place if critical services are disrupted during emergencies (Whitman et al., 2013).

layer hens will merely be moved from one form of cage to another.[1]

Helping people who have lost animals

The same assumptions and prejudices we have thus far discussed as underpinning the trivialisation of animals affected by disasters, and operating in Western culture more generally, also affect humans who care for other species. The broad societal depreciation of the uniqueness of our relationships with other living beings impacts detrimentally on people's emotional well-being when animals are lost or die. In the introduction to this book, we discussed the notion of disenfranchised grief, the 'unsupported suffering' or 'quiet sorrow' of those who have lost a close relationship with a companion animal (Cordaro, 2012, p. 285). Such sorrow is 'disenfranchised' because it is not socially recognised or validated, typically going unacknowledged by others and unsupported by any public period of mourning (Cordaro, 2012).

The trivialisation of human bereavement for an animal is further demonstrated in the unspoken cultural expectation that guardians quickly overcome grief reactions and replace the deceased animal. Many readers will be familiar with the sometimes well-meaning responses of those who learn of a companion animal's death and then enquire if – or how soon – they are going to get another dog or cat. Psychologist and 'pet loss' therapist, Millie Cordaro (2012) explains: 'The implicit norm that is endorsed is that the bonds forged between people and companion animals do not have the same depth and meaning as bonds between people; therefore, the grief felt when a pet dies should not be as intense as when another person dies' (p. 288). In a more extreme case, grief for an animal will simply not be viewed as legitimate.

Because the presence of animals has been shown to particularly benefit certain demographics of people facing adversity – such as children and the elderly – the absence of companionate interspecies relationships may heighten the sense of loss and bewilderment for individuals in these groups. Children's grief for animals may be further complicated by the fact that society deems children's emotional capacities, like animals', to be undeveloped (or naïve). Canterbury's seismic activity most certainly impacted on the special relationships shared by children and animals. The affection, routine and distraction provided by companion animals both reassured and supported children adjusting to life in a shaking city. However, the close bond between children and animals also means that

---

1   With respect to intensive egg and chicken meat (broiler) farms, United States poultry health expert Julie Helm has devised an Emergency Preparedness document outlining essential ways for factory farmers to prepare for emergencies. This is accessible online at http://www.clemson.edu/public/lph/ahp/disease_links/images/poultry_prepared.pdf.

when animals are missing or have to be relinquished as a repercussion of natural disaster, the child (and animal) will experience confusion and distress. When complicated by the disorientation accompanying loss of routine and unfamiliarity of environment, the sense of suffering may be exacerbated.

This was also the case for those elderly residents of Christchurch who suddenly found themselves evacuated from the homes they knew and living in unfamiliar surroundings without the company of loved and sometimes long-term feline, canine or avian friends who may have been lost or relinquished due to the change of circumstances imposed by the quakes. Hayley Squance (2011) recommends the return of companion animals to elderly people as quickly as practicably possible following disasters, in order to improve their resilience and long-term recovery.

Grief can also be complicated by guilt and regret when animals are euthanised. Because the healthcare of companion animals is not subsidised in New Zealand, the costs of on-going veterinary care for chronically ill or stressed animals becomes untenable for those in lower socioeconomic households. A decision to euthanise, based on such financial restrictions, compounds the experience of remorse when a human companion 'cannot afford to save the pet's life' (Meyers, 2002, p. 370).

Neinmeyer and Jordan (2002) employ the term 'empathic failure' to theorise the interpersonal processes that result in disenfranchised grief and to discuss this phenomenon with bereaved guardians of deceased companion animals. They describe to their clients four levels or domains in which their experiences of grief are disqualified or marginalised through societal and familial expectations: the first they label 'self with self', where bereaved guardians feel they need to minimise or deny the emotional impact of losing a beloved animal; the next domain is 'self with family', where members of the bereaved person's family fail to empathise (mainly because mourning for a non-human is outside the family's 'normal' patterns of grief). The third level is called 'self with larger community' (in this case the bereaved may not tell work colleagues about their grief, anticipating a trivialising response, and bereavement leave is not usually an option as it would be for a human death). Finally, Neinmeyer and Jordan discuss a level they call 'self with transcendent reality', which alludes to the ways in which certain belief systems and orthodox religions deny the presence of a soul or afterlife to beings other than humans.

When assisting those who have lost cherished companion animals, professionals need to examine their own attitudes, prejudices and assumptions about animals and human–animal relationships. People often feel they must either justify or avoid discussion of their close relationships with animals. When mourning an animal's absence, it may be difficult to talk about this loss due to a fear of stigmatisation. In such cases, counsellors can openly discuss the phenomenon of 'socially unspeakable losses', and also explain the ways in which people can fail to empathically understand the meaning and experience of another (Cordaro, 2012, p. 290). Mourners also need help identifying and responding to those who trivialise their grief for an animal. Cordaro (2012) proposes the bereft may benefit from gaining the confidence to 'confront or even reevaluate relationships with those who ridicule or minimize the loss' (p. 261). It may also be useful to practice self-protection. For example, if human–animal relationships are not respected in a workplace, then it may be best to avoid specifics and instead request time off to deal with 'a family bereavement' or other matter. Luckily, every animal death will bring to light those people who are reliably or unexpectedly kind and empathetic; these encounters are welcomed and valued.

Some animals' behaviours may change in response to trauma: dogs may develop aggressive behaviour or refuse to enter a house that is associated with fear or injury; alternatively, a cat may refuse to leave the house, becoming an 'inside' animal (as Pinky did in chapter 3). Sometimes, personality or behavioural changes in companion animals can trigger a grief response in a guardian due to the impact on their shared relationship. Sustained disasters – such as the protracted seismic events in Canterbury – are more likely to produce this distressing outcome (Evans, 2011). It is also important to realise that the spaces once shared as part of a human–animal companionship may be permanently or temporarily damaged in disasters. This includes usual walking routes for people and dogs, territories for cats, paddocks for horses, and so on. As Evans (2011) claims, disruptions to the land and well-known places may bring further distress to companion animals and their guardians.

Get ready, get through[1]

It is clear from the accounts in this book that different species (and even individual animals within species) react in different ways when faced with unexpected or dramatic changes in their environment. When earthquakes and aftershocks strike, many cats and dogs, if able to do so, will run (cats may also hide); caged birds such as cockatiels may panic, particularly if disturbed by tremors at night-time. We have heard from the Heathcote Riding School that horses in herds may act collectively but not necessarily consistently – for example, when faced

---

[1] This is a reference to the New Zealand government's emergency preparedness campaign 'Get Ready, Get Thru' (see http://www.getthru.govt.nz/).

with one earthquake the school's horses bolted in fright together but when experiencing another they all stood still and turned their backs to the tremor as one. Chickens who are free to roam appear unfazed by seismic activity, while giraffes lock their legs together and male kiwis incubating chicks try to stay positioned on their eggs. Knowing how a certain species is likely to react when afraid assists in the preparation of individualised animal emergency plans; knowing how your unique companion animal responds helps to fine-tune any plan.

The issue was raised in chapter 4 of how best to protect companion animals left at home in our absence in order to maximise safety should adverse events occur. Of course, various environments will affect animals differently, and the risk to each pet will depend on their temperament, the type and location of the dwelling, and the magnitude of the earthquake. However, some things can be done to promote greater safety. Inadequate fencing surrounding yards containing companion dogs dramatically increases the risk of escape should a significant earthquake strike. While this may suggest that leaving dogs indoors is the safest option, this too presents some risk. To reduce the chances of harm to animals, it is important to examine any rooms they have access to when left at home alone. Potential hazards such as large objects, if not secured, can fall and 'spook' and injure dogs. In one case described in this book, falling objects prompted a dog to jump through an external plate-glass window. Such danger can be mitigated by fastening household furniture to walls, and fixing ornaments to surfaces with special anti-shake wax or glue.

While it could be argued that leaving dogs in cages can protect them from falling objects or prevent them from running away, caging (or 'crating', as this practice is more euphemistically referred to) is not recommended. Dogs restricted to cages are unable to move independently and are therefore at risk of quake-related issues such as liquefaction, crushing and panic. Earthquakes notwithstanding, leaving dogs confined in cages throughout the day restricts their freedom. The philosophy behind crates, as often stated, is that they provide a safe space for a dog to retreat to and relax in, just as they would naturally desire the sanctuary of a den if living in the wild. However, pet dogs are not wild dogs: they are domesticated and accustomed to living in family homes. Furthermore, it is all too common that these wire cages are used as a means to control dogs for human convenience; to contain the dog so as to prevent destructive or undesirable behaviour in the home or elsewhere. Dogs confined to locked crates cannot make independent choices about whether to move, run or hide, at any time, let alone during an earthquake. It is our contention that the increasingly common practice of crating dogs needs to be critically examined before these cages become routinely employed in our relationships with canines. Inevitably, all conditions contain potential risk, but what is most important is that guardians of companion animals assess their home and pay careful consideration to where and how each animal is left.

We have also learned from canine experts that following major upheaval caused by events like earthquakes dogs require routine in order to maintain psychological equilibrium and good health. Canine friends become confused and anxious when home environments and everyday schedules are frequently changed. Reassurance, treats, positive attention and maintaining some schedule regarding walks, food, company and sleep will help dogs cope with unpreventable changes in the home environment resulting from adverse events. Dogs may also become apprehensive or fretful in response to the nervous behaviours of a stressed or worried guardian, so helping ourselves to relax when under pressure has transferable benefits for our companion canines.

We have heard from rescue agencies that feline companions whose usual homes are damaged, may, on the other hand, sometimes be best left *in situ* rather than moved from their familiar territories to short-term accommodation with their human companions. If it is possible for guardians to return daily or there are neighbours who can feed and care for cats in their own home environments, some professionals endorse this as being a less traumatic option for these animals than relocating them (this also depends of course on the nature of the individual cat).

Turtles, fish, rabbits, rats, mice, guinea pigs and birds require their homes to be securely fastened to prevent injury in case of an earthquake. Those who care for these types of captive animals stress the need to ensure that their homes are carefully secured, before earthquakes or other emergencies occur. Typically, this entails fastening cages or tanks to strong structures so that, in the event of a severe tremor (or, for that matter, a tornado or cyclone), the animals inside these spaces stand a better chance of survival, and are not crushed or otherwise injured by their cages or tanks collapsing or falling. Aquarium tanks should be constructed of material able to withstand severe shaking so their walls do not explode. Avian experts have also suggested that caged birds such as cockatiels would benefit from safe night-lights in areas prone to tremors because they can panic when frightened in darkness.

The value of the micro-chip

Guardians who have their animals micro-chipped will be most assured of reunion with dogs and cats who have fled during a natural or anthropogenic disaster. Animals without micro-chips are much less likely to be returned home quickly and easily, if ever. In New Zealand it is now mandatory for dogs to be micro-chipped when registered for the first time. However, micro-chipping is only effective if contact details of guardians are kept up to date. The current existence of both local (City Council) and national (New Zealand Companion Animal Register, NZCAR) registers complicates the process of reunification, particularly if an animal is only associated with one of these domains. After the Canterbury quakes, for example, some guardians whose dogs were only registered to the local authority had longer to wait for reunification as power and phones were affected in the city. Although one system would be more user-friendly, at this stage, since New Zealand operates both local and national systems, guardians are advised to register animals with both.

Appendix I: Guide to protecting pets during disasters, by Steve Glassey, provides advice on how to prepare in order for your companion animals to remain safe, healthy and cared for in the event of an emergency. Appendix II lists some online resources that are focused on the prevention of harm to non-human animals caught in adverse events. In particular we draw your attention to the website of the New Zealand branch of the World Society for the Protection of Animals (to be renamed World Animal Protection), which features an online guide called *Protect Your Pet in a Disaster*. This site includes free downloadable disaster packs for a range of species, and offers disaster-specific information for companion animals affected by storms, floods, landslides, intense heat, snowstorms, thunderstorms, tsunami, volcanic activity and earthquakes (see http://protectyourpet.worldanimalprotection.org.nz/).

Looking ahead

One of the more positive developments to emerge from the trauma of the Canterbury earthquakes is that, as described in chapter 1, New Zealand – the country with the highest number of companion animals per capita in the Western world – will very soon become one of a handful of nations or regions globally that have committed to take animal welfare in emergencies seriously.

The government's decision to amend Civil Defence policy accordingly has undoubtedly been influenced by the experiences associated with the Canterbury earthquakes and other recent climatic events such as tornadoes and flooding. It is also in large part the result of lobbying from the dedicated co-chairs of NAWEM, Bridget Vercoe and Wayne Ricketts, and the advisory group's other members; local research and awareness-raising by animal welfare emergency experts such as Steve Glassey, Hayley Squance, and Roger Poland; and campaigning from numerous animal welfare and advocacy agencies. As of 2015,

New Zealand's Civil Defence Emergency Management policy will be amended to include non-human species. This involves a government department acting as the official coordinator to ensure that animals are given the best protection prior to emergencies, that whenever possible they are evacuated alongside humans during disasters, and that they are provided with veterinary care and shelter if required. (While this constitutes significant progress at this stage, we might hope in the future to see responsibility for the welfare of animals in emergencies – and in everyday life – delegated to a body whose interests are strongly and solely focused on animals' safety and wellbeing, and separated from the economic objectives of the Ministry of Primary Industries. Animal advocates in New Zealand have for decades drawn attention to the conflict of interest inherent in the Minister for Primary Industries, who oversees intensive farming practices in this country, also being the person responsible for animal welfare matters. Ideally animal welfare issues should be managed by an independent Commissioner for Animal Welfare).

The kind of animal welfare shelters established by Christchurch City Council's Animal Control unit post-quakes will in future become important fixtures at any human welfare centres set up in response to local disasters. Official support agencies will be enlisted from other organisations and experts, such as the Animal Rescue Unit, New Zealand Veterinary Association, SPCA, WSPA, Animal Control units, New Zealand Companion Animal Council and Federated Farmers. NAWEM will continue in a vital advisory and guidance role.

The earthquakes affecting Christchurch and its environs provided many lessons for disaster-management planning for the nation as a whole, not least that animals matter greatly in times of emergency. Untold numbers of animals were killed during the major tremors, while the lives of numerous others have been profoundly altered, but if we learn from these lessons, their distress and suffering will not have been entirely in vain. We thank the people who have contributed to this book for sharing their advice and their stories:

Alison and Gracie; Emma Anderson; Gina Armon, Jamie Armon-Rangi and Shelter; Sue Barr and Petra; Di Barritt and Smudge; Karena Brown; Alison Chambers and Bonnie; Jan Cole and Milly, Molly and Pudding; Constable Pamela Cox and Bobby; Kathleen Crisley, Bracken, Daisy and Trick; Paul Dahl; Ritchie Dawson; Kelly Donaldson; Heather and Brett Douglas and Olive; Sacha Dowell; Bethan FitzGerald, Solomon and Icarus; Aaron Gilmore; Steve Glassey; Becky Hadfield, Jo Harris and Poppy; Rosie and Dave Halligan and Andre; Jennifer Hamlin;

Vanessa Hampton; Mandy Harrington, Tyson and Rocky; Nathan Hawke; Barry Helem; Blair Hillyard; Douglas Horrell and Tui; Pam Howard; Inez and Chippy; Sandra James and Louie; Mallori Kaminski and Keiko; Harry Kerr, Jill Vosper and Robbie; Hans and Nichola Kriek and Presto; Jasmine Lewis; Sandra Leys; Rae Magson, Chelcee and Celcee; Sharon McFarlane and Pinky; Charmaine (Charlie) McLaren; Carolyn Press-McKenzie; Melissa Miles; Donna Moot; Ingrid Morris; Tarn Mullaly and Pudd; Jo Nicol; Jenny Nixey; Karla and Nathan Osmer, Echo and Stella; Fred Pauwels; Diane Provost and Romeo; Janis Richards; Alyssa Salton; Lyane and Paul Scarlett; Sean Scully and Guinness; Judith Shakespeare; Hayley Squance; Janetta Stead; Rachael Stratton; Rachael and Barney; Robyn Stewart, Charlie and Russell; Geoff Sutton; Anthony Terry; Robin Thomson; Bridget Vercoe; Mark Vincent; Sara Wagstaff, Andy Parker and Pussdah, Lilly and Sydney; Alex Walker; Jacquie Walters and Stormy; Patricia (Trish) Waters and Pickle; Debbie Yates; Linda Zampese, Alan McGregor, Lara, Luca and Aja; Lisette Zwarts and Maggie.

Postscript

A disturbing update from the SPCA suggests that the earthquakes' repercussions are still having an impact on the city's animal residents four years later. SPCA Canterbury's inspectorate reports a 92% increase in complaints over the eight months from January to August 2014, compared with the same period in 2013. These complaints cover a range of animal welfare issues from neglect on lifestyle blocks to companion animal abuse. Especially worrying is the dramatic increase in notifications to the SPCA of abandoned dogs. SPCA Canterbury Chief Executive Officer Barry Helem maintains these perturbing statistics should be considered in tandem with reported increases in mental health issues, suicides and domestic violence affecting communities in the wake of the region's disaster. The troubling numbers of abandoned animals are, he believes, closely linked to ongoing tenancy issues in the city. Similar social ills – including a housing crisis and associated abandonment of companion animals – were shown to affect the communities involved in the Black Saturday Bushfires of 2009 in Victoria, Australia (Barry Helem, personal communication, September 2014).

Appendix I
Guide to protecting pets during disasters

by Steve Glassey

Take your pets when evacuating

If you are asked to evacuate, make sure you take your pets too. Leaving them at home or inside with food and water is not sufficient protection as there have been many cases where owners have subsequently been unable to return. Even in a disaster you are responsible for the care and attention of your animals.

Micro-chip all your pets

Micro-chipping is probably the most critical precaution you can take to protect your pets in a disaster. Although all newly registered dogs in New Zealand are now required to be micro-chipped, you should ensure all your pets, including cats, rabbits and other species, are micro-chipped. In the case of dogs, they are added to the national dog identification database; however, such records are generally restricted to local council Animal Control services. If your dog is micro-chipped as part of dog registration, he or she may not necessarily be added to the larger national database called the New Zealand Companion Animal Register (NZCAR). It is therefore best to ensure you register your pet's micro-chip with NZCAR too (http://www.animalregister.co.nz/), as this database is accessible to animal welfare agencies beyond local authority Animal Control. Be sure to provide details for a secondary contact who lives outside your area in case you are unable to be contacted during a local emergency. Also, take care to keep your dog registration and micro-chip contact details up to date.

Make sure your dogs have an identification tag

Ensure your dogs have a name and phone number tag, in addition to their mandatory dog registration. This should have your mobile phone number on it because if you are evacuated you will generally be unable to answer calls made to your home.

Disability Assist Dogs should have the new Civil Defence tag too

If you are the guardian of a certified Disability Assist Dog, you should apply for the Civil Defence Disability Assist Dog identification tag, which is available through your certifying organisation (for example, the Royal New Zealand Foundation of the Blind). This ensures that in the event of separation, your dog will be treated for priority reunification; and in an evacuation it makes it easier for emergency workers to validate you have a bona fide Disability Assist Dog permitted to accompany you into evacuation shelters. This special tag has the Civil Defence logo on one side and the dog's details on the other. As it uses the Civil Defence logo, its use is protected by the Civil Defence Emergency Management Regulations 2003. Further information is available from the Department of Internal Affairs (Dog Control Policy) website at www.dia.govt.nz

Family emergency plan

Ensure your family has an emergency plan that includes the care of your pets. Copies of family emergency plans are available from www.getthru.govt.nz (Ministry of Civil Defence and Emergency Management). Speak to your local Civil Defence Emergency Management Office and ask what local animal emergency plans have been developed, including the location of pet-friendly evacuation shelters.

Pet evacuation kit

Just as you should have a family or personal evacuation kit (also known as a get-away kit), a small kit should be prepared for your pets. This should include vaccination and micro-chip cards, as well as food and water. For each dog, you should have a muzzle. Each cat should have his or her own pet carrier. A simple alternative to wire cages are cardboard (disposable) cat boxes, which are ideal for owners of multiple cats. Ensure all cages are labelled with information about the animals inside them, as well as your contact details.

Some items you may wish to put in your pet evacuation kit (depending on animal type/quantity):

- Muzzle
- Pet collar, lead or harness
- Dry or canned food for seven days (and can opener if required)
- Water for seven days
- Vaccination card with local veterinary clinic contact details
- Photo of your pet
- Pet and owner details
- Critical pet medication for at least seven days (if prescribed)
- Pet carrier (with familiar blanket or liner if time permits)
- Litter tray and litter (for cats)
- Plastic bags for animal waste

Store in a backpack or other suitable container that can be easily carried.

Photographs

Some guardians already keep photos of their pets on social media channels such as Facebook. However, it is a good idea to have several digital photographs stored online (e.g. in a webmail folder or in cloud storage) in case you need them for lost and found advertisements.

New technology

New radio frequency identification (RFID) technology such as TrackR allows the attachment of small tiles to objects in order to track their location through crowdsourcing applications. Although this technology is rather new, its potential is promising for the tracing of missing pets. If the small tile is attached to an animal's collar, for example, this permits guardians to track pets at all times.

For further information on pets in disasters visit:
www.animalsindisaster.com

Steve Glassey
Masters in Emergency Management (Charles Sturt University)
Associate Director, Centre for Risk, Resilience and Renewal, and Programme Director, Public Safety Studies, University of Canterbury
Fellow, Emergency Planning Society (UK)

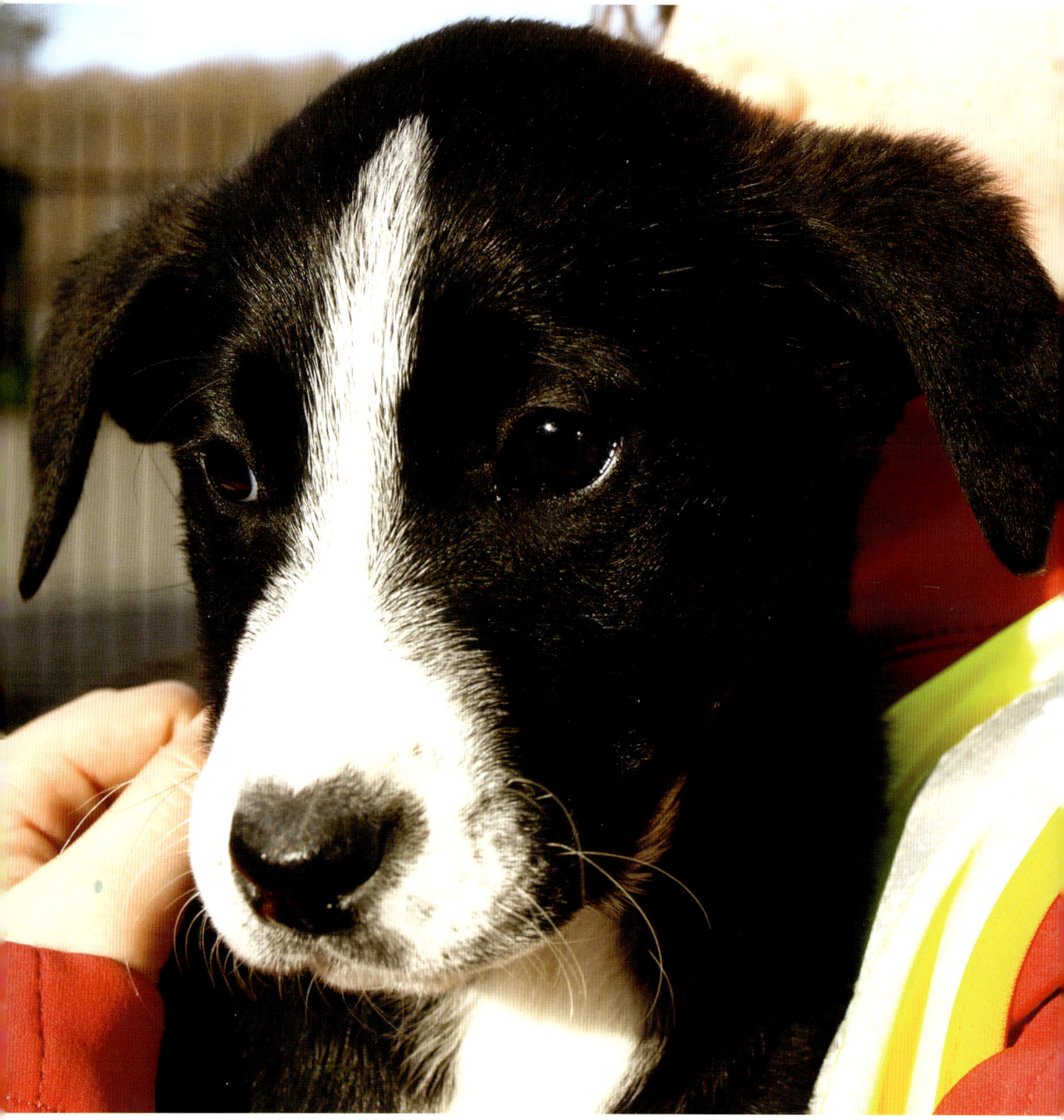

Appendix II
Online resources

New Zealand resources

Ministry of Civil Defence and Emergency Management: 'Animal Welfare':
http://www.civildefence.govt.nz/cdem-sector/welfare/national-welfare-arrangements/animal-welfare/

National Animal Welfare Emergency Management (NAWEM) advisory group: 'Coordinating Welfare Response to Natural Disasters':
http://www.biosecurity.govt.nz/publications/biosecurity-magazine/issue-75/national-animal

New Zealand Companion Animal Register:
www.animalregister.co.nz

Pets on the Net: Lost and found companion animal service:
http://www.petsonthenet.co.nz/

SPCA Canterbury: 'Pet Emergency Plan':
http://www.spcacanterbury.org.nz/assets/Forms/PET-EMERGENCY-PLAN.pdf

World Society for the Protection of Animals (to be renamed World Animal Protection): 'Animals in Disasters':
(http://protectyourpet.worldanimalprotection.org.nz/).

Opposite page: A puppy waits for foster care after arriving on the Cook Strait ferry with HUHA volunteers, June 2011 (see chapter 2).

Jo Moore

Global resources

Advanced Aquarist: 'Emergency Protocols for Home Aquariums':
www.advancedaquarist.com/2008/4/aafeature1

Helm, J. D.: 'Emergency Preparedness for Commercial Poultry Farmers':
http://www.clemson.edu/public/lph/ahp/disease_links/images/poultry_prepared.pdf

The Horse Fund: 'Disaster Preparedness for Horses':
http://www.horsefund.org/resources/Disaster%20Preparedness%20for%20Horses.pdf

The Humane Society of the United States: 'Disaster Preparedness for Farm Animals':
http://www.humanesociety.org/issues/animal_rescue/tips/disaster_preparedness_for_livestock.html

PetMD: 'Top Ten Pet Emergency Kit Items':
http://www.petmd.com/dog/care/evr_multi_top10_emergency_pet_kit_items

United States Department of Agriculture National Agriculture Library: 'Companion Animals: Emergencies and Disaster Planning':
http://awic.nal.usda.gov/companion-animals/emergencies-and-disaster-planning

The University of Vermont: 'Emergency Preparedness – Disaster Planning for Livestock':
http://www.uvm.edu/~ascibios/?Page=Emergency/Disaster_Planning_for_Livestock.html&SM=submenuemergency.html

World Parrot Trust: Emergency plan for parrots: 'Plan Your Escape: Protect Your Parrot in Times of Emergency'
http://www.parrots.org/pdfs/all_about_parrots/reference_library/beginners_guide_to_parrots/Protect_Your_Parrot_in_Times_of_Emergency.pdf

References

Allen, C. & Bekoff, M., (1999), *Species of Mind: The Philosophy and Biology of Cognitive Ethology*, MIT Press, Cambridge, Massachusetts.

Allen, K., Blascovich, J. & Mendes, W. B., (2002), 'Cardiovascular reactivity and the presence of pets, friends, and spouses: The truth about cats and dogs', *Psychosomatic Medicine*, vol. 64, no. 5, pp. 727–739.

Allen, K. M., Blascovich, J., Tomaka, J. & Kelsey, R. M., (2006), 'Presence of human friends and pet dogs as moderators of autonomic responses to stress in women', *Journal of Personality and Social Psychology*, vol. 61, pp. 582–589.

Anderson, A. & Anderson, L., (2006), *Rescued: Saving Animals from Disaster*, New World Library, California.

Armstrong, P., (2008), *What Animals Mean in the Fiction of Modernity*, Routledge, London.

Ascione, F. & Weber, C. V., (1996), 'Children's attitudes about the humane treatment of animals and empathy: One year follow up of a school-based intervention', *Anthrozoos*, vol. 9, pp. 188–195.

Balcombe, J. P., (2007), *Pleasurable Kingdom: Animals and the Nature of Feeling Good*, Palgrave Macmillan, New York.

Barnett, N., (2010), 'Pets and the quake', retrieved 30 November 2012 from http://www.stuff.co.nz/life-style/blogs/four-legs-good/4098123/Pets-and-the-quake

Baum, M., (2011), 'Room on the ark? The symbolic nature of US pet evacuation statutes for non-human animals', in C. Freeman, E. Leane & Y. Watt (eds), *Considering Animals: Contemporary Studies in Human-Animal Relationships*, Ashgate, Surrey, pp. 105–118.

Beck, A. & Katcher, A., (1996), *Between Pets and People: The Importance of Animal Companionship*, Purdue University Press, West Lafayette.

Bekoff, M. & Goodall, J., (2003), *Minding Animals: Awareness, Emotions and Heart*, Oxford University Press, Oxford.

Bekoff, M., Allen, C. & Burghardt, G. M., (eds), (2002), *The Cognitive Animal: Empirical and Theoretical Perspectives on Animal Cognition*, MIT Press, Cambridge, Massachusetts.

Binning, E., (2010), 'Missing pets add to post quake stress,' *The New Zealand Herald*, 6 September 2010, retrieved 23 April 2014 from http://www.nzherald.co.nz/nz/news/article.cfm?c_id=1&objectid=10671385

Birke, L., (2004), 'Who – or what – are the rat (and mice) in the laboratory?', *Society & Animals*, vol. 3, pp. 207–224.

Brackenridge, S., Zottarelli, L. K., Rider, E. & Carlsen-Landy, B., (2012), 'Dimensions of the human-animal bond and evacuation decisions among pet owners during Hurricane Ike', *Anthrozoos*, vol. 25, no. 2, pp. 229–238.

Bullard, R. D. & Wright, B., (2010), *Race, Place, and Environmental Justice after Hurricane Katrina: Struggles to Reclaim, Rebuild, and Revitalize New Orleans and the Gulf Coast*. Westview Press, Boulder, Colorado.

Burgess, D., (2011), 'Owners breach cordons for pets', *The Dominion Post*, 26 February 2011, retrieved 14 June 2014 from http://www.stuff.co.nz/national/christchurch-earthquake/4706624/Owners-breach-cordons-for-pets

Cain, A. O., (1991), 'Pets and the family', *Holistic Nursing Practice*, vol. 5, no. 2, pp. 58–63.

Carville, O., (2012), 'Pets at risk as rental scarcity hits home', *The Press*, 27 April 2012, retrieved 1 September 2014 from http://www.stuff.co.nz/the-press/news/christchurch-earthquake-2011/6814421/Pets-at-risk-as-rental-scarcity-hits-home

Carville, O., (2014), 'Pets quake victims, too', *The Press*, 18 May 2014, retrieved 4 June 2014 from http://www.stuff.co.nz/the-press/news/christchurch-earthquake-2011/10057290/Pets-quake-victims-too

Chur-Hansen, A., (2010), 'Grief and bereavement issues and the loss of a companion animal: People living with a companion animal, owners of livestock, and animal support workers', *Clinical Psychologist*, vol. 14, no. 1, pp. 14–21.

Cordaro, M., (2012), 'Pet loss and disenfranchised grief: Implications for mental health counseling practice', *Journal of Mental Health Counseling*, vol. 34, no. 4, pp. 283–294.

Cusack, O., (1988), *Pets and Mental Health*. Haworth Press, New York.

Davis, H. L., (2011), 'Death of a companion animal: Understanding human responses to bereavement', in C. Blazina, G. Boyra & D. Shen-Miller (eds), *The Psychology of the Human-Animal Bond: A Resource for Clinicians and Researchers*, Springer, New York, pp. 225-242.

Department of Conservation, (2014), 'New Zealand fur seal/kekeno', retrieved 4 June 2014 from http://www.doc.govt.nz/conservation/native-animals/marine-mammals/seals/nz-fur-seal/

Dickison, M., (2010), 'Flooding and animal sickness hit farmers after Canterbury earthquake', *The New Zealand Herald*, 13 September 2010, retrieved 14 June 2014 from http://www.nzherald.co.nz/nz/news/article.cfm?c_id=1&objectid=10672979

Dyer, A., (2012), *Impact of the Recent Earthquakes on the Christchurch Animal Research Area*, University of Otago, Christchurch. (pdf)

Environment Canterbury, (2011), *Ecological Effects of the Christchurch February Earthquake on our City Rivers: Summary and Management Recommendations*, Environment Canterbury report no. U11/6. (http://ecan.govt.nz/publications/Reports/eq-effects-summary-river-lowres.pdf)

Evans, C. S., (2002), 'Cracking the code: Communication and cognition in birds', in M. Bekoff, C. Allen & G. M. Burghardt (eds), *The Cognitive Animal: Empirical and Theoretical Perspectives on Animal Cognition*, MIT Press, Cambridge, Massachusetts, pp. 315–321.

Evans, C. S. & Evans, L., (1999), 'Chicken food calls are functionally referential', *Animal Behaviour*, vol. 58, no. 2, pp. 307–319.

Evans, N., (2011), 'The dynamics of animal-human relationships during and following a natural disaster', *Te Awatea Review*, vol. 9, no. 2, pp. 35–40.

Evans, N. & Perez-y-Perez, M., (2013), 'Will Marley come home? An exploration of the impacts of the Canterbury earthquakes on people's relationships with their companion animals, *Aotearoa New Zealand Social Work Review*, vol. 25, no. 2, pp. 7–17.

Field, M., (2011), 'Brave Kiwi saves master', retrieved 27 April 2014 from www.stuff.co.nz/national/christchurch-earthquake/4736593/Brave-Kiwi-saves-master

Fox, M., (2010), 'Shaken chickens lay again', *The Press*, 9 September 2010, retrieved 28 April 2014 from http://www.stuff.co.nz/the-press/news/christchurch-earthquake-2011/canterbury-earthquake-2010/4109899/Shaken-chickens-lay-again

Franklin, A., (1999), *Animals in Modern Cultures*, Sage, London.

Friedman, E., Thomas, S. A. & Eddy, T. J., (2000), 'Companion animals and human health: Physical and cardiovascular influences', in A. L. Podberscek, E. S. Paul & J. A. Serpell (eds), *Companion Animals and Us: Exploring the Relationships Between People and Pets*, Cambridge University Press, Cambridge, pp. 125–142.

Gates, C., (2012), 'Wildlife returns to abandoned suburbs', *The Press*, 13 August 2012, retrieved 31 May 2014 from http://www.stuff.co.nz/the-press/news/christchurch-earthquake-2011/zonelife-stories/7456141/Wildlife-returns-to-abandoned-suburbs

Giroux, H. R., (2006), 'Reading Hurricane Katrina: Race, class, and the biopolitics of disposability', *College Literature*, vol. 33, no. 3, pp. 171–196.

Glassey, S., (2010), *Recommendations to Enhance Companion Animal Emergency Management in New Zealand*, Mercalli Disaster Management Consulting, Wellington.

Glassey, S. & Wilson, T., (2011), 'Animal welfare impact following the 4 September 2010 Canterbury (Darfield) earthquake', *Australasian Journal of Disaster and Trauma Studies*, pp. 49–59.

Goldman, J. G., (2011), 'Impact of the Japan earthquake and tsunami on animals and environment', *Scientific American*, 22 March 2011, retrieved 20 April 2014 from http://blogs.scientificamerican.com/guest-blog/2011/03/22/impact-of-the-japan-earthquake-and-tsunami-on-animals-and-environment/

Hall, M. J., Ng, A., Ursano, R. J., Holloway, H., Fullerton, C. & Casper, J., (2004), 'Psychological impact of the animal-human bond in disaster preparedness and response', *Journal of Psychiatric Practice*, vol. 10, no. 6, pp. 368–374.

Heath, S. E., (1999), *Animal Management in Disasters*, Mosby, St Louis, Missouri.

Heath, S. E., Kass, P. H., Beck, A. M. & Glickman, L. T., (2001), 'Human and pet-related risk factors for household evacuation failure during a natural disaster', *American Journal of Epidemiology*, vol. 153, no. 7, pp. 659–665.

Horowitz, S., (2010), 'Animal-assisted therapy for inpatients: Tapping the unique healing power of the human-animal bond', *Alternative & Complementary Therapies*, vol. 16, no. 6, pp. 339–343.

Houghton, R., Wilson, T., Smith, W. & Johnston, D., (2010), '"If there was a dire emergency, we would never have been able to get in there": Domestic violence reporting and disasters', *International Journal of Mass Emergencies and Disasters*, vol. 28, no. 2, pp. 270–293.

Hunt, M., Al-Awadi, H. & Johnson, M., (2008), 'Psychological sequelae of pet loss following Hurricane Katrina', *Anthrozoos*, vol. 21, no. 2, pp. 109–121.

Hyde, K. R., Kurdek, L. A. & Larson, P., (1983), 'Relationships between pet ownership and self-esteem, social sensitivity, and interpersonal trust', *Psychological Reports*, vol. 52, no. 1, pp. 101–110.

Irvine, L., (2006), 'Animals in disasters: Issues for animal liberation activism and policy', *Animal Liberation Philosophy and Policy*, vol. 4, no. 1, pp. 2–16.

Irvine, L., (2007), 'Animals in disasters: Responsibility and action', *Animals and Society Institute Policy Paper*, Animals and Society Institute, Ann Arbor.

Irvine, L., (2009), *Filling the Ark: Animal Welfare in Disasters*, Temple University Press, Philadelphia.

Kurdek, L. A., (2008), 'Pet dogs as attachment figures', *Journal of Social and Personal Relationships*, vol. 25, no. 2, pp. 247–266.

Laska, S. & Morrow, B., (2006), 'Social vulnerabilities and Hurricane Katrina: An unnatural disaster in New Orleans', *Marine Technology Society Journal*, vol. 40, no. 4, pp. 16–26.

Leonard, H. A. & Scammon, D. L., (2007), 'No pet left behind: Accommodating pets in emergency planning', *Journal of Public Policy & Marketing*, vol. 26, no. 1, pp. 49–53.

Lindell, M. K., Lu, J.-C. & Prater, C. S., (2005), 'Household decision making and evacuation in response to Hurricane Lili', *Natural Hazards Review*, vol. 6, pp. 171–179.

Lowe, S. R., Rhodes, J. E., Zwiebach, L. & Chan, C. S., (2009), 'The impact of pet loss on the perceived social support and psychological distress of hurricane survivors', *Journal of Traumatic Stress*, vol. 22, no. 3, pp. 244–247.

Lucas, C., (2009), 'Swine flu: is intensive pig farming to blame?', *theguardian.com* Tuesday 28 April 2009, retrieved on April 29 2014 from http://www.theguardian.com/commentisfree/2009/apr/28/swine-flu-intensive-farming-caroline-lucas#

Lynch, K., (2011), 'After hours vets had to carry on', *The Press*, 7 April 2011, retrieved 1 September 2014 from http://www.stuff.co.nz/the-press/news/christchurch-earthquake-2011/4858788/After-hours-vets-had-to-carry-on

McCutcheon, K. A. & Fleming, S. J., (2001), Grief resulting from euthanasia and natural death of companion animals', *Journal of Death and Dying*, vol. 44, no. 2, pp. 169–188.

Meyers, B., (2002), 'Disenfranchised grief and the loss of an animal companion', in K. J. Doka, (ed.), *Disenfranchised Grief: New Directions, Challenges, and Strategies for Practice*, Research Press, Champaign, Illinois, pp. 207–226.

Muir, J., (2010), 'Christchurch earthquake: Puppy stitched up after night of panic', *The New Zealand Herald*, 8 September 2010, retrieved 20 March 2012 from http://www.nzherald.co.nz/nz/news/article.cfm?c_id=1&objectid=10671835

National Animal Ethics Advisory Committee, (2013), Annual Report 1 January to 31 December 2012. Ministry of Primary Industries, Wellington.

Neimeyer, R. A. & Jordan, J. R., (2002), 'Disenfranchisement as empathic failure: Grief therapy and the co-construction of meaning', in K. J. Doka (ed.), *Disenfranchised Grief: New Directions, Challenges and Strategies for Practice*, Research Press, USA, pp. 95–117.

New Zealand Companion Animal Council (NZCAC), (2011), *Companion Animals in New Zealand July 2011*, Publicis Life Brands, Australia. (pdf)

New Zealand USAR Search Dog Association, (2012), '*Pawprint Special Edition: Christchurch Earthquake February 22 2011*', retrieved 20 April 2014 from www.usardogs.org.nz/articles/newsletters/Pawprint-Earthquake-edition2.pdf

O'Connor, S.-J., (2013), 'Illegal "pet bonds" charged on rentals', *The Press*, 26 August 2013, retrieved 14 June 2014 from http://www.stuff.co.nz/the-press/news/9085200/Illegal-pet-bonds-charged-on-rentals

Orana Wildlife Park, (2011), 'End of an era for Southern Encounter Aquarium and Kiwi House', 2 March 2011, retrieved 13 July 2013 from http://www.oranawildlifepark.co.nz/end-for-southern-encounter/

Paul, E. S. & Serpell, J., (1993), 'Childhood pet keeping and humane attitudes in young adulthood', *Animal Welfare*, vol. 2, pp. 321–337.

Perry, N., (2011), 'New Zealand goldfish survive 134 days without food', *The New Zealand Herald*, 27 July 2011, retrieved 23 April 2014 from http://www.highbeam.com/doc/1A1-0fad4bf6864240cc94a83117610a0914.html

Pets Evacuation and Transportation Standards (PETS) Act, (2006), Public Law 109-308, United States House of Representatives (HR3858).

Plec, E., (ed.), (2013), *Perspectives on Human-Animal Communication: Internatural Communication*, Routledge, London.

Podrazik, D., Shackford, S., Becker, L. & Heckert, T., (2000), 'The death of a pet: Implications for loss and bereavement across the lifespan', *Journal of Loss and Trauma*, vol. 5, no. 4, pp. 361–395.

Potts, A., (2012), *Chicken*, Reaktion, London.

Potts, A., Armstrong, P. & Brown, D., (2013), *A New Zealand Book of Beasts: Animals in our Culture, History and Everyday Life*, Auckland University Press, Auckland.

The Press, (2012), 'Distressed spoonbill captured', *The Press*, 29 February 2012, retrieved 31 May 2014 from http://www.stuff.co.nz/the-press/news/6495812/Distressed-spoonbill-captured

The Press, (2013), 'Rare birds on the rise', *The Press*, 18 February 2013, retrieved 31 May 2014 from http://www.stuff.co.nz/the-press/news/8315917/Rare-birds-on-the-rise

Press Reporters, (2013), 'Thousands of chickens die in fire', *The Press*, 12 January 2013, retrieved 27 April 2014 from http://www.stuff.co.nz/the-press/news/8169750/Thousands-of-chickens-die-in-fire

Quackenbush, J. E. & Glickman, L., (1984), 'Helping people adjust to the death of a pet', *Health & Social Work*, vol. 9, no. 1, pp. 42–48.

Rad, S., (2011), 'One handler's story', *Pawprint Special Edition: Christchurch Earthquake February 22 2011*, www.usardogs.org.nz/articles/newsletters/Pawprint-Earthquake-edition2.pdf

Ross, I., (2012), 'Disaster management session, New Zealand Veterinary Association Conference', 19-22 June 2012, http://www.nzva.org.nz/sites/default/files/mediareleases/christchurch%20earthquakes%20provide%20lessons%20for%20veterinarians.pdf

Royal New Zealand Foundation of the Blind (RNZFB), (2012), 'Quake guide dogs retrained', retrieved 23 April 2014 from http://www.fetchmag.co.nz/ARTICLES/TRAINING++SKILLS/Quake+guide+dogs+retrained.html

Sachdeva, S., (2012), 'Disease outbreak kills more birds than Rena', The Press, 25 February 2012, retrieved 1 September 2014 from http://www.stuff.co.nz/the-press/news/6478379/Disease-outbreak-kills-more-birds-than-Rena

Serpell, J., (1986), *In the Company of Animals: A Study of Human-Animal Relationships*, Cambridge University Press, Cambridge.

Sessions, L. & Bullock, C., (2013), *Quake Dogs: Heart-Warming Stories of*

Christchurch Dogs, Random House New Zealand, Auckland.

Sharkin, B. S. & Knox, D., (2003), 'Pet loss: Issues and implications for the psychologist, *Professional Psychology: Research and Practice*, vol. 34, no. 4, pp. 414–421.

Shiley, M., (2006), *Dark Water Rising: Survival Stories of Hurricane Katrina Animal Rescues*, Shidog Films, United States of America. (DVD)

Squance, H., (2011), *Animal Welfare Emergency Management: Educational Needs*, Master's Thesis, Massey University, Palmerston North.

Squance, H., Hill, K. E. & Bridges, J., (2013), *Evaluation of Morbidity and Mortality of Animals Post Canterbury Earthquakes*, Massey University pdf report. Massey University, Palmerston North. (pdf)

Television New Zealand (TVNZ), (2010), 'Many pets still missing following quake, 2010', One News, retrieved 23 May 2104 from http://tvnz.co.nz/national-news/many-pets-still-missing-following-quake-3832993

Thomas, A. E., (2009), *Pet Loss: A Study of Grief and Bereavement*, Christchurch. http://202.49.69.9/PetLoss.pdf

Wells, D. L., (2009), 'The effects of animals on human health and well-being', *Journal of Social Issues*, vol. 65, no. 3, pp. 523–543.

Whitehead, N. & Ulusoy, Ü., (2013), 'Macroscopic anomalies before the September 2010 M=7.1 earthquake in Christchurch, New Zealand', *Natural Hazards and Earth System Sciences*, vol. 13, no. 1, pp. 167–176.

Whitman, Z., Wilson, T., Seville, E., Vargo, J., Stevenson, J., Kachali, H. & Cole, J., (2013), 'Rural organizational impacts, mitigation strategies, and resilience to the 2010 Darfield earthquake, New Zealand', *Natural Hazards*, vol. 69, pp. 1849–1875.

Wilson, T., Dantas, A. & Cole, J., (2009), 'Livestock evacuation or not: An emergency response assessment of natural disasters', *Proceedings of the Eastern Asia Society for Transportation Studies*, vol. 7: https://www.jstage.jst.go.jp/article/eastpro/2009/0/2009_0_8/_pdf.

Wise, S., (2003), *Rattling the Cage: Science and the Case for Animal Rights*, Basic Books, New York.

World Society for the Protection of Animals (WSPA), (2013), *The case for preparedness: Quantification of production losses due to livestock deaths from disasters in New Zealand,* Paper by Emma Coll for the World Society for the Protection of Animals.

Zogby International, (2005), 'Poll in the wake of Hurricane Katrina shows majority want furry friends rescued during emergency evacuations', retrieved 10 April 2012 from www.zogby.com/templates/printnews.cfm?id=1029

Zottarelli, L. K., (2010), 'Broken bond: An exploration of human factors associated with companion animal loss during Hurricane Katrina', *Sociological Forum*, vol. 25, no. 1, pp. 110–122.

Further reading

Appleby, M. C. & Stokes, T., (2008), 'Why should we care about nonhuman animals during times of crisis?' *Journal of Applied Animal Welfare Science*, vol. 11, pp. 90–97.

Bekoff, M., (2007), *The Emotional Lives of Animals: A Leading Scientist Explores Animal Joy, Sorrow, and Empathy, and why they Matter*, New World Library, Novato, California.

Best Friends Animal Society, (2006), *Not Left Behind: Rescuing the Pets of New Orleans*, Yorkville Press, New York.

Crisp, T., (2000), *Emergency Animal Rescue Stories: True Stories about People Dedicated to Saving Animals from Disasters*, Prima, Roseville, California.

Farrell, F., (2012), *The Quake Year*, Canterbury University Press, Christchurch.

Helm, J. D., (2004), *Emergency Preparedness for Commercial Poultry Farms*, Clemson University, Columbia.

King, B. J., (2013), *How Animals Grieve*, University of Chicago Press, Chicago.

Lee, J.-T., (2013), *Effects of the Christchurch Earthquakes on Cats and Dogs: The Owners' Perspectives*, Research project completed for Bachelor of Applied Science (Animal Welfare and Management), Unitec, Auckland.

Millman, S. T., (2008), 'Caring during crisis: Animal welfare during pandemics and natural disasters', *Journal of Applied Animal Welfare*, vol. 11, pp. 85–89.

Ministry of Civil Defence & Emergency Management, (2008), *National Civil Defence Emergency Management Strategy 2007*, Department of Internal Affairs, Wellington.

Ministry of Civil Defence & Emergency Management, (2009), *CDEM Exercises: Director's Guidelines for Civil Defence Emergency Management (CDEM) Groups [DGL 10/09]*, Ministry of Civil Defence & Emergency Management, Wellington.

Ministry of Civil Defence & Emergency Management, (in progress), *Draft Director's Guideline: Planning for Companion Animal Welfare in an Emergency*, Ministry of Civil Defence & Emergency Management, Wellington.

Scott, C., (2008), *Pawprints of Katrina: Pets Saved and Lessons Learned*, Wiley Publishing, Hoboken.

Swarbuck, N., (2013), *Creature Comforts: New Zealanders and their Pets*, Otago University Press, Dunedin.

University of Florida, (1998), 'Maintaining livestock health after a flood', in *The Disaster Handbook – National Edition*, Institute of Food and Agricultural Sciences, University of Florida, Gainesville, Florida.

Van Beynen, M., (2012), *Trapped: Remarkable Stories of Survival from the 2011 Canterbury Earthquake*, Penguin, Auckland.

White, S., (2012), 'Companion animals, natural disasters and the law: An Australian perspective', *Animals*, vol. 2, pp. 380–394.

Wood, L. J., Giles-Corti, B., Bulsara, M. K. & Bosch, D. A., (2007), 'More than a furry companion: The ripple effect of companion animals on neighbourhood interactions and sense of community', *Society & Animals*, vol. 15, pp. 43–56.

Wright, B., (2009), *Race, Place, and Environmental Justice After Hurricane Katrina: Struggles to Reclaim, Rebuild, and Revitalize New Orleans and the Gulf Coast*, Westview Press, Boulder, Colorado.

Contributors acknowledge their supporters

One name recurs in contributors' lists of gratitude: Anthony Terry. Anthony is thanked by numerous agencies and individuals for so promptly creating and effectively coordinating the Animal Aid website that linked welfare and advocacy agencies with helpers and supporters during Canterbury's time of need.

Blair Hillyard from the Animal Rescue Unit (ARU) wishes to acknowledge the expertise and camaraderie of the other ARU team members deployed to Christchurch post-quakes: Kelly Adams, Jill Brakensiek, Samantha Hughes, Shamus Jackson, Olena Khytko, Emily Meilink and Alicia Sloan. ARU also thanks the Royal New Zealand Air Force Museum, Wellington SPCA, RNZSPCA, Canterbury Civil Defence Emergency Management, their sponsors and donators, and the public of Canterbury for the support that allowed their deployment to be so successful.

Christchurch Cat Rescue thanks HUHA (Helping You help Animals) volunteers for collecting donations of cat food and equipment.

Mark Vincent from Christchurch City Council's Animal Control unit sincerely thanks all the animal shelter staff, as well as Clare Milne of CCC's Civil Defence logistics team, Dakins (who provided working facilities to staff), Wellington SPCA's ARU, Ritchie Dawson, Dogwatch, Cats' Protection League, and all the other animal welfare agencies who made such a difference to quake-affected animals and their families.

Pamela Howard, Manager of Dogwatch, is grateful to HUHA, Master Pet, Nestle Purina, Paw Justice, The Natural Pet Treat Company, all the kind individuals who dropped off food and water for the kennels, and the wonderful women who provided home baking for the Dogwatch volunteers.

Kathleen Crisley from Canine Catering is grateful to Lucy Sandford-Reed, guardian of Bracken (whose story appears in chapter 4: Canine tales) and her many other customers who trusted her to help their quake-affected dogs.

HUHA Sanctuary thanks Royal Canin; and Vicki Harwood from Wellington City Council's Animal Control unit for allowing use of the Animal Control facilities in order to process dogs into foster or forever homes.

Janetta Stead, wildlife rescuer, is immensely grateful to Irene Chapman, Evelyn Knotts, Peg Logue, Mel Smith and Ian Ross for helping with the animal casualties she cared for.

Hayley Squance, on behalf of the Veterinary Emergency Response Team (VERT), would like to acknowledge the following companies and organisations who made a significant contribution to VERT's deployment: Massey University for releasing team members for 10 days' deployment, SPCA Canterbury; USAR; ARU; SPCA National; Christchurch's veterinary community; staff at the RNZAF Museum; Provet NZ Pty Ltd; Shoof International Ltd; New Zealand Veterinary Pathology and Gribbles Veterinary Pathology; Thrifty car rentals; Christchurch After Hours Veterinary Clinic; Whangaparaoa Vet Centre clients for their generous donation; and VERT's families, friends and colleagues for supporting the team's deployment.

HUHA rescues Dogwatch pup.

Jo Moore

Index

AABH *see* Animal and Bird Hospital
abandonment 28–30, 43, 69, 77–78, 80, 87, 91, 94–95, 101, 103, 107, 137, 146, 191–93, 219, 234, 248
abuse 4–5, 103, 160, 196, 248
accommodation, lack of vii, 80, 100, 164, 236–37, 248
Adams, Kelly 44
adoption 25, 28, 31, 55, 67–68, 72–75, 83, 85, 92, 94, 97, 134, 137, 139, 186, 231
aftershocks 120, 135, 144, 153–55, 157, 196–98, 205, 215, *see also* earthquakes
aggressive behaviour
    dogs 78, 166, 242
    other animals 46, 184, 195, 229
Alexander, Craig 211–12
allergic reactions (in animals) 86, 161–63, *see also* skin irritations
Anderson, Emma 198
Anderson, Lynn 216–17
Angel Horse Sanctuary 204–06
Animal Aid (Facebook site) 29, 73, 77, 85–87, 91–92, 97, 152
Animal and Bird Hospital (AABH) 61–63, 153, 162–63, 187
Animal Control
    Christchurch City Council
        shelter 12, 38–39, 151, 231, 246
        unit 12, 19, 23, 35–40, 72, 168, 238
    Nelson 173
Animal Rescue Unit (ARU) (Wellington SPCA) 23, 41–51, 53, 56, 81, 86, 246

Animal Welfare Act 2002 43, 235
Animal Welfare Emergency Response Team (AWERT) 36–37
animals used in teaching 42, 49, 192, *see also* laboratory animals
anthropocentrism 43, 232–38
anxiety (in animals) 67, 82, 83, 85, 99, 131, 165–71, 182, 199, 229, 244
    chronic 156–58, 166, 176
aquariums *see* tanks/aquariums
Aranui 102
Armon, Gina 160–64
Armon-Rangi, Jamie 160–64
ARU *see* Animal Rescue Unit
Ashburton 92, 108
Auckland 25, 155
Austin, Ruby 96
avian botulism 211–12
aviaries 191, 213, *see also* cages
Avoca Valley 50, 128–30
Avon-Heathcote estuary 211
Avon River 211–12
AWERT *see* Animal Welfare Emergency Response Team

Balclutha 209
Ballantine, Stephanie 49
Balogh, Todd 15
Banks Peninsula 19
Barnett, Nick 108
Barr, Sue 158
Barritt, Di 109–13
Belfast 205

Bexley 231
Bird Rescue Christchurch 212
birds 19, 28, 49, 64–65, 103, 109–10, 112, 179, 187–92, 207, 209, 211–17, 219, 238, 242, 244
    native 213–15, 217
    seabirds 19, 209
    see also blackbirds; brown teal; budgerigars; chickens; Chinese quail; cockatiels; ducks; geese; grey teal; hens; kiwi; mallard duck; paradise shelduck; parakeets; pigeons; pukeko; roosters; royal spoonbills; spotted shags; starlings; turkeys; wax eyes
blackbirds 209
Blanks, Ross 33, 41
blindness (in cats) 96, 120
boarding kennels 156–58, 238
Bradshaw, Dave 183
Brakensiek, Jill 44
Bromley 72, 82
Brook, Kip 152
Brown, Karena 93–95
brown teal 213, 214
brown trout 211
Buchanan, Kim 88
budgerigars 28, 187, 190, 192
Burne, Chris 183
Byfield, Kathy 200

cages 64, 81, 192, 219, 225, 238, *see also* aviaries; crating (of dogs)
Canine Calm Coat 171–72
Canine Catering 165
canines *see* dogs; puppies
Canterbury Bird Supplies 187
Canterbury Earthquake Images, Stories and Media Integrated Collection *see* CEISMIC
Canterbury Television (CTV) Building 52, 86, 149, 152
CARA *see* Christchurch Animal Research Area
Cashmere 153
Cat Care Incorporated 137
Cat Help 19, 71, 90, 93–96, 139
Cat Rescue Christchurch 19, 71, 86, 90–93
cats 2, 19, 24–29, 31, 42, 47–48, 61, 65, 69, 82, 89–103, 107–47, 198, 234, 237, 242, 244, *see also* feral cats; kittens
Cats' Protection League (CPL) 19, 71, 88, 90, 96–100
Cats Unloved 90

catteries 96–97, 129, 238
cattle 56, 179, 224–25, 239
CBD *see* central business district (CBD) Christchurch
CDEM *see* Civil Defence, Emergency Management
central business district (CBD) Christchurch vii, 8, 17, 42–43, 45–47, 53, 57, 72, 149
CEISMIC (Canterbury Earthquake Images, Stories and Media Integrated Collection) vii, 152
Central New Brighton School 141
Chambers, Alison 153
Chapman, Irene 208
cheetahs 216
chickens 19, 28, 48, 50, 56, 83, 103, 179, 187, 190–91, 224, 238, 243, *see also* hens; roosters
    broiler 222–24, 240
Chinese quail 192
Christ Church Cathedral 33–34, 63, 128
Christchurch Airport 124
Christchurch Animal Research Area (CARA) 228–29
Christchurch Bird Club 191
Christchurch City Council 35–36, 245
Christchurch Polytechnic Institute of Technology *see* CPIT
Civil Defence 36, 38, 42–43, 56, 124, 245, 250
    Emergency Management (CDEM) 57, 59–60, 246
    welfare centres 12, 37–39, 77
Close Up (TV programme) 193
cockatiels 19, 187–88
    night fright 189–90, 242
Code of Welfare for Layer Hens 239
Cole, Jan 131–32
compulsive behaviour 91, 170
contaminants *see* sewer damage, pollution; water, pollution of; toxins
Cordaro, Millie 240, 242
Corkery, Pam 174
Costello, Erika 83
cows *see* cattle
CPIT (Christchurch Polytechnic Institute of Technology) 192
    veterinary nursing school 42, 49
CPL *see* Cats' Protection League
crating (of dogs) 155, 238, 243
Crisley, Kathleen 165–69
Cox, Pamela 141–43

CTV *see* Canterbury Television (CTV) Building
cystitis 68, *see also* urinary tract disorders

Dahl, Paul 19, 71, 101–03
Dallington 128
Dalton, Les 58
Darfield 11
Davis, Eleanor 48
Dawson, Ritchie 15, 41, 45, 47, 50, 53, 58, 238
de Fonseca, Lena 155
deaths
    animal 5, 12, 56–57, 68, 139, 190, 192, 197, 211, 223–25, 228, 239, 246
    human vii, 72, 149–50, 152, 212, 224
Department of Conservation 180, 211
Department of Internal Affairs 58
dehydration 53, 94, 133, 137
depression (in animals) 53
desexing 25, 34, 72, 79–80, 92, 93, 132–33, 137, 235
Diamond Harbour 131–32, 156
Disability Assist Dogs 12*fn*, 151, 250
disease (in chickens) 239
Dog Control Act 2002 12*fn*
dogs 2, 12, 17, 19, 24–25, 27–30, 35–40, 48, 57, 61–63, 65–66, 69, 72–84, 90, 102, 112, 149–77, 224, 234, 238, 242–45, *see also* puppies
    police dogs 61
    USAR dogs 52–54, 57, 61, 149–51, 172
Dogwatch (Bromley) 19, 38, 71–83, 86, 93, 151, 231, 235
Donaldson, Kelly 194–96
donations 43, 82, 102, 174
    food 31, 38, 42–43, 73, 82, 93, 102, 133
    money 30, 38, 42, 73, 96, 155
    time and service 30–31, 73, 183, *see also* volunteers
Douglas, Brett 119
Douglas, Heather 119
Dowell, Sacha 86–88, 91–93
ducks 209, 211–12, 238, *see also* brown teal; grey teal; mallard duck; paradise shelduck
Duckworth, Janine 212
Duff, Lisa 74
Dunedin 75, 92
discospondylosis 166
Dyer, Aaron 228

Earthquake Commission (EQC) 12, 68, 94, 164
earthquakes
    Christchurch
        September 2010 11, 17, 23, 37, 62, 94, 108–09, 111, 115, 120, 131, 139, 150, 152–53, 156, 170, 211, 214, 224–25, 228, 231, 239
        February 2011 vii, 7, 17, 23–24, 28, 48, 50, 53, 56–57, 60, 62, 68, 71–72, 81, 92–93, 96–97, 101, 116, 121, 124, 128, 132–33, 135, 140, 144, 149, 151, 154–55, 157, 161, 167, 195, 199, 216
        June 2011 19, 100, 135
        December 2011 19, 113, 153, 200
    Izmit, Turkey 111
    Kobe, Japan 111
    lights 111
    see also aftershocks
educational initiatives (in animal welfare) 35, 72, 74, 81, 200, 237
eels 211, 217
elderly
    animals 42, 47–48, 67, 98, 119, 144–46
    people 29, 93, 99, 102–03, 240–41
electricity outages 12, 60, 62, 64, 72, 96, 199, 213, 228
emergency procedures, recommendations 56–58, 61
entertainment, animals used in 59
Environment Canterbury 211
EQC *see* Earthquake Commission
euthanasia 5, 67–68, 77, 120, 157–58, 176, 237, 241
evacuation 7–8, 11, 13, 48, 50, 60–61, 77, 129, 184, 233, 236, 241, 249, 250
Evans Pass 102
eye irritations 53, 66

Facebook 152, 155
factory farms *see* intensive farming
farm animals 16, 28, 56, 59, 179, 221–25, 237–40, *see also* cattle; goats; horses; pigs; sheep
fatigue 53
Federated Farmers 58–59, 238, 246
Federation of New Zealand Aquatic Societies 179
felines *see* cats; kittens
feral cats 94, 133, 137, 235

Index   269

Ferrymead 200, 204
Fetch (magazine) 74
Field, Michael 151
fish 2, 28, 43, 48–49, 179, 211, 217, 222, 224, 228, 238, 244
    tropical 228
    see also brown trout; eels; goldfish; mudfish; sharks
Fisher, Glenis 48
FitzGerald, Bethan 197–98
fleas 66, 91
Fleetwood, Caroline 153
flight response 65, 72, 90, 107–08, 113, 115–18, 121, 129–30, 133, 144, 152, 170, 189, 199, 204, 242
flooding 124, 198, 202, 207
Four Legs Good (blog) 108
fostering 68, 72, 78, 83–84, 91–92, 94, 137, 195, 231
fur seals 211

Gadenne, Donelle 234*fn*
Gap Filler vii
gastroenterological ailments 65, 237
Gates, Charlie 212
geese 103
GeoNet 154
Gilmore, Aaron 214, 216
giraffes 213, 216, 243
Gisborne 25
Give a Little (website) 88
Glassey, Steve 13, 15, 52, 234, 245, 251
goats 28, 48, 102, 179
Golden Bay 158–59
goldfish 43, 48–49, 102
Governors Bay 180
Greendale fault 166
grey teal 212
Greymouth 25
grief (due to loss of companion animal) 1, 5–6, 158, 240–42
guide dogs *see* Disability Assist Dogs
guinea pigs 63, 197–98, 244, *see also* hamsters

Hadfield, Becky 171
Hagley Community College 36
hair loss 83, 155
Halligan, Dave 113
Halligan, Rosie 113
Hamlin, Jennifer 179
Hampton, Vanessa 26–27, 33
hamsters 48, *see also* guinea pigs

Harrington, Mandy 198–201
Harris, Bev 97–98
Harris, Jo 171–72
Hawke, Nathan 215, 217–18
Hay, Andrew 61
Hazlitt-Black, Trudi 194–96
Heathcote 121, 128–30, 156, 186, 202
Heathcote Riding School 87, 198–204, 242–43
Heathcote Valley 51, 107
hedgehogs 19, 207–10
Helem, Barry 248
Helm, Julie 240*fn*
hens 82, 102–03, 239
    battery 56, 222–26, 240
    free range 62, 191, 225–26
    see also chickens
Hill, Kate 57*fn*
Hillsborough 115
Hillyard, Blair 44–47, 50–51
Hokitika 25
Hororata 225
Horrell, Douglas 169
horses 19, 179, 198–206, 219, 238, 242
Hothouse Turtles (Hawkes Bay) 183
Housing New Zealand 43
Howard, Pam 72–73, 78–81
Hughes, Samantha 44
HUHA (Helping You Help Animals) 19, 71, 81–86, 93
Hullet, Lea 108
Humane Society 96
Huntsbury 140
Hurricane Katrina 1, 7–11, 16, 36, 51, 223, 227, 232, 236

injuries
    external 27, 53, 61, 63–65, 122, 133, 140, 153, 182, 204, 207, 224–26
    internal 27, 170, 224
intensive farming 8, 19, 56, 221–25, 238–39, 246
Irvine, Leslie 8–11, 221–23, 227, 229
Izmit, Turkey (earthquake) 111

Jackson, Shamus 44, 51
James, Sandra 128–30
Johnston, Kirsty 108

Kaiapoi 137–38
Kaikoura 45
Kaminski, Mallori 194–96
Kerr, Harry 75–76

Khytko, Olena 44
kittens 25, 41, 91–94, 96, 101, 137–38, 146, *see also* cats
kiwi 214–15, 217, 243
Kobe, Japan (earthquake) 111
Kriek, Hans 82, 86, 88–90
Kriek, Nichola 82, 86–87, 89–90

laboratory animals 8, 19, 59, 193, 221–22, 227–29, 238, *see also* animals used in teaching
Landcare Research 212
Latimer Square 46
Latter Spur Track 154
legislation
    animal welfare 2, 12–13, 43, 56, 59, 235, 239
    civil defence and emergency 7, 12–13, 56, 58–59
    local 71
lemurs 214, 224
Lewis, Jasmine 24–25, 30–32
Leys, Sandra 96–100
lions 214–15
liquefaction 19, 65–66, 68, 86, 96, 100, 152, 155, 192, 207, 211, 237, 239, 243
livestock *see* farm animals
Lynch, Keith 60–61
Lyttelton 17, 19, 71, 101–02, 144, 191, 199
    Recreation Centre 101
    tunnel 42, 50, 102
    Volunteer Fire Brigade 101

McClean, Tania 161
McConnell, Blair 151
McFarlane, Sharon 144–45
McGregor, Alan 173
McLaren, Charmaine (Charlie) 72–73, 82
McLean's Island 213
McMurtie, Penny 108
McNab, Danielle 109
Magson, Rae 108
Mainfreight 183
mallard duck 212
Manchester Street 90, 192
Manley, Stephanie 193
Marlborough 192
massage therapy 166
Massey University 58–59, 237
    Centre for Service and Working Dog Health 57*fn*
    Institute of Veterinary, Animal and Biomedical Sciences 52

Veterinary Emergency Response Team (VERT) 19, 23, 45, 52–57, 68, 233
mastitis (in cows) 226
MCDEM *see* Ministry of Civil Defence and Emergency Management
Meadow Mushrooms 31
Meilink, Emily 44, 50
mice 222, 228–29, 244
Miles, Melissa 204–06
micro-chipping 13, 28, 34, 39, 63, 69, 72, 80, 87, 92–93, 95, 98, 136, 141–43, 151, 153, 168, 244–45, 249
Ministry for Primary Industries (MPI) 58–60, 246
Ministry of Civil Defence and Emergency Management (MCDEM) 58–60
Molloy, Paul 58
Moot, Donna 179–87
Morris, Ingrid 27
mudfish 217
MPI *see* Ministry for Primary Industries
Mullaly, Tarn 124

'Nana Pam' 209
Napier 17
National Animal Welfare Advisory Committee (NAWAC) 239
National Animal Welfare Emergency Management (NAWEM) 2, 15, 23, 42, 52–53, 58–60, 239, 245–46
National Aquarium (Napier) 183
native species 211, 213–17, 243, *see also* brown teal; eels; fur seals; grey teal; kiwi; mudfish; paradise shelduck; pukeko; royal spoonbills; spotted shags; wax eyes
NAWAC *see* National Animal Welfare Advisory Committee
NAWEM *see* National Animal Welfare Emergency Management
neglect 29, 80, 91, 101, 103, 194, 196, 236, 248
Nelson 92, 138
neutering *see* desexing
New Brighton 102, 209
    Police Station 141–43
New Zealand Animal Welfare Strategy 60
New Zealand Civil Defence Emergency Management Act 2002 12, 58
New Zealand Companion Animal Council (NZCAC) 2, 34, 58–59, 246
New Zealand Companion Animal Register (NZCAR) 34, 168, 245, 249

New Zealand Veterinary Association (NZVA) 58–59, 61, 246
Nicol, Jo 93–95
Nixey, Jenny 53–54, 56–57
North Canterbury 137
NZCAC *see* New Zealand Companion Animal Council
NZCAR *see* New Zealand Companion Animal Register
NZVA *see* New Zealand Veterinary Association

Ohoka 142
Orana Wildlife Park 19, 112, 212–18, 224
    endangered species 213–15
    exotic species 212–16
    ZooDoo 213*fn*
    see also cheetahs; giraffes; kiwi; lemurs; lions; rhinoceroses; spider monkeys; tigers; waterbuck
Osmer, Karla 120–23
Osmer, Nathan 121–23
Otago 25
Our Vets 133

paradise shelduck 209, 212
parakeets 188
Parker, Alan 135–36
Pauwels, Fred 53
Paw Justice 88, 93, 102–03
Pawprint (New Zealand USAR Search Dog Association newsletter) 150
pet emergency/evacuation kit 85, 250–51
pet stores 43, 238
Pets on the Net 29, 88, 90, 117, 130, 152
Petrova, Maria 30
Phillipstown 139
PGC *see* Pyne Gould Corporation (PGC) building
phobias 67
pigeons 33–34
pigs 48, 238
PlaceMakers (Cranford Street) 133
poisons *see* sewer damage, pollution; water, pollution of; toxins
Poland, Roger 58, 60, 245
pollution *see* sewer damage, pollution; water, pollution of; toxins
ponies *see* horses
Port Hills 129, 173
possums 212
Potts, Annie 58, 144–45, 153, 191

pound *see* Animal Control, shelter; shelters, animal
Press, the (Christchurch) 60, 97, 130, 211–12, 225
Press-McKenzie, Carolyn 81–85
psychological trauma *see* trauma
Provost, Diane 115
pukeko 209
puppies 79–80, 93, *see also* dogs
Pyne Gould Corporation (PGC) building 149

QEII fitness complex 101
quail *see* Chinese quail
Quail Island 101
Quake Dogs (book) 150*fn*, 155, 164
Quake pets (Christchurch *Press's* lost and found registry) 152
QuakeStories vii, 152
Quantum Chartered Accountants 48*fn*
quarantine 54

rabbits 28, 48–50, 197–98, 222, 228, 239, 244
Rad, Sara 150
radio frequency identification (RFID) 251
Rangiora 137
Rat Club 195
Rat Rescue 192–96
rats 19, 49, 187, 192–96, 219, 228, 244
RD1 (rural supplier) 200
Red Cross 38
red zone 8, 43, 45–46, 52–53, 57, 82–83, 86, 137–38, 186, 212
Redcliffs 77, 191
rehoming *see* adoption
release into wild (of domesticated animals) 180, 196, 209, 219
reptiles 179, 217; *see also* turtles
rescue (of animals) 7, 12, 43–52, 56, 94, 200, 217
research and testing (animals used for) *see* laboratory animals
respiratory issues 53, 66
RFID *see* radio frequency identification
rhinoceroses 216
Richards, Janis 93
Ricketts, Wayne 58–59, 245
ringworm 96
RNZFB *see* Royal New Zealand Foundation of the Blind
rock falls 50, 56, 129, 136, 150, 161, 199, 210–11

rodents 179, 229, 238; *see also* hamsters; guinea pigs; mice; rats
Rolleston 225
roosters 82, *see also* chickens; hens
Ross, Ian 60–61
Ross, Mark 58
Royal New Zealand Air Force Base (Wigram) 46, 53
Royal New Zealand Foundation of the Blind (RNZFB) 151*fn*, 250
royal spoonbills 212
runaways *see* flight response

Sabin, Robyn 155
SAFE (Save Animals from Exploitation) 19, 29, 71, 77, 82, 85–90, 96–97
Salton, Alyssa 213
Saunders, Stephanie 41
Save Animals from Exploitation *see* SAFE
Scarborough Cliffs 104–05, 210
Scarborough Hill 135–36
Scarlett, Lyane 187–92
Scarlett, Paul 187–92
Scully, Sean 174–75
seismic sensing 110–13, 131–32, 174, 198, 216
sewer damage 48, 72, 209
    pollution 207, 209–12
Shakespeare, Judith 97–98, 100
sharks 48
sheep 56, 102, 179, 228, 238
shelters, animal 82, 139, *see also* Animal Control, shelter
skin irritations 66, 114, 132, 161–63, *see also* allergic reactions
Sloan, Alicia 44
social media 77, 97, 152, 155, 251
Society for the Prevention of Cruelty to Animals *see* SPCA
Song, Lily 193
South Brighton 210
Southern Encounter Aquarium and Kiwi House 183, 213, 216
Southland 25
Southshore 171
SPCA (Society for the Prevention of Cruelty to Animals) 4, 52, 58–59, 233, 246
    Canterbury 13, 19, 23–36, 41–45, 53, 56, 66, 77, 87–88, 116, 125, 130, 138, 168–69, 180, 184, 186, 235, 238, 248
    South Canterbury 25, 28
    temporary care of animals 28
    Wellington 15, 19, 81
SPCA Rescue (TV programme) 42–43, 47–49
spider monkeys 214
spoonbills *see* royal spoonbills
spotted shags 105, 210
Squance, Hayley 52–58, 68, 233, 237, 241, 245
St Albans 86
St Andrews Hill 99, 124, 126
Star, the (Christchurch) 141
starlings 209
Stead, Janetta 104–05, 207–10
sterilisation *see* desexing
Stewart, Robyn 139–41
Stratton, Rachael 52–54, 57
strays 28, 38, 92–93, 101, 133, 137, 146, 235
stress (in animals) 27, 61, 80, 93, 114, 165, 182, 244
stroke 120
Student Volunteer Army 81, 175
Sumner 27, 77, 102, 116–17, 135, 150, 160, 210
surgical operations (during earthquakes) 64
Sutton, Geoff 23–25, 27–29, 31–32, 34–35, 41, 45

tanks/aquariums, fish and turtle 181, 187, 219, 238, 244
Tauranga 92
TC3 zone 96, 137
Telecom Exchange Building 151
territorial bonds and behaviour 107, 114–18, 185
Terry, Anthony 73, 85–86
The Palms shopping mall 81
therapy, human–animal interaction in 3–4, 55, 173–75, 180, 202, 231–32, 240
Thomson, Robin 96–97, 100
tigers 215
Timaru 25, 28, 92, 108
TNR (trap–neuter–return) 91, 93
toxins, exposure to 54, 57*fn*, 211, *see also* sewer damage, pollution; water, pollution of
Track A Pet 12, 29
Trade Me 29, 31, 80, 88, 90, 97, 117, 122, 130, 152, 180
trap–neuter–return *see* TNR
trapped animals (result of earthquake) 133, 200

trauma 83, 85, 91, 96, 107, 120, 131, 146, 155, 157–58, 168, 172, 194, 200, 224, 242
turkeys 179, 238
Turtle Rescue 179–87
turtles 9, 82, 179–187, 219, 223, 238, 244
TV3 News 97

University of Canterbury vii, 228
Urban Search and Rescue (USAR)
    Australia 51, 54, 149
    Japan 54–55, 149
    New Zealand 45–46, 48–49, 52–54, 57, 149–51
    Singapore 54, 149
    United States 51
urinary tract disorders 61, 68, 237
USAR *see* Urban Search and Rescue

vaccination 28, 72, 92, 137
Vercoe, Bridget 58–60, 245
VERT *see* Massey University, Veterinary Emergency Response Team
veterinarians 13, 55, 68, 103, 122, 126, 176
veterinary clinics 55, 191, 210
    Animal and Bird Hospital 61–63, 153, 162–63, 187
    Christchurch After Hours Veterinary Clinic 60
    Halswell Veterinary Clinic 61
    Hornby Veterinary Centre 61
    Our Vets 133
    Vets for Pets 100
veterinary nurses 55, 81, 87, 187
veterinary treatment 122, 126, 132–33, 157, 161–63, 165, 186
Vets for Pets 100
Victoria Park 154
Vincent, Mark 35–39
volunteers 39, 52, 56, 69, 71–72, 81–82, 85–88, 90–92, 95, 102, 180–81, 206, 231, *see also* donations, time and service
Vosper, Jill 75–76

Waayer, Leonie 58
Wagstaff, Sara 135–46, 199
Wainoni Fish and Chips shop 95
Walker, Alex 24, 34
Walters, Jacquie 116–18
water
    lack of 12, 60, 62, 64, 96, 183, 199–200, 205
    pollution of 12, 65, 209, 211
waterbuck 112, 216
Waters, Trish (Patricia) 156
wax eyes 209
Weedons Poultry Farm 224, 239
weight loss 158, 170, 199
Wellington 81–84, 125, 192
West Melton 206
Weiros *see* cockatiels
wildlife, urban 179, 207–12, 231, *see also* blackbirds; feral cats; ducks; hedgehogs; pigeons; starlings
Wilson, Tom 13
wing damage 65, 189
Woolston 91, 100, 109, 187
    fire service (Ferrymead) 200
World Society for the Protection of Animals (WSPA) 16, 41, 52, 58–59, 226, 245–46
WSPA *see* World Society for the Protection of Animals

Yates, Debbie 19, 23, 61–68, 191, 225–26

Zampese, Linda 173–74
zoo animals *see* Orana Wildlife Park
Zumbraegel, Susie 162
Zwarts, Lisette 193–94

Pet memorial photographed 30 June 2011, near the CBD.

Nixx Doms